LIFE WITHOUT MEDIA

This book is part of the Peter Lang Media and Communication list.
Every volume is peer reviewed and meets
the highest quality standards for content and production.

PETER LANG
New York • Washington, D.C./Baltimore • Bern
Frankfurt • Berlin • Brussels • Vienna • Oxford

LIFE WITHOUT MEDIA

Edited by Eva Comas, Joan Cuenca, and Klaus Zilles

PETER LANG
New York • Washington, D.C./Baltimore • Bern
Frankfurt • Berlin • Brussels • Vienna • Oxford

Library of Congress Cataloging-in-Publication Data

Life without media / edited by Eva Comas, Joan Cuenca, Klaus Zilles.
pages cm
Includes bibliographical references and index.
1. Mass media—Philosophy. 2. Mass media—Social aspects. 3. Digital media.
I. Comas, Eva, editor of compilation.
II. Cuenca, Joan, editor of compilation.
III. Zilles, Klaus, editor of compilation.
P90.L44 302.23—dc23 2013005241
ISBN 978-1-4331-2262-0 (hardcover)
ISBN 978-1-4331-2261-3 (paperback)
ISBN 978-1-4539-1090-0 (e-book)

Bibliographic information published by **Die Deutsche Nationalbibliothek.**
Die Deutsche Nationalbibliothek lists this publication in the "Deutsche Nationalbibliografie"; detailed bibliographic data is available on the Internet at http://dnb.d-nb.de/.

The paper in this book meets the guidelines for permanence and durability of the Committee on Production Guidelines for Book Longevity of the Council of Library Resources.

29 Broadway, 18th floor, New York, NY 10006
www.peterlang.com

Printed in the United States of America

Table of Contents

Part Two. Parenting, Schooling, and Socializing: Youth Mediatization Gone Wrong?

Part Three. Mediated Life and Death in Arts and Entertainment

Part Four. Journalism and Public Relations in a Changing Media Sphere

Acknowledgments

The contributions of several friends and colleagues were essential to the completion of this project. We wish to thank our former Dean, Miquel Tresserras, who entrusted us with the organization of the Life Without Media conference, and our current Dean, Josep Maria Carbonell, with whose support we saw the project to its conclusion. We are grateful to Albert Saéz and Joan Sabaté, who were instrumental in conceiving of, and conceptualizing, the original conference theme. Thanks are due to Sue Aran for her help in formulating the final call-for-papers. The Life Without Media conference would not have been possible without the assistance of the technicians in the IT and audiovisual departments, and the student volunteers and graduate students, who performed many of the logistical tasks essential to any successful conference.

Introduction: Life Without Media

EVA COMAS, JOAN CUENCA, AND KLAUS ZILLES

In ancient Greece, Hermes was the messenger of the gods—the god of communication, if you will—but he was also the god of thievery. Mythology preserved in ancient papyri recalls that Hermes's first exploit, right after birth, was the theft of Apollo's immortal cattle, herding them back to Greece backwards to throw his pursuers off their tracks. We have acted in a manner similar to Hermes when in June 2011 we hosted an international conference at the Blanquerna School of Communication in Barcelona with the theme "Life Without Media." By dint of this provocative title, we stole—albeit figuratively and conceptually—the media away from contemporary life in order to try and understand the importance and value they have in current society.

The result of hypothesizing the total disappearance not only of newspapers, but of all traditional media as they have come to be understood in the past two centuries, suggests that the privileged position these media have lain claim to in the collective and conceptual imagination may have come to an end. What triggered our basic hypothesis was the sheer quantity of messages issued in various media outlets that augured, or at least hinted at, the demise of the printed news, or the end of pretty much all traditional media. It was striking that the communication media themselves were creating a narrative of their own decease. For instance, as early as March 2005 the journal *Wired* envisaged the disappearance of radio as the universal, ubiquitous medium of the western world. The front page of the issue featured a small red transistor radio being shattered to pieces by a bullet emerging from its frontal speaker, suggesting that the device (and by extension, the medium as a whole) had been shot in the back. The headline read "The End of Radio (As We Know It)." On a similar note, on February 27, 2010, Spanish Public Television (Televisión Española) aired a report called "Paper Storm" (Rodicio & López, 2010), in which they called attention to the fact that in the first two months of that year, sales of printed newspapers had dropped by 30 percent. Indeed, increasingly the messages reporting or presaging the media's decline were corroborated by hard data. In the case of the mainstream media, we are seeing a profound crisis that goes far beyond the economic crisis that broke on September 15, 2008. According to data provided by the World Association of Newspapers (WAN) at their annual conventions, the crisis manifests itself in a general decrease in the print publications, and in consequence, dwindling advertising revenue that affects the major part of the printed press in industrialized nations.

Deplorably, this crisis also results in general downsizing and layoffs of media professionals who research, compile, and edit daily newsworthy information in many prestigious media outlets. A case in point is none other than the *New York Times*, which early in 2010 made some thousand jobs in their newsroom redundant. This trend affects not only print media, but also such pillars of the traditional audiovisual communication media as the BBC, which has suffered several waves of downsizing personnel in recent years. Everything points to the fact, then, that the hypothesis of the end of the traditional media is not a fanciful or short-lived idea, and that many high-ranking editors, directors, and media executives have interiorized the notion of the downward spiral and make their decisions regarding budgeting and human resources accordingly.

Thus we started wondering, in the face of these palpable predicaments, what it would actually look like were newspapers and other communication media indeed to cease their existence. In a manner of speaking, we contended that a thought experiment based on an antithesis would help us ascertain the core functions of the traditional mainstream media in the heart of our society up to now.

But first we must clarify that the traditional mass media do not arise from a purely technological rationale. The first medium, the newspaper, was not born simply because the printing press was invented in the mid-15th century. Indeed, there lapsed a period of almost two centuries between the emergence of the technology that made the printed press possible, and the advent of the actual medium. Thus, even though the technologic circumstances are indispensable, they alone are not sufficient for a communication medium to emerge. Other factors, such as the necessity of social organization and a clear function of the medium within the human community are critical also.

One might say that the traditional media materialized thanks to the occurrence of three revolutions that took place in western societies almost simultaneously two centuries ago. The first of these is of a political nature and it resulted in the genesis of modern representative democracies. The United States of America in 1776, France between 1789 and 1799, and various European countries in successive surges (1820, 1830, and 1848) exemplify a concerted struggle to afford sovereignty to all the citizens of the western nation states, which henceforward availed themselves of the political and legal instruments in order to govern themselves through systems of representative democracy.

As Alexis de Tocqueville declared in the mid-19th century in his landmark work *De la démocratie en Amérique*, the newspapers and communication media that provide accurate and impartial information are one of the crucial pieces in the intricate workings of representative democracy. Democracy is a political system in which the citizens elect their representatives, which in turn necessitates a well-informed electorate. Over the past 200 years, other prominent writings on political theory and sociology have drawn attention to the weight the transmission of information through the media carries in the structuring and functioning of public life in western society. Some of these are *Public Opinion* by Walter Lippmann (1922), *The Fall of Public Man* by Richard Sennett (1977), *Media Events: The Live Broadcasting of History* by Daniel Dayan and Elihu Katz (1992) and *Media and Modernity: A Social Theory of the Media* by John B. Thompson (1995). All of them, albeit from different perspectives, bestow a central place upon the communication media in the construction of what is called "the public sphere." Needless to say, our approach to the notion of communication owes much to the discipline of sociology, following in broad strokes the methodology submitted in 1966 by Peter Berger and Thomas Luckmann in their seminal work *The Social Construction of Reality: A Treatise in the Sociology of Knowledge.*

Transcending the notion of the physical public meeting place, for 200 years the media have constituted a shared conceptual forum, a gathering place that allows the citizens to make their own decisions and conduct their business. Thus did Walter Lippmann define this public sphere in 1922:

> Those features of the world outside which have to do with the behavior of other human beings, in so far as that behavior crosses ours, is dependent upon us, or is interesting to us, we call roughly public affairs. The pictures inside the heads of these human beings, the pictures of themselves, of others, of their needs, purpos-

> es, and relationship, are their public opinions. Those pictures which are acted upon by groups of people, or by individuals acting in the name of groups, are Public Opinion with capital letters. (p. 7)

The second of the three revolutions mentioned previously that mark the emergence of the traditional communication media is the one that occurred in the realm of knowledge, namely, the Enlightenment. Before the advent of the Enlightenment in the 17th century, with its struggle for literacy and emancipation, the cultural conception of European countries was profoundly theocratic. Any work of a scientific nature had to undergo the scrutiny and approval of the religious authorities. There abound cases like that of Giordano Bruno, whose writings, and indeed the author, perished because they would not bow to the religious rulers. In the west, it is Immanuel Kant's famed dare "*sapere aude*" that irrevocably broke with theocratic tradition, defining Enlightenment as mankind's finally coming of age, the emancipation of the human consciousness from an immature state of ignorance and error. Pamphlet writers and early newspapers performed their duty in the spreading of knowledge, and the enlightened used the forums of their papers to proclaim that humans must think for themselves and use their powers of reason without heeding the religious dogma. In fact, the very conceptualization of "medium" as an vehicle for spreading knowledge and learning is showcased in the threefold mission of the BBC: "inform, educate and entertain," articulated by Lord Reith in the 1920s, and that still endures as a common dictum for public communication media in Europe.

Finally, the third revolutionary movement that concurs with the appearance of representative democracy and the Enlightenment is the economic reform triggered by the Industrial Revolution, which utterly transformed and modernized Europe and North America from the 18th century on. Industrialized production processes are dependent on the creation of new, larger markets and new consumers to whom information about new commodities must be communicated incessantly and effectively. Thus, the need for advertising is a result of the dynamics of the industrialized marketplace, and advertising revenue will eventually constitute the financial foundation of the traditional communication media. In this manner, it transpires that whereas the media are at once the result of social change caused by the three revolutionary movements discussed here, they are also the driving forces that have played a part in forging and consolidating not only western political systems, but also the market economy that arose out of the Enlightenment movement and the growing literacy of the general population.

Nonetheless, owing to the crisis of the traditional media and the radical changes resulting from the advent of the Internet and social media, the cherished epistemological certainties regarding the core functions of the media and the information they transmit are suddenly under scrutiny. The central question that we will eventually have to answer is whether the virtual space and the new media will be able to take on and carry out to some extent the core functions the traditional media have performed until recently in representative democracies, namely the campaign for literacy and the enlightenment of the populace in a market economy.

While newspaper sales dwindle, and their capacity to influence shrinks, voices of alarm are heard cautioning us that this is not just a profound crisis, or even the impending death, of our capitalist market economy. Many feel that the repercussions have a much greater impact. Thus, in *El País* of February 18, 2010, the writer Gustavo Martín Garzo reminded us that the press is a bastion of morality "of responsibility and commitment."

Alarmed by the rapid and deep transformations affecting the printed press, in 2009, Leonard Downie Jr., former executive editor of the *Washington Post* and professor of journalism at the Walter Cronkite School of Journalism and Mass Communication at Arizona State University, and Michael Schudsen, professor at Columbia, published a report entitled *The Reconstruction of American Journalism.* They present data that shows "the economic foundation of the nation's newspapers, long supported by advertising is collapsing, and the newspapers themselves, which have been the country's chief source of independent reporting, are shrinking—literally."

Similarly, a survey carried out by the Pew Research Center's Project for Excellence in Journalism, which examined the communication media in Baltimore throughout the year 2009, revealed how the mainstream press generated 48 percent of the information they themselves published, whereas the so-called new media only produced 4 percent of the information. Thus, according to this study, the online press and the social media are extraordinarily fast in spreading and publishing information, but their capacity to investigate and generate the news is disproportionally inferior. According to José María Álvarez Monzonillo, who is the chair for Audiovisual Communication at Universidad Rey Don Juan Carlos, this is mainly due to the fact that generating information is currently not a lucrative business for the new media.

On a similar note, Christopher Caldwell (2009) points out that the revenue grossed by online outlets is not sufficient to sustain the investigative and rigorous journalism as we have come to understand it. Indeed, according to his article in the *Financial Times*, the online media and social networks exploit the moral and educational capital built laboriously over a long time by the traditional media, and it predicts that this knowledge capital will not be replenished in the generations to come.

The "digital natives," as Marc Prensky (2001) labeled the first generations of Internet users, have now come of age and may exercise their right to vote in many western nations. It is begging the question, we feel, whether the online media and the social networks, which are after all the digital natives' natural habitat, provide an equally appropriate forum for controversial, responsible debate, which the traditional media have prided themselves on throughout the 20th century. And taking our inquiry one step further, we deem it vital to probe into the possibility of whether it is not just the gatekeeper role of the traditional media that is being under threat. Rather, we feel that it is the political, economic, and cultural underpinning, which ultimately facilitated a common cultural ground, that is now undergoing a radical transformation from the roots up.

Perhaps we are traversing a period of transition between one power constellation to another, from an established power to a counter-movement. Manuel Castells in *Communication and Power* (2009) finds that power goes beyond communication, and communication transcends power, but power resides in the control of communication, and counter-power can only arise when it succeeds in triumphing over the established controlling power.

Be that as it may, up until very recently the ground was "worked" by information and communication professionals who investigated, and answered for, their own contents, which were cross-referenced, fact-checked, and certified by a culture of professional ethics and expertise. In the new media environment, however, this practice is increasingly replaced by obtaining information and contents that must be, albeit not firsthand, released and aired at a breathtaking speed and instantaneity thanks to social networks and powerful search engines.

In the face of these bewildering developments and constellations in the new mediascape, we wished to confer with academics and media practitioners about what might happen if the media as we know them really were to disappear; that is to say, envisaging a world without the by now well-established mediacentrism in terms of public life, politics, economy, and knowledge: in short—life without media. If indeed we were to cease taking the communication media for granted as an intrinsic, fundamental element in our daily lives, perhaps we might reconsider its value and core functions. The present volume of texts authored by media scholars and practitioners, both veteran and novice, is essentially the outcome of the thought experiment of imagining life without media.

Contents and Contributors

Upon reading the chapters of the researchers and scholars who contribute to this volume, and who have embraced the premise of "life without media," one senses skepticism toward the radical hypothesis of the death of the media. And yet, at the same time, one also observes a mounting concern regarding the changing media space(s) and the relevance of the media's roles and places in different and diverse social spheres. Unanimously, they find that while these roles and places have changed, the difficulty lies in where and how to delineate them. The chapters that constitute this volume provide some answers to these questions, and in many instances raise new questions and doubts.

A series of general theoretical reflections that explore and respond to these initial questions make up Part One of the volume entitled "Exploring New Perspectives on Life and Media." The opening text by Mark Brewin examines the conspicuous changes in the relationship between individuality and community as a result of the Internet's impact on the public sphere. Brewin's text, entitled "The Public Sphere in a Networked Age," compellingly asserts that what we have so far understood as the human subject's sense of self is now being re-imagined in ways that shift toward a more and more porous idea of the self. This emerging "porous self" is capable of connecting directly to various communities, thus linking media users together without the need of intervening media institutions like television networks or newspapers. To Brewin, the creation of identity has ceased to follow the guidelines established by the 18th-century Enlightenment ideas, and has changed from a centralized mediascape into a system that lacks a center, allowing a more uninhibited, unmediated flow of information along a multitude of channels.

Indeed, the idea of the media as a central locus of life and living, and the pitfalls of this model, is also at the core of Nick Couldry's chapter, "Life Without Media: Or, Why Mediacentrism Is Bad for You." The British researcher calls into question that the media are, or should be, regarded as the epicenter of social life. He therefore proposes a decentralized approach through which the specific contributions of the media to society can be described and assessed. The chapter "Life Without Democracy, Life Without Citizenship, Life Without Media" by Richard Maxwell and Toby Miller concludes the broad-spectrum theoretical reflections on life without media and explores the concepts of democracy and citizenship by emphasizing the impact of technological change and mediatized cultures on the environment and in the social sphere. This impact appears characterized by a decline in traditional media, media convergence, and hybridization of genres, formats and technological elements, but above all by an increased spending of energy.

When we deliberated on "Life Without Media" as an admittedly provocative title for our conference, we meant to call attention to the fact that the media are key in the functioning of the representative democratic system, the education of the population, and the free-market economy. Thus, if we attempt to redefine henceforth the media and their position, we must also contemplate redefining, at least in part, our political, educational, and economic models. This redefinition seems to impinge on two areas in society in particular, in which the changing role and place of the media are experienced with particular sensitivity. These are, first, the early formative years of media consumers, and, second, the world narrative fiction writing. A significant number of researchers who attended the conference turned their thoughts to these areas, and to them we have dedicated the two central sections of the book.

Thus, Part Two, "Parenting, Schooling, and Socializing: Youth Mediatization Gone Wrong?" focuses on childhood and adolescence, striving to explore how the young are affected by the media in terms of economic, societal, and educational conditions. David Buckingham, in "Life Without Markets? Childhood and Consumer Culture," conducts an in-depth study of the various ways in which children are conceptualized as consumers. Taking a different view at young media consumers, in the following chapter, Jordi Busquet and Ana Cynthia Uribe, aided by a team of 12 researchers, examine the cultural distance between adolescents and adults following the evolution from written culture and book culture to audiovisual and online media.

Further to the impact of the media on adolescents, Michael Walrave, Wannes Heirman, and Ellen Van Gool present an empirical study entitled "Connecting and Protecting? Adolescents, Social Network Sites, and Privacy," conducted on a sample of 350 Belgian preadolescents and adolescents aged 10 to 19. The study is concerned with the extent to which teenagers disclose personal data and use privacy settings when posting personal information on social network sites. Targeting a slightly older demographic, the chapter "Hyperreal Higher Education" brings to a close this section on media consumers in their formative stages. In this chapter, James Moir scrutinizes the unbridled trend towards media use in university teaching from a critical perspective and alerts us to such consequences as the demise of slow and thorough reading and comprehension for the sake of flexibility, constant re-skilling, and increased employability.

Indeed, the practice of unhurried and thorough reading of texts is at the heart of Part Three of the present volume. The arts and literature manifest a profound awareness regarding the new media environment. This may be due to the repeated crises and redefinitions experienced by this sector through the impact of the

Internet. It is equally likely, though, that the reason for this heightened attention lies in the fact that arts and entertainment provide spaces for a kind of creativity that is able to serve both as catalysts and as meta-media through which to explore and reflect on the new customs and social attitudes that emerge. Thus, Part Three of our volume, entitled "Mediated Life and Death in Arts and Entertainment[L7]," opens with Martin Lüthe's "'Infinite Deaths': The Death of and by the Media in David Foster Wallace's *Infinite Jest*," which examines the ways in which a truly original work of fiction may serve to show up the dynamics of addiction and, much more to the point here, the schizophrenic intricacies and insidious addictiveness of the entertainment media. In fact, the novel's message, made more poignant by the early death of its author, seems to presage nothing less than the demise of the mass media, along with its audiences, as we have known them thus far.

Literature is also the subject of Chapter 9, though with a significantly different focus on both literature and the audiovisual media. In "The Big Screen in the Transnational Novel," Jenine Abboushi submits an analysis of new ways to pen novels with "the big screen already written in." While her subject is not screen adaptation per se, she analyses a series of transnational novels by writers such as Somerset Maugham, Aravind Adiga, Jhumpa Lahiri, Hanif Kureishi, or Khaled Hosseini. She compellingly shows that many of these writers' novels were clearly conceived with the big screen adaptation in mind, owing to the desire to reach a wider, multicultural audience, a trend that portends the impending demise of the traditional conception of the novelistic genre.

Throughout the 20th century, the various disciplines of social communication have staked their respective claims and have established boundaries between the academic fields. The new media environment has deepened these divisions, and the various academic fields have found themselves compelled to thoroughly rethink their disciplines from the roots up. In the last section of our volume, we have included two chapters that examine these redefinitions in different media genres: journalism and public relations. In "Life Without a 'Liberal Representative' Journalism: Towards a Professional Deontology with a Deliberative Turn," María Lamuedra Graván conducts a field study in the area of public service broadcasting and assesses its possible role in an practicable form of deliberative democracy. The author asks whether the democratic political system ought to become less representative and more deliberative, and examines the relevance of public broadcast journalism in this context.

In the concluding chapter, Kathy Matilla and Guillem Marca provide an exhaustive state of the question on the management of potential conflicts, which they examine from a public-relations angle in their text "Issues Management as a

Mediated Activity in a Changing Media Sphere." From an initial panoramic vista, the discussion homes in on a specific idea, namely that for "issues management," it is imperative to review its theory and practice as soon as there are any significant changes in the nature of any of the four actors that make up the system. Indeed, the very *raison d'être* for this particular communication discipline lies in the internal dynamics among organizations, public authorities, citizens, and the media.

As did our conference, this volume took its inspiration from the current apocalyptic scenarios auguring that some media are destined to disappear. And through reductio ad absurdum we have taken the apocalyptic discourses of many media experts to a deliberately challenging extreme: Life Without Media. Imagining the death of the media has helped us see that they retain their vital force, but oftentimes they do change their behavior and their place and role in contemporary societies. Perhaps the deftness at thievery of the Greek messenger god has aided us in realizing the value and importance of what we have, but are in danger of losing.

References

Álvarez Monzonillo, J. M. (2010, January 8). Incertidumbres de la web 2.0. El País.

Berger, P., & Luckmann, T. (1966). *The social construction of reality: A treatise in the sociology of knowledge.* New York, NY: Doubleday Anchor Books.

Caldwell, C. (2009, October 23). The state and journalism. *Financial Times.*

Castells, M. (2009). *Communication power.* New York, NY: Oxford University Press.

Dayan D., & Katz, E. (1992). *Media events: The live broadcasting of history.* Cambridge, MA: Harvard University Press.

Downie, L., & Schudson, M. (2009, March 19). *The reconstruction of American journalism. Columbia Journalism Review.* Retrieved from http://www.cjr.org/reconstruction/the_reconstruction_of_american.php?page=all

Lippmann, W. (1922) *Public opinion.* New York, NY: Macmillan.

Martín Garzo, G. (2010, February 18). Elogio de la prensa escrita. *El País.*

Norris, P. (2000). *A virtuous circle: Political communications in postindustrial societies.* Cambridge, United Kingdom: Cambridge University Press.

Prensky, M. (2001, October). Digital natives, digital immigrants. *On the Horizon,* 9(5). Retrieved from http://www.marcprensky.com/writing/prensky%20%20digital%20natives,%20digital%20immigrants%20-%20part1.pdf

Rodicio, A., & López, C. (2010, February 27). *Informe semanal: Tormenta de papel. RTVE.* Retrieved from http://www.rtve.es/alacarta/videos/informe-semanal/informe-semanal-tormenta-papel/706730/

Sennett, R. (1977). *The fall of public man.* Cambridge, United Kingdom: Cambridge University Press.

Thompson, J. B. (1995). *Media and modernity: A social theory of the media.* Stanford, CA: Stanford University Press.

Tocqueville, A. (1992) *De la démocratie en Amérique* (1st ed. of Part 1, 1835, Part 2, 1840). Paris, France: Gallimard.

Wired. (2005, March). *The end of the world (as we know it).* Retrieved from http://www.wired.com/wired/archive/13.03

Part One. Exploring New Perspectives on Life and Media

1

The Public Sphere in a Network Age: Rethinking the Relations Between Self, Media, and Political Community

MARK BREWIN

Introduction

Theories of the modern public sphere assume a certain understanding of the self, one that more or less resembles what Charles Taylor has called the "buffered self" (2007): autonomous and rational, with the boundary between self and environment clearly defined. It also assumes a certain model of the media, in which a group of media producers (such as journalists) produce a message or set of messages for an audience of more or less autonomous, more or less rational citizens. These assumptions, taken together, led media scholars to ask a whole series of questions related to both the quality of the messages produced in the public sphere (for example, are they truly informative?) and to the competence of the political selves—that is to say, citizens—who were receiving those messages (for example, are they as rational as they should be?). The rise of new media technologies has changed the model of the public sphere, since the distinction between media producer and audience is no longer as clear as it once was. At the same time, cultural and economic changes have led to a different construction of the self, what we might call a postmodern or networked self, in which the boundaries between the individual and the environment are no longer so sharply defined. Taken together, the new social constructions of the self and of the media result in a new set of questions for media scholars in the 21st century.

In 1672, the English nobleman Roger L'Estrange, who was both an early Tory journalist and the king's censor, had this to say about the new information technology of his day: "A public mercury [a newspaper] should never have my vote, because I think it makes the multitude too familiar with the actions and counsels of their superiors, too pragmatical and censorious, and gives them not only an itch, but a kind of colourable right and licence to be meddling with the government" (quoted in Society for the Diffusion of Political Knowledge, 1833, p. 14). L'Estrange was only one of the earliest to voice concerns about the modern public's use (and misuse) of media. Over 300 years later, the American journalist Christopher Hedges was still worrying:

> The worse reality becomes, the less a beleaguered population wants to hear about it, and the more it distracts itself with squalid pseudo-events of celebrity breakdowns, gossip, and trivia. These are the debauched revels of a dying civilization. The most ominous cultural divide lies between those who chase after these manufactured illusions, and those who are able to puncture the illusions and confront reality. . . . This is the divide between a literate, marginalized minority and those who have been consumed by an illiterate mass culture. (2009, p. 190)

Hedges and L'Estrange are separated by time, politics, religion, and much else, and it is worth pointing out that they were critiquing very different kinds of media cultures. What the two men share is the clear understanding that a modern public is a mediated public: it depends upon the media for its sense of identity and its sense of power. Perversions in the media will ultimately result in a perverted politics. They also assume a similar outline to this public: a mass, or multitude, or population of individuals, some with greater or lesser abilities of discernment, and potentially critical of power and of power's representations.

In this paper, I take the notion of "life without media" to signal a changed social landscape in which traditional mass media play an increasingly less important role in the lives of individuals, and what Manuel Castells has called "mass self-communication" (2009, p. 55) plays an increasingly more important one, with media technologies understood here primarily as a set of *cultural practices* rather than an array of *artifacts* (see Marvin, 1990, p. 4). I hope to show that the arguments we've had about the public sphere in the past hundred years or so make sense, only given some important assumptions about the human subject, and that subject's relationship to the world and to other people, which were the result of the intersection of specific technological, cultural, political, and economic regimes. Predictions of the rise of the "network society" (Castells, 2000a, 2000b, 2004) and the "networked self" (Wittel, 2001; Papachirissi, 2010), suggest a radical re-visioning of public life, but my primary interest here is not with empirical claims about how people may be using communication technologies in the 21st century. It is, rather, about the ways in which we mentally construct our media cultures. Thus my focus will be on dominant intellectual constructions, and how changes in these constructions can be expected to change the questions that we ask about ourselves as political animals and media users.

The Individual, the Public, and the Media

It is common within modern social theory to posit a tension between the individual and society. On the one hand, many critics have been worried that modern culture is overly solicitous of the needs of the individual subject, often driven by the imprecations of modern consumer culture and its focus on individual desire and egoistic fulfillment. The fear has been that the modern subject is so concerned with her personal moral and material happiness that any sense of the larger good disappears (Bellah, Madsen, Sullivan, Swidler, & Tipton, 1985; Lasch, 1979; Macpherson, 1962; Pooley, 2010; Putnam, 2000; Taylor, 1992; Sennett, 1976). Fairly early on, Alexis de Tocqueville predicted that modern individualism, if left unchecked, would confine the modern democratic subject "wholly in the solitude of his own heart" (2000, p. 484). But Tocqueville was also anxious over the way in which the democratic community could overwhelm the individual and force her into conformity, through the "tyranny of the majority" (2000, pp. 239–242), a concern echoed in Søren Kierkegaard's essay on *The Present Age* (1962). In the 20th century, the two phenomena—excessive egoism and excessive conformity—were combined in the concept of mass society (Horkheimer & Adorno, 1944/2002, p. 95).

This tension between the individual and the group should not, however, blind us to the fact that the distinctiveness of the democratic public lies precisely in it being a *community of individuals*. To be more precise, it is a community of what Charles Taylor has described as "buffered selves" (Taylor, 2007, pp. 37–41, see also Taylor, 1992). The buffered self is one that sees a clear distinction between its own moral and physical boundaries and those of the world. It is, or at least conceives of itself to be, autonomous, and thus issues of personal freedom, self-expression, and personal enlightenment and fulfillment are keys to what this self understands as "the good life." The moral superiority of the modern democratic public supposedly lies in its ability to protect and encourage the conditions of life that allow for individual flourishing along these lines: the group exists for the sake of the individual, not the other way around.

Modern democracy connects disparate individuals through cultivating an awareness that by joining together, they are best able to promote their individual freedoms, security, property, and happiness. Thus, the modern democratic citizen faces her fellow citizens as a separate but equal person, cooperatively and freely engaged on the common project of protecting the liberty of each person within the community. The similarity between this model of political life and the emerging theory of a capitalist economy, in which individual subjects confront one another in the marketplace to barter and exchange money, goods, and services, is surely no accident. The modern subject *possesses* rights and freedoms, just as he *possesses* property and labor (Macpherson, 1962). An economic system built upon a series of contracts between individuals is consequently able to develop.

This theory of the modern public is at the same time a theory of the modern media. Media are essential to the proper functioning of the public because the modern media allow the individuals who make up the modern public to communicate with one another and to coordinate their actions. They provide modern citizens with information about their outside environment and about the actions of the state: in the formulation of midcentury functionalists, the media perform the duties of correlation and surveillance (Wright, 1986). They do more than this, however. As Gabriel Tarde notes, the modern press actually creates the public, insofar as this public is brought together by shared beliefs and interests, and in the *awareness* of these shared beliefs and interests (Tarde, 1969, p. 278). A theoretical ancestor to Benedict Anderson's (2006) imagined community, Tarde's public only comes into existence once its members are able to connect themselves spiritually without ever physically meeting one another, although Tarde adds the necessity for these mass-mediated messages to enter into, and provide the spark for, interpersonal communication. The member of the modern public not only reads what is in the newspaper (or watches what's on the television), she talks about it—at the office, or in the coffee shop, or on the subway, or at the dinner party. Public opinion is thereby created. (Tarde thus combines the notion of the imagined mediated community with a theory of media's effects interacting with interpersonal networks, presaging the work of the Columbia school some 40 years later [Katz, 1996]). One implication of this argument is that the public cannot have existed prior to the invention of the printing press.

Once we realize that the theory of the modern public is also a theory of the modern media, we can see the parallels between the public and the media audience (in English, at least, the term *public* can often serve as a synonym for *audience*, as when we speak of the "listening public for NPR," or "the public for serious literature.") Like the public person, the audience member presents herself as a private individual: as a citizen or a consumer (within mainstream discourse these are often, importantly, conflated), and also, potentially, as a critic. She reads her newspaper silently to herself at the morning table, or listens to the radio in the car, or watches television in her living room. The text confronts her as a thing apart from her, but one that nevertheless makes a claim upon her for its relevance to her life. Ideally, she is meant to think about the message, to weigh it, to determine for herself its truth value. If she is convinced, she acts. She votes, or writes a letter to her representative, or goes to the mall. And where does she find the resources to make a reasoned decision on the text? From qualities arising within her own self, and obtained through natural gifts or through education and socialization: a minimum level of intelligence, a set of commitments to the public welfare, an ability to gauge the veracity of a source, a critical ability to consider various elements of the question.

The media's public role also comes through the notion of critical reflection. The ideal modern public exercises a critical reason on all aspects of public life, and it is this exercise of individuals reasoning together in public that justifies the modern political regime (Habermas, 1962/1989, p. 28). Thus there are no formal boundaries to public discussion. Anything is open to critical scrutiny. This leads soon enough to self-criticism, both on the part of the public and of the various individuals who compose it. The reader of the text is able to stop, reflect, criticize the thoughts put forth on the page in a way that is much more difficult to do with a speech, or a song, or a rite. The modern technology of reading encouraged the development of the sense of self separate from the outside world, a subject more prone to think about itself in a critical or reflective manner (Ong, 1982, p. 129). Within the cultural moment of early modern life, given an economic, religious, and cultural context already predisposed to emphasize the importance of the buffered self and that self's duty to reflection and internal criticism, the printed text presents itself as a tool through which to accomplish these tasks. On a related point, Michael McKeon has argued that a central change in public life during the early modern period was the move away from tacit knowledge toward explicit knowledge. The mystical, tacitly assumed unity of the secular and the sacred through the kingship falls into question the moment that such a theory is explicitly articulated. As McKeon notes, "Print is the very mechanism by which the tacit is made explicit" (2005, p. 49; see also Gouldner, 1976, pp. 39–44). It is precisely this moment that Roger L'Estrange fears in 1672: not the specific questions aimed at the government, but the very act of questioning itself, which leads to the creation of a critical public.

Debates Over the Modern Public Sphere

The brief argument sketched out above is not meant to provide a full theory of the modern liberal public or the modern self, but rather to suggest that a certain way of thinking about selves has implications for a certain way of thinking about public life, and also for how we think about media. The crucial role of media in the equation explains why criticisms of modern democratic politics so often turn into mass-media critiques. Indeed, this model of the public has provided the framework for much debate over media in the past century, and has driven a good deal of media research as well. Generally, these debates and this research revolve around two questions. First, is the media audience *competent* to perform the sort of critical, public-minded responsibilities that are required of them for the theory to make sense? Second, are media texts the kinds of texts that can create an active, democratic public such as theorized by Tarde and others?

We can see elements of both these concerns in the quote from Chris Hedges given at the beginning of the paper. Hedges makes an explicit distinction between two types of media audience, or mediated public. There are on the one hand those who "chase after . . . manufactured illusions," who are part of an "illiterate mass culture." On the other, there are those who are "able to puncture the illusions and confront reality." The latter group, according to Hedges, is a "marginalized" minority: the larger and more influential group consists of those people too lazy and/or too stupid to see through the mediated mess of the present moment. Such a concern has a long history, and comes in both conservative and radical variants (Lippmann, 1922/1997; 1925/1993; Marcuse, 1964).

The other element of modern media critique—which often goes hand in hand with worries over the audience—focuses on the shortcomings of the mass-mediated text itself. The emphasis here is on the issue of what Jürgen Habermas and others term "systematically distorted communication" (Crossley, 2004), which refers to the fact that the modern mass-mediated text does not and perhaps cannot provide the kind of information that a democratic public requires. This is due to the domination of corporate or state interests, whose power would suffer irreparable harm if modern media audiences gained access to the truth about economic, political, and social inequalities in the modern world. The structure of the mass media, in which a single entity is able to control the flow of information by establishing control over the central source through which information must pass—be this a television station, a movie studio, or a printing press—allows for this de facto censorship to take place. Sometimes the media simply withhold information; sometimes they twist it, so that the information is turned to the advantage of the status quo or framed in such a way as to neuter the message's political effects; but the most popular method of dealing with politically sensitive news is simply to overwhelm it with consumer culture and celebrity gossip. The literature that addresses this broad style of media critique is vast, but examples would include the work of Noam Chomsky (2003), Herbert Schiller (1973), Armand Mattelart (1996), Guy Debord (1967/1994), and Manuel Vázquez Montalbán (2008).

The Liberal Self Re-examined

Given that the modern constructions of public and private self are so closely related, and that the role of media is central to any understanding of the modern democratic public, and given the way our conceptions of our political lives are so intimately tied up with our understanding of our economic situations, it stands to reason that a change in the understanding of the individual subject—particularly as a political being—a change in economic conditions, or a change in the dominant technological regime, will result in important changes in our theories of public life as well. In fact, in the past 30 years, modern societies have seen shifts in all three of these realms of human experience.

Take the refashioning of the political subject. Since the advent of structuralist thought, an important alternative conception of the self has begun to take shape in modern life, competing with the older idea of the buffered or liberal subject. Within a world that could only be approached via a series of signifiers, playing off one another and forming, in the intersections between terms, a set of meanings that constantly shifted as the language itself evolved, often in highly complex and unpredictable ways, the human self became simply one more sign in a series of signs. The self was the product of a set of semiotic differences or, as Michel Foucault would later have it, the various strategies of channels of power pulsing through modern social networks. At about the same time, cybernetic theory was attempting a somewhat similar deconstruction of modern notions of the autonomous self. The initial aim of theorists like Norbert Wiener was probably to work on behalf of the liberal conception of society, as N. Katherine Hayles (1999) has suggested. Under the onslaught of cybernetics proponents like Warren McCulloch, however, the idea of the autonomous liberal self became increasingly tenuous, as the traditional barriers that defined that self—such as the distinction between human mind and machine—came to be questioned: the mind was mechanized (Dupuy, 2000). With the advent of second-order cybernetics, and the inclusion of the theorist herself into the system she was attempting to objectively describe (Krippendorff, 2009), the concept of an autonomous self receded ever farther into the distance.

No longer was the human individual seen as radically separated from the environment, attempting to critically understand something fundamentally other. Rather, humans were conceptualized as elements within a system, interacting with other elements, constantly affecting and being affected, not only by other people but all other beings, whether "conscious" or not. When he attempted to explain the workings of consciousness, Gregory Bateson (1972) labeled his work an "ecology of mind," signaling the operation of human thought could no longer be considered separately from the environments in which it existed.

In sum, social theory was leading us away from the buffered self, back to a sense of a more porous self, a move summarized by the following comment from anthropologist Victor Turner:

> Members of our species are peculiarly festooned with prepositions, with relational and functional connectives. If we are, visibly, islands, we are genetically and culturally linked by ties of love and hate, by the pleasure bond, by the pain bond, by the duty chain, by noblesse oblige, or by innate or induced needs for dominance or submission. We are for, against, with, toward, above, below, against, (sic) within, outside, or without one another. If we could make a psychosomatogram of a member of our species, it would not be smoothly nude but sprouting with prepositional lines and plugs, and pitted with prepositional holes (1984, p. 19).

Turner's argument here suggests influences both from the structuralist/post-structuralist literature (the references to "prepositional lines and plugs") and to cybernetic ideas of connectivity to others and to the environment. It also makes a nice fit with the image of the modern media user, constantly in contact with others through a series of information lines sprouting, not literally from the body (at least not yet), but from smart phones, iPads, netbooks, and computer terminals. In such a world, the Enlightenment citizen, bravely confronting tradition and superstition with his individual reason and moral sensibility, no longer makes much sense. Nor does a theory of the public that both depends upon the efforts of these various reasoning, autonomous individuals to devise a way forward, and depends as well on the sense of individual freedom to ultimately justify itself.

This is significant, because about the same time as the modern self was being re-imagined, important changes were taking place in mediated communication. One aspect of this related to how messages were stored and transferred. New technologies allowed for greater manipulation on the part of the users, and allowed as well for the possibility of technological "convergence," that is, for media devices that could combine features of earlier media forms. While possibilities for the manipulation of media messages existed long before this, what the new technologies did was allow for this manipulation to become a popular option: no longer limited to computer programmers or television producers but to high school students and stay-at-home moms. The second important element to the changes was the development of networks that could link media users together without the need of intervening media institutions like television networks or newspapers. The creation of the modern imagined community was once unthinkable without the mass media. Now, people could create their own community through newsgroups, chat rooms, and other forms of online communication (Rheingold, 2000).

In an earlier age, the idea of creating a genuine or "authentic" community that lacked personal interaction or shared physical space would have been regarded with some suspicion. But the skepticism that postmodernism, poststructuralism, and deconstruction had introduced toward all manner of social institutions made for a more welcoming atmosphere to these new publics, which existed *only* in mediated space. If individuals could not find the sort of support and human connection that they needed through more traditional forms of public gathering, then the online community seemed a reasonable and humane alternative (Turkle, 1997). This could be the case in particular for members of groups who felt themselves isolated within their physical locales: secular-minded individuals living within fundamentalist religious environments, for example, or gay men and women living in strongly conservative communities. In such cases, the possibilities offered by online communication offered a freedom and potential for honest expression outside traditional media forms. Throughout the course of the 1990s and into the early 2000s, as more and more people become more familiar with the online world, the potential for the development of public identity through participation in online communication became increasingly manifest: witness, for example, how opponents to the war in Iraq used communication such as blog sites and chat rooms to create, from a nearly taboo set of propositions, a significant protest voice against the Bush administration's efforts to silence them.

So too, the fluid nature of information online made a nice fit with the postmodern understanding of personal identity as a shifting, ambiguous, unstable set of attributes. Poststructuralists had attacked what they saw as the overly rigid understanding of modern subjectivity, the notion that one had a stable "self" that lasted over the course of a lifetime, which confronted the world as a free, autonomous and independent being. Such a self-conception, again linked to Enlightenment thinking, was taken to be not only insufficiently attuned to the ways in which the world makes up one's sense of self, but also a method for controlling the subject: by defining individuals as unchanging and unchangeable, modern institutions could better control them. A more fluid understanding of subjectivity allowed people to escape labels and categories into which they were previously forced. Given the unstable nature of information on the Internet, the ways in which it allowed users to construct a new identity for themselves online (changing gender, race, class, even species), new media was a natural fit for this newer understanding of identity. An early exploration of this came in Sherry Turkle's (1997) *Life on the Screen.* Through ethnographic research and interviews conducted with computer users in the early 1990s, Turkle provided an image of a world in which people no longer had to accept the identity that society, or their parents, or their peers, had decided for them. They could choose to be someone or something else online.

If modern media practices encouraged users to think of their identities in a less rigid fashion, it also highlighted the fact that they were not isolated individuals living alone in an urban jungle, but rather members of dense, extensive personal and technological networks. From the beginnings of the ARPANET in the 1960s, digital technology promoted the sharing of information and the development of relationships across space, first through email and Usenet groups, then through the World Wide Web and the various forms of information sharing—personal web pages, blogs, social networking sites—that it has spawned. The web does not merely allow for the creation of networks: it requires the existences of strong networks in order to reach anything like its full potential. Thus for the media user of the 21st century, the notion of a cybernetic system of various elements operating closely in connection with one another and constantly impacting each other through exchanges of information makes intuitive sense. The idea of the heroic lone individual, doing his or her own thing, does not last long on the Internet.

To the extent that the modern citizen is a member of a network, engaged in the co-construction of media texts (Wikipedia, Facebook "wall" pages, Twitter feeds) or media forms (Linux and other forms of open-source software), then she is no longer part of the public audience that consumes media that elite producers create (Bruns, 2008). The barrier between the individual user and the medium dissolves—she is now part of the mediating process, and some modern news sites, such as the short-lived Soitu site in Spain, have made it a policy to recruit users as co-producers of content (González, 2010). In such cases, each node on the network—the figure that might once have been represented variously by terms such as *consumer* or *critic*—contributes part, but only part, of the whole. This style of community begins to look a great deal like Durkheim's notion of organic solidarity, with each part of the organism differentiated but dependent upon the other elements within the system (Durkheim, 1984). Just as Durkheim's organic sociability did not do away with individuality but rather required it, built upon it, so too does the network. The communal form introduced by the modern multimedia is no "hive mind," but rather a vast interconnection of individuals, each dependent upon one another and aware of that dependency.

The background to all of this has been an ongoing shift in the modern capitalist economies, toward an increasingly globalized market and production process, and the growing importance of the so-called information or knowledge economy, i.e., an economy based on the production of and manipulation of symbols rather than of material goods. This economic shift may have encouraged the changes in technology and the social imaginary just described: certainly it made a good fit with them. The affinity between postmodern culture and the postmodern notion of the self, and a late capitalist global economy, had been noted as early as the 1980s by cultural critics such as Fredric Jameson (1991) and Terry Eagleton, the latter suggesting in a 1985 essay that late capitalism had deconstructed the subject much more efficiently than poststructuralist meditations on the literary text (1985, p. 71). Likewise, Castells has noted the way that technological advances in computing technology allowed modern businesses to adapt to a shifting economic landscape: industry innovations pushed technological innovation, and vice versa (2000a, pp. 184–186).

To sum up, then, both the new media environment and the new economic environment allowed members of the postmodern public to put into practice a number of the ideas that had already achieved a kind of intellectual currency by the time that computers, the Internet, and then later mobile devices and social networking sites had become popular media forms. These new media, at least in the manner in which they eventually came to be used, made a good fit with many of the alternative models of public life that had sprung up in the wake of growing dissatisfaction with the modern media, and with the relationship between individual and group that these older media had seemed to presume. This affected not only how we thought about media, but how we used it. By the millions, new media users, particularly the young, who had never known alternative ways of public life and public discourse, were enacting the sort of shifting and highly integrated social identities that social critics of the 1970s and 1980s had been promoting.

From the Public Sphere to the Network Society

What are the implications of these changes for how we think about public life? To begin to answer that question, we need to start with the idea of separation. The citizen as autonomous, buffered individual is both part of, but at the same time separate from, the public. His identity as citizen derives from his membership in the group—hence its importance, and the moral demand to accede to its opinion

(Tocqueville's tyrannical public opinion). At the same time, because he is a distinct individual, there is always the theoretical possibility of dissent: the citizen can create some distance from, and criticize, widely held beliefs and assumptions. In fact, the greatest heroes of the democratic age are defined precisely by their ability to stand apart from the crowd, to speak unpopular truths. This holds even more strongly for the member of the mass audience, who consumes the mediated message but is never a part of the message, since that message is created by "experts" like movie directors, journalists, music producers. While the fear is that the audience member will be manipulated by the product (which is alien to the audience but pretends to be part of it, i.e., pretends to be a "popular" message), the potential is there for her to "see through" the media's myths and debunk their pretensions. Consequently, part of media reformers' efforts have always focused on educating the audience, enlightening them, and thereby giving them the tools to engage in a popular critique of the consumerist culture.

For the member of the network, the matter is much different. Somewhat paradoxically, while the network is less central to his moral conception of selfhood, it is also more difficult for him to criticize. It is less central to the construction of self because one is not part of a single network but multiple ones. Indeed, modern social capital increases as the number of one's networks increases (Wittel, 2001). Thus no single network can lay claim to the individual's central allegiances—the way in which, for example, being part of a national, or religious, or class-based public once did. Moreover, as Castells characterizes them (2000a, pp. 180–184), networks are not stable things: they exist for a certain time period, often for the purpose of accomplishing a specific task (or in the case of personal networks, for a circumscribed period of time). This fits, of course, with the unstable postmodern self: as I change, as my needs, desires, interests, and life experiences change, so will my networks.

At the same time, however, the individual is much more important to the proper working of the network: no longer one single member of a "mass" of people, the networked individual is assumed to have distinctive skills that can contribute to the network's success. If she does not produce, or simply leaves the network, it will suffer accordingly. Conversely, the health of the network—its success, its prestige—will reflect on her. In media terms, this can be seen in the way that modern media enlist the audience of content to become producers of content. Indeed, in the most innovative of the new media projects, the distinction between audience and producer disappears. The audience is the producer, or perhaps easier to say, any audience member at one moment can turn into a media producer at the next. This aspect of the new media is generally celebrated for its democratic and creative potential (Kelly, 2011; Shirky, 2010), but it has its dangers as well. It is much harder to see the problematic aspects of a news story when you yourself have been involved in writing it. Where does the criticism come from?

The answer is it comes from other networks, generally competing ones. As they struggle for power within a defined social arena—say for example, politics—members of various networks are assumed to be keeping track of other networks. The most conscientious and effective critics of the excesses of right-wing political blogs are left-wing political bloggers, and vice versa. As a system, therefore, the networked media ensure a kind of self-correction, to replace the correction of the individual critique of public opinion and the mass media (a critique that, alas, only too rarely appeared, and when it did, was all too often and all too easily squelched). The problem with this solution, or at least a tension within it, comes from the fact that this criticism rarely leads to any kind of dialogue. The internal critique of the modern public or of the media audience was also a member of that public or audience, and therefore could find some sense of common ground with opponents. This rarely happens in the blogosphere: what we get instead are flame wars, trolls, and banishments from the site.

If the theoretical problem of internal critique changes with the shift from public to network, so too does the question of power. In the modern mass-mediated system of communication, power was exercised one of two ways—through the central production point, and/or through control of the distribution systems for these centrally produced messages. The only groups wealthy and powerful enough to control such centralized systems were corporations and states, who were therefore often able to exercise a form of censorship (more or less explicit) over what messages made it to the mass media audience. This solar-type of media system is replaced in the modern network age with a system that lacks a center, so various channels of information interweave, pass through and by and over one another (Ramonet, 2011). Such a system makes control of content much more difficult, as modern media corporations and modern states have increasingly discovered. But an end to modern styles of censorship does not mean an end to control. Increasingly in a networked world, power will be exercised in three different ways. The first is the power over code, instead of content. No communication system (at least no system that is popularly used) allows users to send just anything: the most obvious example of this is the number of characters limited to any Twitter post. Controlling the means of text production by laying down the initial rules of the game through the production of control becomes far more important in the networked age than through managing content itself, if only because the decentralized nature of the new media makes the latter so increasingly implausible. The second way of exercising control over messages is through directing users' attention: given the large number of messages that can be accessed by almost any modern media user, and the impossibility of accessing anything more than a minute fraction of these messages, power will accrue to search engines, and information accumulators who can direct users to one message rather than another. Finally, power is exercised through the network itself. In the modern public, a central point of contention centered on who was considered a legitimate player, and who was not. In a networked society, the notion of insider and outsider becomes more complicated. There is no longer a "mainstream" from which one may or may not be excluded. The method of ensuring one's own success relative to others is now to ensure the success of one's network vis-à-vis its competitors.

A Thought Experiment

When we try to get a glimpse of our mediated future, we are peering through a very dark glass indeed, and would do well to remind ourselves of that fact before making overly confident predictions. Ten years ago, Facebook and Twitter did not even exist. Twenty-five years ago there was no such thing as the World Wide Web or an Internet browser. Empirical work that has been done on how people use new media suggests a number of different possible paths to where we might end up, some of which look more like our present age (Hindman, 2009; Webster & Ksiazek, 2012) than others (Benkler, 2006; Prior, 2007; Uricchio, 2009). Thus to posit a world in which the tendencies that I have outlined above have in fact come to fruition—in which digital media networks have more or less entirely replaced mass media, and in which the more porous selves of postmodernity have replaced the buffered selves of the modern age—is less an exercise in futurology than it is an attempt to think through, and to press to their logical conclusions, certain ways of conceptualizing and acting upon the media that exist in the present.[1]

With that understanding, then, let's suppose that in this imagined future, a piece of information is brought forth that suggests some fact of political importance for at least some segment of the population. Say, for example, the minister of health was caught on tape making sexist remarks about a female colleague. In the world of mass media, that sort of information would have come from the press, if it had come from anyone at all. In the world of mass self-communication, the press no longer acts as the Fourth Estate, as gatekeeper and defender of the public interest, because there no longer is a single public whose interests can plausibly be defended. The decline of the general-interest media market means that the economic model of the traditional news media comes under severe stress (Grueskin, Seave,

& Graves, 2011), and the evolution of "the" public into multiple publics results in a splintering of a shared mediated space in which this information would have made sense (Sunstein, 2007). Increasingly lacking any common touchstones, the various members of competing groups within the modern networked society can no longer agree on the facts themselves, a phenomenon recently illustrated in the 2012 U.S. presidential election, when supposedly objective information such as polling and economic data was criticized for partisan bias (Kucinich, 2012; Potter, 2012).

So in the current case, a more likely source for this information would probably be a blog, or perhaps the website of a feminist activist group. Here we run into another important difference between a mass-mediated environment and a networked age. How does information become politically relevant, or how does it fail to? In the mass-media age, the journalist was the person designated to seek out information on behalf of the public. Due to specialized skills, dedicated resources (on the part of the journalistic institution), and distinctive channels of access, as well as a "news judgment" that allowed him to distinguish relevant from irrelevant stories, the journalist was supposed to get to the public what it needed to know. The public would then consider that information, and act on it (or not). Of course, very often information failed to reach the public because of efforts by centralized authorities to bury it. In this particular case, we could imagine that the minister's press office might pressure journalists or editors not to report on the event. Or a shared culture between reporters and politicians—the "old boys" club—would mean that the reporters did not even consider turning the occasion into a story.[2] In the case of digital self-produced media, however, such tactics would be unlikely to work: the political sympathies of the journalists, as well as changing economic logics (such outlets might be nonprofit, or in any case too small to worry about backlash from advertisers), would mean that pressures to keep silent had little or no effect. However, this lack of institutional coercion certainly does not mean that relevant stories would always find their way to citizens. The problem for the new media journalist is not too much control over her activities from on high; rather it is the lack of resources. In the case of activist networks of websites and social media platforms, the reason that the story would fail to reach the public is because these smaller outlets, with more limited means, simply didn't hear about it. The most likely way that the information reached them would be through personal channels (and some luck): perhaps a friend who overheard the remarks passed it on to a blogger, or someone took a video of the minister and posted it online.

In other words, in an age without media, this sort of information would come to light more or less by chance, not by method. If someone did manage to uncover it, however, and if the remarks were considered provocative enough, then the story might start to move. First it would travel through one network of activists, and then to other networks that were connected to the first. That is, various linked sites might start to link to other sites carrying the remarks, or the video. Individual members of the network might remark upon it through social media or via emails to friends. The extent to which the information spread would depend on the network connections, or better yet, the connections established by at least one node along the information path. Still, large segments of the population, not being part of any of the networks involved in the spread of the story, would remain totally ignorant of the remarks and of any anger created by them. A possible exception to this might be networks diametrically opposed to the political sympathies of the original source: politically engaged conservatives. In that case, the information would be used to illustrate the perfidy, or perhaps simply the inanity, of ideological opponents.

In the world of the traditional public sphere, a news story becomes politically significant to the extent that some group of interested citizens can convince a large enough segment of their fellow citizens that the story matters. This is where debate and discussion takes place. Feminist spokespeople in the traditional public sphere might argue that the remarks provide clear evidence of the minister's inability to do his job effectively, and push for his resignation; conservative opponents would then respond that the remarks are a personal affair, or that their meaning is not the one that feminists wish to assign. Both groups would be attempting to sway the larger public opinion. In the world of networks, such debate would be unlikely to take place. Given the political assumptions of the members of the network, which would be obvious simply by the fact that they are members of the particular network, the meaning of the remarks would be taken as self-evident. Moreover, extensive debate of the issue would be constrained by the communication technologies used in the spread of the information. Twitter, Facebook, and other forms of social media that limit the number of words one can use in the transmission of a message are not conducive to nuanced dialogue. For these reasons, we might expect communication to center on the appropriate response to the scandal, rather than a deep investigation into, or interpretation of, the meaning of the event. The question of whether the remarks translate into public action, in other words, depends less on the issue of persuasion than on the issue of connections. If the story can connect to enough nodes along various networks, then members of those networks will agree to take action: perhaps stage a street protest. It may only be at this final moment when the newly formed political group becomes aware of its actual power. That is to say, if enough people are motivated to participate in the action, then members of the various networks involved will see this embodied in the streets.

Here we might note another paradox of the new media age, which is that the city itself becomes both less and more important to politics. At one level, physical space might seem to be less important in the age of the digital network, because community is no longer tied to geography. Networks move past traditional physical boundaries with barely a thought, to the extent that the phrase "global network" is almost redundant. At another level, though, and particularly when we move from discussion to political action, physical space would retain its centrality. In the age of the mass media, the city was only one of the elements that members of the public shared with each other. They also met—imaginatively, if you will, or virtually—through the shared use of media. In an age without media, where mediated forums are no longer shared by the entire population, the city becomes a far more important element in the construction of a political movement or a political body. It remains one of the few, and perhaps in cases of extreme media fragmentation, the only space in which the population as a whole can recognize itself, and realize its own strength.

The result of all this imagined communication are political bodies that are more fractious and active, but less ideologically diverse. More willing to hold power to account, these groups are less able to plausibly do so in the name of some general public interest. They may find it easier to make connections between a public event and their own private lives, as in our imagined case, in which many of the angered members of the network could relate the minister's remarks with events in their own history. However, because these connections are so personal, it may be difficult for others outside their networks, people who do not share the same personal characteristics, to feel similarly affected. The public sphere in the end would be a less stable and less rational space, because conversation and even debate across groups would be more difficult. At the same time, the problem of motivating citizens to act and to challenge power on their own behalf might no longer be as severe as it has traditionally been in most Western, media-saturated societies.

Conclusion

Too often, debates over the democratic potential of modern media are framed as a clash between utopians and dystopians, with the former arguing that new media will bring in a world of equality and true democracy (Kelly, 2011; Shirky, 2010; Rheingold, 2000), and the latter suggesting that they will allow the powerful to exert ever tighter controls over us (Andrejevec, 2004, 2006; Barney, 2000). Historically, these sorts of shifts are rare. More commonly, new technologies provide populations with new opportunities on the one hand, new constraints on the other. Modern democratic populations will continue to face attempts at control on the part of powerful groups and individuals. To the extent that these forms of control are part of a networked society and individualized media, the strategies needed to combat them and the questions our theories address to them will look much different than the ones used in an older world. This chapter has tried to think through how and why these changes might happen, using as an organizing device the relationship between our conceptions of self, of democratic community, and of media use. In order to simplify the comparison, I developed two models, along the lines of Weberian ideal types: on the one hand, the modern individual as member of the political (and mediated) mass; on the other, the networked nodal point of the new media age. These types were unapologetically theoretical—first, because this helped dramatize the differences between the two cultures; second, because the discourse surrounding our use of communication technologies matters when it comes to understanding how real people use those technologies. Fernando Bermejo has observed that it is absolutely essential for communication scholars to study not only communication practices, but also the theories that we create about those practices, since the reflexive nature of the discipline means that "theories and concepts used to describe society and communication re-enter their object of study and contribute to changing it" (Bermejo, 2007, p. 1). As tools for shaping and reshaping our common lives together, the media need to be thought of not simply in terms of their formal capabilities, nor even in terms of their response to a set of social and economic conditions, but in terms of the ways that we imagine ourselves using them.

Such meta-theoretical reflections can lead to constructive and important changes in the sorts of empirical questions we ask. Take for example the well-known media personality and owner, Rupert Murdoch. In the past, Murdoch's relevance to media studies has been due to the fact that he owns so many different kinds of media outlets, and therefore can exert inordinate influence over what kind of information is sent out into the public realm (Sergeant, 2011). This is a legitimate concern in an age of mass media, and Murdoch's power over the images that we see and the words that we read will continue to be an issue for some time. In a life without (mass) media, however, this sort of power becomes increasingly problematic, as Murdoch's own inability to control the discussion surrounding his newspapers' wire-tapping activities suggests. This does not mean that Murdoch becomes less important, but it may mean that he becomes less important as a media mogul. His relevance—or the relevance of people like him—may in the future turn more on his status as a key node within a specific network, or a node that links one network with another (Castells, 2009, p. 429). Along somewhat different lines, the significance of recent populist protests in countries such as Israel, Spain, Greece, and the United States may lie less with their status as outsider groups attempting to break through the dominance of mainstream discourse, and more in their ability (or inability) to craft productive links with other, like-minded groups that could maintain and deepen their activities (Kulish, 2011). Such questions initially may seem strange to communication researchers who have grown up in a mass-mediated universe. Nevertheless, if communication is to continue to speak to the concerns of the present, we need to take them seriously, or risk fundamentally misunderstanding the power dynamics of the 21st century.

Endnotes

1 Some recent work in media archaeology has dealt with the histories of imaginary media. Part of the idea behind this approach is that the discourses surrounding fictional media artifacts can often be as illuminating as discourses surrounding actually existing media (Kluitenberg, 2006, 2011). Something similar is being attempted here, although the imaginary media in this case lies in the future, rather than the past.

2 Moreover, within a culture that clearly delineated the spaces between public and private, it is unlikely that such behavior would have been thought newsworthy in the first place. In the postmodern public sphere, on the other hand, the personal very quickly turns political.

References

Anderson, B. (2006). *Imagined communities: Reflections on the origin and spread of nationalism* (Rev. ed.). London, United Kingdom: Verso.

Andrejevec, M. (2004). The webcam subculture and the digital enclosure. In N. Couldry & A. McCarthy (Eds.), *Mediaspace: Place, scale and culture in a media age* (pp. 193–208). New York, NY: Routledge.

Andrejevec, M. (2006). *iSpy: Surveillance and power in the interactive era.* Lawrence: University Press of Kansas.

Barney, D. (2000). *Prometheus wired: The hope for democracy in the age of network technology.* Chicago, IL: University of Chicago.

Bateson, G. (1972). *Steps to an ecology of mind.* New York, NY: Ballantine Books.

Bellah, R., Madsen, R., Sullivan, W. M., Swidler, A., & Tipton, S.(1985). *Habits of the heart: Individualism and commitment in American life.* Berkeley: University of California Press.

Benkler, Y. (2006). *The wealth of networks: How social production transforms markets and Freedom.* New Haven, CT: Yale.

Bermejo, F. (2007).*The Internet audience: Constitution and measurement.* New York, NY: Peter Lang.

Bruns, A. (2008). *Blogs, Wikipedia, Second Life, and beyond: From production to produsage.* New York, NY: Peter Lang.

Castells, M. (2000a). *The rise of the network society* (2nd ed.). Malden, MA: Blackwell.

Castells, M. (2000b). *End of millennium* (2nd ed.). Malden, MA: Blackwell.

Castells, M. (2004). *The power of identity* (2nd ed.). Malden, MA: Blackwell.

Castells, M. (2009). *Communication power.* New York, NY: Oxford University Press.

Chomsky, N. (2003). *Media control: The spectacular achievements of propaganda* (2nd ed.). New York: Open Media/Seven Stories Press.

Crossley, N. (2004). On systematically distorted communicated: Bourdieu and the socio-analysis of publics. In N. Crossley & M. Roberts (Eds.), *After Habermas: New perspectives on the public sphere* (pp. 88–112). Malden, MA: Blackwell.

Debord, G. (1967/1994). *Society of the spectacle* (D. Nicholson-Smith, trans.). New York: Zone Books.

Dupuy, J.-P. (2000). *The mechanization of the mind: On the origins of cognitive science.* Princeton, NJ: Princeton University Press.

Durkheim, E. (1984). *The division of labor in society* (W. D. Halls, trans.). New York: The Free Press.

Eagleton, T. (1986, July/August). Capitalism, modernism, and postmodernism. *The New Left Review, I*(152), 60–73.

González, J. L. (2010). Auge y caída de Soitu, un ejemplo de medio nativo digital en España. *Comunicación y Sociedad, 23*(2), 267–288.

Gouldner, A. (1976). *The dialectic of ideology and technology.* New York, NY: Oxford University Press.

Grueskin, B, Seave, A., & Graves, L. (2011). *The story so far: What we know about the business of digital journalism.* New York, NY: Columbia Journalism School, Tow Center for Digital Journalism.

Habermas, J. (1962/1989). *The structural transformation of the public sphere: An inquiry into a category of bourgeois society* (T. Burger & F. Lawrence, trans.). Cambridge, MA: MIT Press.

Hayles, N. K. (1999). *How we became posthuman: Virtual bodies in cybernetics, literature, and informatics.* Chicago, IL: University of Chicago Press.

Hedges, C. (2009). *Empire of illusion: The end of literacy and the triumph of spectacle.* New York: Nation Books.

Hindman, M. (2009). *The myth of digital democracy.* Princeton, NJ: Princeton University Press.

Horkheimer, M., & Adorno, T. A. (1944/2002). *Dialectic of enlightenment* (E. Jephcott, trans.). Stanford, CA: Stanford University Press.

Jameson, F. (1991). *Postmodernism, or the cultural logic of late capitalism.* Durham, NC: Duke University Press.

Katz, E. (1996). *Mass media and participatory democracy.* Murfreesboro, TN: Middle Tennessee State University (John Seigenthaler Chair of Excellence First Amendment Studies).

Kelly, K. (2011). *What technology wants.* New York, NY: Viking.

Kierkegaard, S. (1962). *The present age* (A. Dru, trans.). New York: Harper & Row.

Kluitenberg, E. (2006). *The book of imaginary media: Excavating the dream of the ultimate communication machine.* Rotterdam, Netherlands: NAI; London, United Kingdom: Art Data.

Kluitenberg, E. (2011). On the archaeology of imaginary media. In E. Huhtama & J. Parikka (Eds.), *Media archaeology: Approaches, applications, and implications* (pp. 76–101). Berkeley: University of California Press.

Krippendorff, K. (2009). *On communicating: Otherness, meaning, and information.* New York, NY: Routledge.

Kucinich, J. (2012, September 27). Romney's Ohio backers don't believe the polls. *USA Today,* 6A.

Kulish, N. (2011, September 27). As scorn for vote grows, protests surge around the globe. *New York Times,* A1.

Lasch, C. (1979). *The culture of narcissism: American life in an age of diminishing expectations.* New York: W. W. Norton.

Lippmann, W. (1925/1993). *The phantom public.* Piscataway, NJ: Transaction.

Lippmann, W. (1922/1997). *Public opinion.* New York: The Free Press.

Macpherson, C. B. (1962). *The political theory of possessive individualism: Hobbes to Locke.* Oxford, United Kingdom: Clarendon Press.

Marcuse, H. (1964). *One-dimensional man: Studies in the ideology of advanced capitalist society.* Boston, MA: Beacon Press.

Marvin, C. (1990). *When old technologies were new: Thinking about electronic communication in the late nineteenth century.* New York: Oxford University Press.

Mattelart, A. (1996) *The invention of communication.* Minneapolis: University of Minnesota Press.

McKeon, M. (2005). *The secret history of domesticity: Public, private, and the division of knowledge.* Baltimore, MD: Johns Hopkins University Press.

Montalbán, M. V. (2008). *Informe sobre la informacíon.* Barcelona, Spain: Random House Mondadori.

Ong, W. J. (1982). *Orality and literacy.* New York, NY: Routledge.

Papachirissi, Z. (Ed.). (2010). *A networked self: Identity, community, and culture on social network sites.* New York, NY: Routledge.

Pooley. J. (2010). The consuming self: From flappers to Facebook. In M. Aroncyyk & D. Powers (Eds.), *Blowing up the brand: Critical perspective on promotional culture* (pp. 71–89). New York, NY: Peter Lang.

Potter, M. (2012, October 6). Obama hit by jabs on jobs. *Toronto Star,* A21.

Prior, M. (2007). *Post-broadcast democracy: How media choice increases inequality in political involvement and polarizes elections.* New York, NY: Cambridge University Press.

Putnam, R. D. (2000). *Bowling alone: The collapse and revival of American community.* New York: Simon & Schuster.

Ramonet, I. (2011). *La explosion del periodismo: De los medios de masas a la masa de medios* (B. Moreno-Luque, trans.). Madrid, Spain: Clave Intellectual.

Rheingold, H. (2000). *The virtual community: Homesteading on the electronic frontier.* Cambridge, MA: MIT Press.

Schiller, H. (1973). *The mind managers.* Boston, MA: Beacon Press.

Sennett, R. (1976). *The fall of public man.* New York, NY: W. W. Norton.

Sergeant, J.-C. (2011, October). Pourqoui l'empire Murdoch se déleste d'un joyau devenu trop pesant. *Le monde diplomatique,* 22–23.

Shirky, C. (2010). *Cognitive surplus: Creativity and generosity in a connected age.* New York, NY: Penguin.

Society for the Diffusion of Political Knowledge. (1833). *A companion to the newspaper, and journal of facts in politics, statistics, and political economy.* London, United Kingdom: Charles Knight.

Sunstein, C. (2007). *Republic.com 2.0.* Princeton, NJ: Princeton University Press.

Tarde, G. (1969). The public and the crowd. In T. Clark (Ed.), *Communication and social influence.* Chicago, IL: University of Chicago Press.

Taylor, C. (1992). *The ethics of authenticity.* Cambridge, MA: Harvard University Press.

Taylor, C. (2007). *A secular age.* Cambridge, MA: Belknap Press (Harvard).

Tocqueville, A. (2000). *Democracy in America* (H. C. Mansfield & D. Winthrop, trans.). Chicago, IL: University of Chicago Press.

Turkle, S. (1997). *Life on the screen: Identity in the age of the Internet.* New York, NY: Simon & Schuster.

Turner, V. (1984). Liminality and the performative genres. In J. J. MacAloon (Ed.), *Rite, drama, festival, spectacle: Rehearsal toward a theory of cultural performance* (pp. 19–41). Philadelphia, PA: Institute for the Study of Human Issues.

Uricchio, W. (2009). Contextualizing the broadcast era: Nation, commerce, and constraint. In E. Katz & P. Scannell (Eds.), *The end of television? Its impact on the world (so far): The annals of the American Academy of Political and Social Science* (pp. 60–73). Thousand Oaks, CA: Sage.

Webster, J., & Ksiazek, T. B. (2012). The dynamics of audience fragmentation: Public attention in an age of digital media. *Journal of Communication, 62*, 39–56.

Wittel, A. (2001). Toward a network sociality. *Theory, Culture & Society, 18*(6), 51–76.

Wright, C. (1986). *Mass communication: A sociological perspective.* New York, NY: Random House.

2

Life Without Media: Or, Why Mediacentrism Is Bad for You

NICK COULDRY

Life *without* media: that is a difficult and unusual theme for a media researcher. Nonetheless, I welcome the opportunity to write on this theme, because all of my research has been opposed to the assumption that media, or a particular *arrangement* of media resources and practices, is automatically necessary or "natural" to social life. We do not need to have the media that we currently have; however, much media tells us that this is the case. My work from the beginning has tried to get a distance from frequent assumptions that media are "the centre" of our life, while studying closely what people actually do with, and around, media! The reference point of a life without media remains vitally important, I will argue. To see why, we must take a journey through social theory before I can return to media at the end of the chapter.[1]

I will not be arguing that life without media is desirable, or even, for many purposes, practically possible. I will be arguing that adequate research into media requires adopting a decentred perspective, that is, a research approach that imagines a life *not* centred on media, a life with purposes and goals beyond media alone.

Three Quotations and a Proposition

Let me start with three representative quotations, which, taken together, illustrate the importance of being able to maintain an analytic distance from media. Here is the first:

> as soon as our call has rung out . . . a tiny sound, an abstract sound—the sound of distance overcome—and the voice of the dear one speaks to us. . . . But how far away it is! How often I have been unable to listen without anguish, as though . . . I felt more clearly the illusoriness in the appearance of the most tender proximity, and at what distance we may be from the persons we love at the moment it seems that we have only to stretch out our hands to seize and hold them. A real presence, perhaps, that voice that seemed so near—in actual separation! (Proust, 1982, pp. 134–135)

This quote is from Marcel Proust's great novel *In Search of Lost Time.* It brings out a contradiction in how media (here the telephone) work at a distance, across distance—a contradiction which, to be sure, we don't now feel in the same way in an age of mobile 3G phones where "connected presence" and the "fantasy of continuous connection" (Licoppe, 2004) seem possible, even necessary. But the idea of a *contradiction* in the dynamics of media within our lives has much wider importance, as we shall see.

Here is the second quotation:

> much of the content of modern communications . . . is a form of unevenly shared consciousness of persistently external events. It is what appears to happen, in these powerfully transmitted and mediated ways, in a world with which we have no other perceptible connections but which we feel is at once central and marginal to our lives.(Williams, 1973, pp. 295–296)

Here Williams explores the ambiguity and contradiction of our relationship to media narratives of the world, "at once central and marginal to our lives." As Williams brings out, the ways we are implicated in media—on what scale, on what terms—are never simple.

And here is a third quotation, taken from a much more recent novel than Proust's:

> I watched TV in my motel. I lived responsibly in the real. . . . I believed we could know what was happening to us. We were not excluded from our own lives. That

is not my head on someone else's body in the photograph that's introduced as evidence. I didn't believe that nations play-act on a grand scale. I lived in the real. (DeLillo, 1999, p. 82)

One way of reading DeLillo's wonderful novel is as a set of reflections on the American people's relationship to the sense of shared presence, of co-presence, that national media once gave them or rather appeared to give them. What happened, the novel asks, to that sense of popular community from the 1940s to the late 1980s? How did it change, where did it go? Part of that, as the quotation brings out, is people's commitment to "follow the news," a commitment full of paradoxes. DeLillo's novel was written a few years before the scandal of the declaration of war on Iraq in 2003 and the tortures committed in 2004 at the Abu Ghraib prison in Iraq, by when the *belief* (of the narrator) that "nations [don't] play-act on a grand scale"—the belief that television's "real" secures a hold on the *truth* of what's going on in the world—was becoming more difficult to sustain.

From these quotations, one clear proposition emerges about our relations to the world through media. Put simply, living with media is full of contradictions. This is a variation on the insight of Henri Lefebvre (1971), the French geographer and theorist, that everyday life is full of contradictions and ambiguities. Why? Because both the promise and the banality of everyday life are implicated in the workings of multiple systems—of work, family, culture, economy, government. So "everyday life" for Lefebvre cannot be simple or unified: there is no total social system, but nonetheless we live out the contradictions between multiple competing systems as everyday alienation or pain.

While Lefebvre's view of the contradiction between "modernity" and the promise of "everyday life" may be too stark, too absolute, his sense of the tensions within everyday life is unrivalled; in my view, Lefebvre's is a voice to which we should keep listening. Take this quotation which surely has new resonance today: "a cry of loneliness rises from the depths . . . where, at the heart of everyday life, the most limited and specialized everydayness lies coiled, the intolerable loneliness of unceasing communication and information" (1971, p. 125).

My broader point, then, is that to understand life with media, we need to do much more than just describe the things we do with media. Analytically we need to grasp "life *without* media." For only a *non*-mediacentric approach can help us grasp the complexities and contradictions of life *with* media. That is what I mean by "life *without* media": the sustaining of analytic and potentially normative reference points *not centred in media,* which can guide our priorities for thinking about our continuing life with media, a media-oriented or at least media-related life that is not likely to disappear any time soon. The importance of avoiding a mediacentric view of media might seem obvious, but for reasons that I will explain it is particularly important to insist on this point, at a time when more and more research is becoming trapped in a misleading account of how media work in wider social life. Let me explain.[2]

What Blocks a Non-Mediacentric Account of Media?

A non-mediacentric approach to life with media is not limited to describing media institutions or media contents for their own sake. It has different priorities. A good way of describing those priorities is in terms of certain priority questions which should frame a non-mediacentric approach to researching media. Let me simply list them, with some immediate commentary:

1. What does media-related practice contribute to our *knowledge* of the world in which we live? (Media do many things, but one thing they definitely claim to do, and one thing we need them to do, is to help us know about the world we live in, so it is a relevant criticism of media if they do not provide such knowledge or make no attempt to.)
2. What does media-related practice contribute to our ability to act (our *agency*) in the world? (Again, agency takes many forms—from civic action to developing skills for one's self-respect to just having the chance to have fun and relax. But media research, and social research generally, that was *not* interested in agency at all would be strange. It would also be divorced from how most people think of their lives: who does not want agency?)
3. What does media-related practice contribute to a life which we can value, that is, what is the relationship between media-related practice and *ethics*? (This third question in my view underpins the importance of the first two questions, since a life led without knowledge, or with no sense of agency, cannot be a life that we would call a good one. How in detail we would define a good life is a perennial debate, but the idea that our research priorities should be completely *detached* from our sense of what we value in life is bizarre.

If the priorities of media research are so simply stated, what then is the problem that this chapter is trying to address? I am concerned that an increasing number of approaches to media, to communications technology, and to social life generally, are being framed in ways that make it very difficult to address the three basic questions I have just listed. Part of the problem is that these new approaches are either explicitly mediacentric or mediacentric by default. A non-mediacentric approach seems blocked by reductionist accounts that collapse "life with media" into a "media" or a "technological" life. There are three versions of this problem: first a crude version of such accounts; second more subtle versions normally motivated by other priorities, but also by some philosophical prejudices which get in the way of seeing media and technology as more than the operations of communication systems; the third version is more disguised, and develops a notion of the "network society" or the "social" that is *apparently* attentive to its changing dynamics of the social world, but in crucial respects thin.

Such reductionist accounts often operate under cover, or with the alibi of something positive: they emphasise their rejection of functionalist accounts of social order, their deconstruction of the idea that "society" is a total social system. Of course I agree with that rejection of functionalism: my work on media rituals (Couldry, 2003) was directed exactly to identifying and deconstructing functionalist accounts of how media and society "fit together," both in media discourse and media practice. But as I will show later, there is no reason why a rejection of functionalism must lapse into a different sort of reduction, a technological functionalism that insists that the only "stuff" worth paying attention to in sociology is what happens through or around "technology."

A crude version of the reductionism that troubles me is contained in Mark Deuze's provocative recent article, "Media Life" (2011). Although Deuze's subsequent development of his argument (Deuze, 2012) is more sustained and much richer—and deserves more extended treatment than I have space for here—the rhetorical verve of his original piece is so intoxicating that it deserves its own response. When I say that original argument is crude in this context, I mean that it is quite directly mediacentric. Indeed Deuze wants, it seems, to abolish the distinction between mediacentric and non-mediacentric, insisting in an echo of Baudrillard's philosophical theory of simulation from 30 years ago that "our life is lived *in*, rather than with, media—we are living a media life" (Deuze, 2011, p. 138). Or, put another way, that "people produce themselves (and therefore each other) in media." Or that "the increasing invisibility of media . . . makes media indivisible from (all aspects of everyday) life. The moment media become invisible, our sense of identity, and indeed our experience of reality itself, becomes irreversibly modified, because mediated" (2011, p. 140).

There is a positive spin to Deuze's argument: a Nietzschean vision of "us" as newly creating ourselves through media, a society where "reality is, like many if not most websites, permanently under construction not only by . . . governments and corporations . . . but also by all of us" (2011, p. 145). What is strange is that Deuze replays Lefebvre's sense of everyday life as creative without *any* sense of the constraints and pressures that power and system seek to and actually do place on that creativity. The analytic distance from everyday life upon which Lefebvre insisted is collapsed here into a reified notion of "media life."

Some of the problems this raises are obvious: first, what about the digital divide? Access to media and enhanced media platforms are not evenly distributed even in the richest countries. Second, people make choices, and one person, as Liz Bird (2003) pointed out, may not be as media-saturated as others—this surely is a basic fact and difference even in societies with very high levels of individual connection. Third, what of the complex values people have *about* media which emerge from work on religious media consumers by Stewart Hoover and others (see, for example, Hoover 2006), but clearly are not confirmed to just those media users? Fourth, what about people's own reflections on their life with and in media: are those reflections simple, can they be critical? If they *are*, what happens to the concept of "media life"? Meanwhile the value that seems to animate Deuze's own position—a general value of freedom and self-creation—appears just as contradictory as the original version in Nietzsche that Michel Foucault developed, and which the philosopher Charles Taylor deconstructed 25 years ago in his powerful essay "Foucault on Freedom and Truth" (Taylor, 1986).

There are also more subtle forms of reductionism, which block us from getting analytic distance from how media and media technologies work in the world. Matt Fuller in his book *Media Ecologies* (2005) tries to develop a materialist account of media "systems" and media "objects" via the concept of "media ecologies." Fuller's term "media ecology" is designed "to indicate the massive and dynamic interrelation of processes and objects, beings and things, patterns and matter" (2005, p. 2). Clearly there is scope for looking in this way at the "systemness" of media's contribution to daily life, but there is no space in Fuller's approach for patterns of use or interpretation. Fuller's detailed analysis focuses largely on software and technical architecture, and so leaves unanswered and unexamined questions of social effect. So Fuller ends up assuming at a general level the very social "effects" that the connective concept of ecology is designed to address.

Jussi Parikka's book *Insect Media: An Archaeology of Animals and Technology* (2010) is a subtly written and highly original book that argues for a view of media which is decentred certainly—but decentred from any notion of the human subjects who might interpret media or act in relation to it. In an effort to get away from any fixed characterisation of what media are capable of, Parikka sees media technologies "as a realm of affects, potentials and energetics" (2010, p. xx). Parikka shares with Deuze a celebration of "creative forces," but definitely not at the level of the human subject. For, as Parikka emphasises, his is "a nonrepresentational cultural analysis" which is "not about imitation and representation of forms or actors (2010, p. xxvi). Parikka has nothing against human actors in particular. Instead his approach rejects the idea of *any* "actualized entity" at all (p. 231, n58).

Behind these media-focussed approaches lie some important positions taken up in wider social research. First, Bruno Latour's argument in his book *Reassembling the Social* (2005) for a shift from sociology of "society" to one of "associology" that traces associations as they are made from place to place and between place to place. Here Latour returns to a dispute of early 20th-century sociology and backs Gabriel Tarde versus Emile Durkheim in their dispute over how social order is made. Latour's rejection of Durkheim's functionalist view of a single society cohering around certain shared values is now common ground—it is certainly crucial to the approach I have taken to media rituals—but Latour goes much further, rejecting *any* interest in the social, any notion of social resources, social context, or whatever, at least in any stable form.

The geographer Nigel Thrift (2008) in his book *Non-Representational Theory* follows Latour's account of society and association, but draws more explicitly on a Deleuzian language of "affect" and "sensation." The emphasis on continual transformation, which is the philosophical basis of Latour's highly provocative approach to how the social is built, is made quite explicit by Thrift and in a way that takes a particular view of media. Let me quote Thrift: "the contours and content of what happens continually change. . . . There is no stable 'human' experience because the human sensorium is constantly being reinvented as the body continually adds parts to itself' (2008, p. 2). It is difficult to know what sense to make of this—it is clearly not literally true, or anything like it. It is difficult to see how it is even a useful approximation of the practical and political realities that make up the material conditions of most people's lives. In addition, like Parikka, although not quite so drastically, Thrift questions the notion of "the [human] subject," at least as an important perspective on what it is sociologists have to understand. Thrift is interested in practices that go on in the world, but insists that "practices are not . . . the practice of actors but of the practices themselves" (2008, p. 8), so there is little scope for raising questions of knowledge or agency.

As to "non-representational theory," Thrift strikingly never explicitly *defends* the claims he implies—the claim either that representations don't matter or that media or other institutions and technologies don't make representations (when he briefly discusses media, it is only in terms of "affects"). Thrift implies that everything is changing so fast that to attribute any causal power to "representation" (or to any other aspect of what media contents do) is like trying to stand on water—

impossible, inconceivable. A strange notion, surely, to any consumer of Fox News or a U.K. tabloid newspaper!

Underlying these positions is a profound suspicion of all representation, including the representations made in the course of academic analysis, and a trust instead in what Deleuze called "immanence." To quote Parikka again, such an approach is interested in "a mode of intensive abstract or spiritual materialism in which everything remains immanent to material substances yet irreducible to any actualized entity" (2010, p. 213). We see similar moves in Hardt and Negri's poetic reflections in their book *Multitude* on "the flesh of the multitude" as "pure potential" (2005, p. 191). A paradox of that book is that it is both inspirational in orienting us to a radically different political future and impoverished in its version of social theory and social reality.

The problem here is not that all these accounts of the world show some interest in media and communications technology: that is, of course welcome, indeed one might say, how could they not? The problem is that these writers frame their whole approach to what's worthy of study in the social sciences and humanities in ways that reject the languages that motivated earlier critical approaches to media and informational technology. I mean specifically the language of *agency* (and its unequal distribution—through the stratification of life changes by class, gender, ethnicity, sexuality). I mean the language of *knowledge*, both its unequal distribution—through the political economy of production, and network dominance, media's involvement in the reproduction of elite power, and so on—and, opposed to this, media's possible role in the knowledge required for resistance to power. Knowledge for resistance is not acquired by abstract subjects or through technology plug-ins; knowledge is acquired and used by real individuals under particular material conditions, with particular sets of resources, connections, and needs. I mean also the language of *ethics* (I'll come back to that later).

A roadblock to a genuinely non-mediacentric approach to contemporary media also arises from the limitations within the most serious recent attempt to grapple with digital media's implications for social and political life: Manuel Castells' work on the "network society" (2009). There is no doubt that Castells makes a convincing and influential argument for the importance of networks in destabilising many of the boundaries on which power structures previously relied. But when we evaluate his work as a positive argument about the nature of contemporary power, it is uncertain on a number of key points. First, how exactly does power *over* and *within* networks translate into other forms of power beyond the flow of networks, and vice versa? Castells insists that "whoever holds power decides what is valuable" and value is generated in networks, while also insisting on individuals' ability to interpret, use, and "reprogram" the meanings that circulate in networks. Indeed his account of news' influence emphasises the context of daily life, showing that people only pay attention "to news about significant topics that clearly relate to their lives and experiences" (2009, p. 205). So the context of everyday action is, Castells acknowledges, not simply reducible to the operations of networks or people's positioning within networks: what then *is* the relative causal weight of "context" versus "networks" in the explanation of social and political process?

Second, there is the issue of time: Castells does not discuss the contexts and resources needed to sustain networks, for example, of political mobilization, in time. Third, it remains unclear from Castells' book how exactly societies are "configured" by communication networks. Crucial resources (economic power, military power, legal authority) cannot simply be reduced to network operations: the state for example, is clearly more than a network operation, it involves the use of various forms of force and the workings of force affect the possibilities of meaningful political action. Finally, what of the time and other resource constraints that may block many from being politically active and what we might call, echoing Marx, the "dull compulsion of *media* life," or at last media-saturated life?

The broader question is as yet unanswered, in Castells or anywhere else: what are the long-term social contexts that sustain individual political action? The individual cannot put together such sustaining contexts on her own. As Danilo Martuccelli argues in his book *La Consistance Du Social* (2005, pp. 81–82), the notion of flow in Castells' work seems to replace any substantive account of social life. But this foreshortening of the social is not unique to Castells. It is common to all the writers I have been discussing, and typical, as Peter Wagner (2008) notes, of political theory's long-term neglect of the social conditions of political mobilization; indeed it is symptomatic of the neglect of the social in recent *social* theory.

This foreshortening of the social in social theory is the unintended effect of something good: a re-examination in contemporary sociology of the nature of social life, and an insistence on recognising its real complexity, uncertainty, instability, and *dis*order. Scott Lash (2009) argues sociology should turn away from the "rationalism" of classical social theory—based on Durkheim's notion of social "facts"—and turn instead towards a different type of "empirical": a "social process [that] rarely stands still long enough to congeal into 'facts.'" The choice for Lash becomes not "how is [social] order possible?" but "what is this social stuff we are experiencing?" (2009, p. 178). Lash's earlier argument in *Critique of Information* (2002) was that the intensity of our embedding in technological systems ensures that "there is no time, no space . . . for reflection" and so no role for representation within our social ontology. Indeed for Lash "the dualism of epistemology and ontology is flattened into the radical monism of technology" (Lash, 2002, pp. 18, 16). In other words, there is technology, and there is "us," and no reflexive space between them exists that is not already captured by the flows and demands of technology. But this, in a much more sophisticated form, takes us back to the problem of Mark Deuze's term "media life": that is, the reduction of life to technology, and specifically to media.

A Way Forward

We can start disentangling the problems here by returning to Henri Lefebvre, whom I quoted earlier. In the later version of his critical reflections on everyday life published in 1968 in French and 1971 in English—*Everyday Life in the Modern World*, which explicitly rejected some of the arguments in his earlier book, *Critique of Everyday Life* from the 1940s—Lefebvre defended an interesting position. First, that there is no total social system (1971, p. 27) because the plurality and mobility of everyday life is always in principle able to exceed any system. But second, for that reason—that is, *because* modern society has no unity and in fact is riven with contradictions between multiple "subsystems" such as work, consumption, governance, desire—the necessity from many institutional perspectives increases to try and control everyday life, to systematize it. This means that "everyday life" both remains an underlying source of inspiration and yet is never a simple site of "pure potential." Everyday life is a site of continual contradiction, that is "cut up and laid out . . . to be put together again like the pieces of a puzzle" (1971, p. 58). So we can't just point to everyday life, or media life, and say "that's how it is."

As a result, for Lefebvre, the deconstruction of the ambiguities and contradictions of everyday life is of crucial importance. We have to be vigilant of exactly those categories in everyday practice that *do the work of ordering* everyday life into something that is *not* ambiguous or contradictory. To quote Lefebvre again: "what we want to demonstrate is the fallacy of judging society according to its own standards, because its categories are part of its *publicity*" (1971, p. 71). And so the response to Scott Lash's reduction of the social to a play of technology, stripped of reflexivity and of representation, is to argue that even if there is no natural social order, let alone a social order neatly focussed on social "centres" and media "centres" such as the nation (as assumed by structural functionalism), nonetheless systematic attempts to order the social go on and they are consequential. "Social functionalism" remains an important force *within* the social: indeed media institutions are active in promoting their supposedly natural role in sustaining a social order. If so, a media theory without a theory of representations *or* social ordering *or both* is missing some key tools.

I am arguing that we need to look much more closely and critically at the assumptions about social ontology, and about media's consequences for social ontology, on which accounts of our life with media are based. The starting points for any such account of our more or less media-saturated life are difficult, contentious. Some approaches are helpful; some approaches, including some fashionable ones, are definitely unhelpful. To make progress we need to reboot media research *and* social theory, reorienting ourselves to some underlying priorities.

For this, we don't need philosopher mentors (and here I find common ground with the founder of non-representational theory, Nigel Thrift, 2008, p. 18). It is important to look at our own resources, as media researchers, for reorienting critical media research towards our needs as citizens, as human beings: our need to act in the world (agency); our need to act in particular on the basis of facts and not illusion, and so to grasp the embedding of knowledge, imagination, and action in material conditions, processes, and infrastructures (knowledge); and our need, through that understanding, to address the work of power and to understand the contradictions between the work of power and a life that we might choose to value (ethics).

So how does media research look once we reject a reduced notion of "media life" and reflect on our life "with" media, while retaining the perspective of a life without media? The following themes seem important to me.

First we need to grasp the multiple forces (technological, economic, social, political, cultural) that intersect in the question of whether what we have known as media institutions ("the media") have a future. For ease of reference, I condense those struggles into the idea that we are witnessing, and will for some time go on witnessing, a contest over the "myth of the mediated centre" (Couldry, 2009). For all the hype about decentred production and a more democratic media, we should remember that a relatively centralized media still provides the "space of appearances" in Hannah Arendt's term (1998) on which many institutions, including governments, depend.

Second we need to look with an open mind, and without the celebrationism of some recent writing in media studies, at the sheer diversity of media-related practice today; not only does the digitalization of media massively increase that diversity, but we cannot any more draw the boundaries of media research around what once constituted media studies: production, texts, and reception. People are showing themselves, archiving themselves, connecting and *dis*connecting, through media, in ways that are new, although, considered as practices, they may have interesting parallels in other eras. Today we have Facebook; 19th-century European elites had something called "society" (one theme in Proust's great novel, *In Search of Lost Time* (1982), is the replacement of "society" by a mass-mediated public space and public sphere).

Third, we need to understand how the vast and expanding domain of media-related practice (what we do with media) remains available to be focussed for purposes of power, whether economic and corporate power or political power. In my work, I have approached this through the concept of media's rituals and processes of ritualization. Crucial here is the work that the regular categories of media discourse do. Remember the Lefebvre quote earlier about categories being society's publicity, not its truth—then think celebrity culture.

Fourth, and relatedly, we need to think about the long-term consequences (for the shaping of individual and social agency) of living in societies focussed still, very much, around large-scale media institutions, and particularly media institutions facing the type of intense competitive pressures faced by today's global media industries. Particularly interesting here are the claims of "reality media" over the past 20 years across the world to present "reality," to show "reality," to teach "reality," claims that play out very differently in different parts of the world. Exemplary here are Graeme Turner's book *Ordinary People and the Media* with his analysis of the social "ideology without intent" that is at work in today's television entertainment industries, and Marwan Kraidy's fine book *Reality Television and Arab Politics* on the Arab world.

We also need to examine more closely the frequent claims that the resources of digital media will of themselves shift the balance of political processes in favour of democratization. This takes us, as we saw, into some very difficult questions about the social resources necessary for sustaining political action, while exposing some problems with current theorizations of social life in terms of networks. Rather than abandon entirely the theory of network society, we have to place it in the context of a much richer account of how mediatization works—one possibility is to look more closely at how different fields of competition (from politics to art) are shaped by media pressures, the pressure to get media exposure, and so on. This casts a new light back onto optimistic readings of digital media's implications for popular politics (all the talk of Twitter revolutions and the like).

We must also understand better how our lives with media—wherever we are—are shaped by pressures that are not those of media: communication needs are driven by deeper forces. For example, economic need: the need, as for China's 150 million internal migrants or the millions of Mexican migrants who regularly cross the U.S. border, in order to earn enough for their families to survive. Or religious need: the need of believers to use digital media resources in particular ways to further their religious practice. Or social need: the need for young people in the U.S. to find space where they can achieve, or be credited with, some public agency which, as danah boyd (2008) argues, is one of the deep reasons for the huge take-up of social networking sites.

The question of need takes us finally back to ethics. It is no accident, I think, that some writers about digital media have recently begun to introduce a note of ethical concern into their work: Sherry Turkle in her book *Alone Together* (2011); Siva Vaidyanathan in his book *The Googlization of Everything* (2011); Bernard Stiegler and Katherine Hayles in their 2009 essays for the journal *Theory Culture and Society*; Jaron Lanier in his book *You Are Not a Gadget* (2011); and Joseph Turow's (2011) book *The Daily You* (which was paralleled in more journalistic form by Eli Pariser's *The Filter Bubble*). A key question to be asked, Turkle notes, about our increasingly intense, multilevel, and multidirectional links with media is whether digital media, are "offering us lives we want to lead" (Turkle, 2011, p. 17). This is not so much a new question about media, as a neglected one. Too little time, in my view, has been spent asking whether, for example, the tabloid press culture of Britain or Spain provides a public culture that is consistent with the lives their populations want to lead. Too much "analysis" of contemporary public culture starts from a fatalism about media; to his credit, Mark Deuze in the full version of his "media life" argument (2012) provides a spirited rejection of fatalism about media, insisting on our capacity to continually transform media and our "media lives." The relentless disinvestment in news gathering in so many parts of the world, however, generates an even more urgent question: whether we *can* live lives we want to lead without being able to rely on some trustworthy sources of news, and whether existing trends in journalistic culture (especially the economic conditions which are shaping them) can any longer meet that need.

These are enough examples, I think, of the questions that we need to address in relation to our lives with media. But my main point is not about those specific questions—you may well have other priorities for media research. I have been arguing, however, that we can only hold onto these and similar questions if we frame them in a way that goes beyond the fiction that our lives are just and automatically "media lives." We need to frame our research about media within a social, political, and ethical perspective that is richer and broader than "whatever it is that we happen to be doing with media right now." And that is because our practice with media, whether we are journalists or not, whether we work in media institutions or not, is important for something beyond media, for a whole range of things that cannot be reduced to the dynamics of media or technology. Our practice with media matters for our possibilities of acting in the world with knowledge, with care, and with some sense of what life it would be good for us to lead.

So let me end these reflections with one final quotation, which comes from a response to some pilot research questions I posed to Britain's renowned Mass Observation Archive back in 2002. Asked whether media provide the resources for a full and active involvement in democratic society (something the theorists tell us media are meant to support), one member of the panel, a 22-year-old student, wrote back: "We live in a media world. There are eyes everywhere but we still know nothing. We still see nothing" (quoted in Couldry & Langer, 2005).

As throughout 2011 we watched people gathering in streets and squares across Europe and the Arab world to refuse the political settlements that they were told were their fate, this final quotation captures the sort of ambiguity onto which, as media scholars and citizens, we must keep hold.

Endnotes

1 For a broader argument about media analysis' relation to social theory, see Couldry (2012).

2. Arguments for the importance of a non-mediacentric approach to media go back originally to Martin-Barbero (1993); see subsequently Couldry (2005, pp. 185–186 and 2006, pp. 13–15), Morley (2007). For an important recent statement, see Moores (2012).

References

Arendt, H. (1998). *The Human condition.* (2nd ed). Chicago: University of Chicago Press.

Bird, S. E. (2003). *The audience in everyday life.* London, United Kingdom: Routledge.

boyd, d. (2008). Why youth social network sites: The role of networked publics. In D. Buckingham (Ed.), *Youth, identity and digital media* (pp. 119–142). Cambridge, MA: MIT Press.

Castells, M. (2009). *Communication power.* Oxford, United Kingdom: Oxford University Press.

Couldry, N. (2003). *Media rituals: A critical approach.* London, United Kingdom: Routledge.

Couldry, N. (2005). Transvaluing media studies: Or, beyond the myth of the mediated centre. In J. Curran & D. Morley (Eds.), *Media and cultural theory* (pp. 177–194). London, United Kingdom: Routledge.

Couldry, N. (2006). *Listening beyond the echoes.* Boulder, CO: Paradigm Books.

Couldry, N. (2009). Does "the media" have a future? *European Journal of Communication, 24*(4), 437–450.

Couldry, N. (2012). *Media, society, world: Social theory and digital media practice.* Cambridge, United Kingdom: Polity.

Couldry, N., & Langer, A. (2005). Media consumption and public connection: Towards a typology of the dispersed citizen. *The Communication Review, 8*(2), 237–258.

DeLillo, D. (1999). *Underworld.* London, United Kingdom: Picador.

Deuze, M. (2011). Media life. *Media Culture & Society, 33*(1), 137–148.

Deuze, M. (2012). *Media life.* Cambridge, United Kingdom: Polity.

Fuller, M. (2005). *Media ecologies.* Cambridge, MA: MIT Press.

Hardt, M., & Negri, T. (2005). *Multitude: War and democracy in the age of empire.* New York, NY: Penguin.

Hayles, N. K. (2009). RFID: Human agency and meaning in information-intensive Environments. *Theory Culture & Society, 26*(2–3), 47–72.

Hoover, S. (2006). *Religion in the media age.* London, United Kingdom: Routledge.

Kraidy, M. (2010). *Reality television and Arab politics: Contention in public life.* Cambridge, United Kingdom: Cambridge University Press.

Lanier, J. (2011). *You are not a gadget.* New York, NY: Vintage Books.

Lash, S. (2002). *Critique of information.* London, United Kingdom: Sage.

Lash, S. (2009). Afterword. In praise of the *A Posteriori*: Sociology and the empirical. *European Journal of Social Theory 12*(1), 175–187.

Latour, B. (2005). *Reassembling the social.* Oxford, United Kingdom: Oxford University Press.

Lefebvre, H. (1971). *Everyday life in the modern world.* London, United Kingdom: Allen Lane.

Licoppe, C. (2004). "Connected" presence: The emergence of a new repertoire for managing social relationships in a changing communication technoscape. *Society and Space, 22,* 135–156.

Martin-Barbero, J. (1993). *Communication, culture and hegemony.* London, United Kingdom: Sage.

Martuccelli, D. (2005). *La consistance du social.* Rennes, France: Rennes University Press.

Moores, S. (2012). *Media, place and mobility.* Basingstoke, United Kingdom: Palgrave Macmillan.

Morley, D. (2007). *Media modernity and technology.* London, United Kingdom: Routledge.

Parikka, J. (2010). *Insect media: An archaeology of animals and technology.* Minneapolis: University of Minnesota Press.

Pariser, E. (2011). *The filter bubble.* New York, NY: Penguin.

Proust, M. (1982). *In search of lost time. Volume 1: Swann's Way* (C. Scott Moncrieff & T. Kilmartin, trans.). Harmondsworth, United Kingdom: Penguin.

Stiegler, B. (2009). Teleologies of the snail: The errant self wired to a Wimax network. *Theory Culture & Society, 26*(2–3), 33–45.

Taylor, C. (1986). Foucault on freedom and truth. In C. Taylor, *Philosophy and the human sciences: Philosophical papers* (Vol. 2). Cambridge, United Kingdom: Cambridge University Press.

Thrift, N. (2008). *Non-representational theory.* London, United Kingdom: Routledge.

Turkle, S. (2011). *Alone together: Why we expect more from technology and less from each other.* New York, NY: Basic Books.

Turner, G. (2010). *Ordinary people and the media.* London, United Kingdom: Sage.

Turow, J. (2011). *The daily you.* New Haven, CT: Yale University Press.

Vaidyanathan, S. (2011). *The Googlization of everything (and why we should worry).* Berkeley: University of California Press.

Wagner, P. (2008). *Modernity as experience and interpretation.* Cambridge, United Kingdom: Polity.

Williams, R. (1973). *The country and the city.* London, United Kingdom: Hogarth Press.

3

Life Without Democracy, Life Without Citizenship, Life Without Media

RICHARD MAXWELL AND TOBY MILLER

What can we possibly be thinking of with this title? It is monstrous to ponder an undemocratic world, one without citizenship and the media. Yet just such a monster is proposed by this very book, which postulates the decline of conventional media forms because the political economy underpinning TV drama, event cinema, print journalism, sport, music, advertising, and so on is undergoing unprecedented change: black-box techniques and technologies, once set away from audiences, are increasingly part of public debate and use. Consumer electronics connect to information and communication technologies and vice versa; televisions resemble computers; books are read on telephones; newspapers are written through clouds; and so on. Genres and gadgets that were separate are now linked, and the mystification of conventional media is supposedly undermined. It is human, all too human (Malmodin, Moberg, Lundén, Finnveden, & Lövehagen, 2010).

In this chapter, we provide a cautious welcome to a life without media—and we include new as well as ancient and middle-aged media in that speculative fiction. Why? Both utopic advocates and dystopic critics have failed to consider the ecological impact of past, present, and future media. This should be a principal concern of both discourses, since the phrase "life without media" presumes disposability. Despite the environmental benefit of a life without media, we query such a future, given the role they have played in democratization.

For true believers, the decline of the traditional media is entirely welcome. They argue that the culture industries are being overrun by individual creativity as new media technologies obliterate geography, sovereignty, and hierarchy in an alchemy of truth and beauty. This deregulated, individuated, technologized world makes consumers into producers, frees the disabled from confinement, encourages new subjectivities, rewards intellect and competitiveness, links people across cultures, and allows billions of flowers to bloom in a post-political cornucopia. It's a kind of Marxist/Godardian utopia. People fish, film, fornicate, and finance from morning to midnight. Consumption is privileged, production is discounted, and labor is forgotten. In *Cyberspace and the American Dream*, for instance, Dyson, Gilder, Keyworth and Toffler propose that the political-economic transformations towards democracy since the 13th century have been eclipsed by technological transformations:

> The central event of the 20th century is the overthrow of matter. In technology, economics, and the politics of nations, wealth—in the form of physical resources—has been losing value and significance. The powers of mind are everywhere ascendant over the brute force of things. (Dyson et al., 1994)

Time magazine exemplified this love of a seemingly immaterial world when it chose "You" as 2006's "Person of the Year," because "You control the Information Age. Welcome to your world" (Grossman, 2006). This discourse buys into individualistic fantasies of reader, audience, consumer, and player autonomy—the neoliberal intellectual's wet dream of music, movies, television, and everything else converging under the sign of empowered and creative fans. The New Right of media and cultural studies invests with unparalleled gusto in Schumpeterian entrepreneurs, evolutionary economics, and creative industries. It's never seen an "app" it didn't like, or a socialist idea it did. Faith in devolved media-making amounts to a secular religion, offering transcendence in the here and now via a "literature of the eighth day, the day after Genesis" (Carey, 2005). Machinery, not political-economic activity, is the guiding light.

This discourse says that the new media fulfill basic human needs, bestowing plenitude and pleasure in place of scarcity and dross. As a consequence, the planet must be comprehensively wired, every child must have a laptop, cell phones must proliferate, and we must all become cultural producers.

A very different cry can also be heard. This dystopic alternative laments a lost world of expertise, certainty, truth, and knowledge, where journalists practised a craft, audiences dozed in armchairs, activists organized through leaflets, unions spoke for the disadvantaged, children began working life delivering newspapers, cultural imperialism was challengeable, and rebelion.org gleamed in Buenaventura Durruti's eye. This position criticizes the equation of technologies and texts with human welfare and a cultural logic of computation that reduces people to calculating machines (Golumbia, 2009).

In William Gibson's novel *Pattern Recognition*, Hubertus Bigend, founder of the Blue Ant advertising agency, says life is changing so quickly that "[w]e have only risk management" (2003, p. 57). Such calculated risk takes the gloss from libertarian and libertine utopias alike and suggests a very managed world. And this is not only an anxiety expressed by leftist political economists. Lapsed sacerdotal zealots of the new media Chris Anderson and Michael Wolff (2010) from *Wired* magazine say the web is dead, because its social networks and software applications are supplanting the old fantasy of an open frontier with a new hegemony of guides and leaders operating inside a small number of institutions. Another former true believer, Andrew Keen, argues that the anything-goes ethos of the Internet generates a cacophony of noise and ignorance rather than quality and knowledge. He is equally aghast at what the web has become (2007, p. 12).

It's easy to mock Keen as an elitist who fails to appreciate the revolutionary qualities of new technology. It's not so easy to prove him wrong. Consider the mad opposition to infant immunization that has gathered pace among superstitious segments of the U.S. population. It dominates YouTube videos and responses on the topic. This is just one of countless examples of perilous medical misinformation that circulates irresponsibly on the service (Keelan, Pavri-Garcia, Tomlinson, & Wilson, 2007). Similarly, as fewer and fewer media outlets become available to them, tobacco companies turn gaspingly to the Internet. Medical researchers are concerned at evidence of product placement via "smoking fetish videos." Aimed at under-age drug users under the soubriquet of "community engagement," they draw massively positive reactions. Many old TV commercials for cigarettes are also slyly archived there, new life breathed into their emphysemic messages (Freeman & Chapman, 2007).

And magical freedoms supposedly associated with cell-phone usage have created new dangerous nightmares for public-health professionals, as prostitutes at risk of sexually transmitted disease increasingly communicate with clients by phone and are less easy to educate and assist than when they are at conventional workplaces (Mahapatra, Saggurti, Halli, & Jain, 2012).

Both sides in these debates, the utopians and the dystopians, have things to say. It is true that we inhabit times of remarkable change, and that things are both won and lost for socialists such as ourselves as well as those on other sides of politics. We are torn between the arguments in favor of both utopic and dystopic positions.

For example, we enjoy selecting our "own" music in a trice wherever we go, but deeply regret the absence of great music radio in the places we have lived during this era (London, New York, Mexico City, Brisbane, Chicago, and Los Angeles). The exciting music on radio that we grew up with was selected by others with a desire to promote and challenge as well as to profit and propagandize. Those practices have been overrun by private-sector governmentality, as the medium has been corporatized. In terms of the new freedoms that have supposedly supplanted such centralized taste-making, we have to ask whether it is revolutionary to buy through Amazon, make friends through Facebook, sell on Craig's List, travel with Apple appliances, look for facts on Google, or get news from the BBC. Far from a neoliberal intellectual's wet dream, this is a political economist's arid nightmare of music, movies, television, and everything else converging under the sign of empowered firms.

We also doubt the basic claim underpinning each side of this debate—namely, that the conventional bourgeois media are finished. Consider television and the 2012 U.S. presidential election. Yet again, the election was televisual. Yet again, we were told it was not. No matter how many people followed the election cycle on TV, no matter how much time and money the campaigns spent on it, Internet bores/boors declined to face facts. Their cybertarian obsessions lead them time after time—it's actually decade after decade now—to proclaim that "legacy media" are on the way out. Television's demise, in particular, is routinely announced or predicted. So far that hasn't happened. The Internet isn't taking over. TV matters much more. How many U.S. residents who watched the 2012 U.S. presidential debates between Mitt Romney and Barack Obama preferred the Internet to TV as their source? 3 percent. How many watched on both TV and the Internet? 11 percent. How many people shared their reactions online? 8 percent (Pew Research Center, 2012).

There *has* been a successful cybertarian infiltration of television—a potent sign of their rhetorical success. The very people who make TV walk among these true believers, either sagely or anxiously foreshadowing their own demise. So 2012's U.S. election-night coverage focused on digital imagery and social media as much as human beings and broadcasting (which we assume is part of the "anti-social" media). The *Los Angeles Times* described network TV that evening as "a visual monument to the iPad generation" via "walls and crawls and ever-shifting checkerboards of imagery" (McNamara, 2012). But that was only part of the story. The *Washington Post* actually deemed the networks to be all too human. It highlighted "the crazy coverage of election night across the TV networks, in comparison to which, Comedy Central's election night anchoring by Jon Stewart and Stephen Colbert looked like Chet Huntley and David Brinkley" (de Moraes, 2012). On Fox, serial college dropout Karl Rove fought against statistics to insist that Ohio had not been won by Obama. On ABC, George W. Bush political consultant Matt Dowd advised viewers that 2012 "may be the last election that we see two white men run against each other for president" (Holpuch, 2012). Who knew critical race studies had percolated through the Republican Party in its deconstruction of the 44th president's racial subjectivity? And the social as well as the anti-social media ran hot with unkind claims that ABC's Diane Sawyer was drunk. They Might Be Giants tweeted "Diane Sawyer declares tonight's winner is . . . chardonnay!" Big story: this was re-tweeted by Ricki Lake. Then Sawyer's network was overcome by a power outage as it was declaring the result. CBS, po-facedly but perhaps delightedly, reported these stories ("Election 2012," 2012). Those trivial questions formed part of a landscape that saw US$6 billion spent on political advertising in the bourgeois media in 2012 ("Who's Afraid," 2012).

The contemporary moment in media technology is not an unprecedented eruption of difference. Rather, it joins a long history of ambivalence. Changes to the media are frequently key indices of modernity and its doom-laden portent, a bravura blend of magic and reason, of confidence and hubris. There is a genealogy tying such innovations to millenarianism, science, and religious redemption. In the archives of monks, explorers, inventors, scientists, technocrats, psychologists, and journalists, cultural and communications technologies have repeatedly served as the harbinger of a future that is simultaneously perfect and monstrous, depending on how it is interpreted. Technology brings life, liberty, happiness, death, enslavement, and depression.

In addition to denying the stickiness of the traditional media, seemingly out of time yet remarkably persistent, each side of the utopic-dystopic debate has neglected a key element of the media that threatens the very idea of discourse on which the contemporary left and right hang their ideas of democracy and citizenship.

Because so many prophets of both glory and gloom focus on consciousness, they miss an underlying and supervening material reality. Before there can be a story to analyze, a message to decode, or a social pattern to identify in the collective and individual use of media, there has to be a physical medium, a technical means of communication. Books, magazines, money, and other printed media rely on a chain of production that begins with papermaking and printing. Similarly, radios, televisions, computers, cell phones, and music players arrive in our homes and offices with parts assembled and packaged using materials that have been excavated and manufactured, and the entire process requires an array of electrical and electronic technologies, while cable and airborne networks make the media possible. In short, apart from the immediate surroundings of buildings, classrooms, homes, subways, cars, and campuses where students engage the media, the physical foundation of the media is machinery, which is created and operated through work and leaves an impact on the Earth.

The media are not only means of awareness, analysis, and ecstasy. And in addition to their imperialistic and accumulationist roles, they are also responsible for climate change, pollution growth, biodiversity decline, and habitat decimation—core constituents of our global ecological crisis. We explore that issue here, questioning the environmental costs of the media, be they old, middle-aged, or new, and hence asking not only whether they are over and gone, but what that might imply ecologically and democratically.

The presumption that the media, whether television sets or cell phones, deliver a cleaner, post-industrial, capitalism has been continually reinforced by the "virtual nature of much of the industry's content," which "tends to obscure their responsibility for a vast proliferation of hardware, all with high levels of built-in obsolescence and decreasing levels of efficiency" (Boyce & Lewis, 2009, p. 5).

Producing and powering the media consumes, despoils, and wastes natural resources and exploits human life at an ever-increasing rate. The media contain toxic substances that pervade the sites and environs where they are manufactured, used, and thrown away, poisoning humans, animals, vegetation, soil, air, and water. Rapid cycles of innovation and planned obsolescence accelerate both the emergence of new electronic hardware and the accumulation of obsolete media, which are transformed overnight into junk. Today's digital devices are made to break or become un-cool very rapidly indeed. This planned obsolescence reinforces consumerism and animates the ideology of growth that says technological innovation is necessary and good. Immediacy and interactivity induce ignorance of intergenerational effects of consumption, including long-term harm to workers and the environment. Constant connectedness diminishes the ability to dwell on interconnections between the media and the Earth. Media technology leaves an environmental legacy of poisoned waterways, sickened workers, and toxic habitats. In this very important sense, we might welcome the end of the media, and not only established technologies.

In 2007, a combination of media technologies and production accounted for 3 percent of all greenhouse gas emitted around the world (Malmodin et al., 2010). Between 20 and 50 million tonnes of electronic waste (e-waste) are generated annually, much of it via cell phones and computers, which wealthy people throw out regularly in order to buy replacements. E-waste is historically produced in the

Global North—Australasia, Western Europe, Japan, and the United States—and dumped in the Global South—Latin America, Eastern Europe, Africa, and Asia, in the form of a thousand different, often deadly, materials for each computer, though this is changing with India and China now generating their own media detritus (Robinson, 2009; Herat, 2007).

The Environmental Protection Agency estimates that U.S. residents own approximately three billion electronic devices (2007, p. 1) with well over half such purchases made by women (Twist, 2005). The Consumer Electronics Association says US$145 billion was expended in the sector in 2006 in the U.S. alone, up 13 percent on the previous year. It refers joyously to "the consumer love affair with technology continuing at a healthy clip" (Consumer Electronics Association, 2007). By 2010, three quarters of the population owned a computer and 85 percent had a cell phone. Media ownership varied with age—adults under 45 typically boasted four gadgets; those over 65 made do with one (A. Smith, 2010). In the midst of recession, 2009 saw US$165 billion in sales (Consumer Electronics Association, 2010).

In 2007, "of the 2.25 million tons of TVs, cell phones and computer products ready for end-of-life management, 18% (414,000 tons) was collected for recycling and 82% (1.84 million tons) was disposed of, primarily in landfill" (Environmental Protection Agency, 2008, p. 1). It has been estimated that the 500 million personal computers discarded in the U.S. between 1997 and 2007 contained 6.32 billion pounds of plastics, 1.58 billion pounds of lead, three million pounds of cadmium, 1.9 million pounds of chromium, and 632,000 pounds of mercury (Environmental Protection Agency, 2007; Basel Action Network and Silicon Valley Toxics Coalition, 2002, p. 6). The European Union is expected to generate upwards of 12 million metric tons (tonnes) annually by 2020. While refrigerators and dangerous refrigerants account for the bulk of EU e-waste, about 44 percent of the most toxic e-waste measured in 2005 came from computer monitors, TVs, telecommunications equipment, toys, tools, and anything with a circuit board (Commission of the European Communities, 2008, pp. 17, 31–34).

The material origin and function of media technologies are easily forgotten in today's abundance, because of the symbolic power of the technological sublime: enchantment with the seeming magic of iPhones, flat-screen high-definition televisions, wireless communication, 3-D IMAX cinema, mobile computing, and so on. This technological sublime relates to what Marx called "the Fetishism which attaches itself to the products of labour" once they are in the hands of the consumer, who lusts after them as if they were "independent beings" (1987, p. 77).

In everyday life, the sublime experience of electronic machinery conceals the physical work and material resources that go into them, while the technological sublime makes the idea that more-is-better axiomatic, even sexy. Such symbolic power underlies what Juliet Schor calls "the materiality paradox": the greater the frenzy to buy goods for their transcendent or non-material cultural meaning, the greater the use of material resources (2010, pp. 40–41). Conversely, mentioning the political-economic arrangements that make shiny new things possible, or the environmental consequences of their appearance and disappearance, is unwelcome—no way to describe "cool stuff."

This technological sublime systematically overstates the newness and preeminence of the media. A "cult of the present" is particularly dazzled by the spread of objects through globalization (Mattelart & Constantinou, 2008, p. 22). Fortunately, we have a corrective to the sublime that originates, ironically, from inside this very beguiling discourse.

Testifying before the U.S. Atomic Energy Commission, the noted physicist J. Robert Oppenheimer, who led the group that developed the atomic bomb, talked about the instrumental rationality that animated the people who created this awesome technology. Once these scientists saw that it was feasible, the device's impact lost intellectual and emotional significance for them. They had been overtaken by what he labeled its "technically sweet" quality (United States Atomic Energy Commission, 1954, p. 81). Just such technical saccharine is the lifeblood of the technological sublime. And there are intriguing ties between this instrumental pleasure and exhilarating utopias.

"Technically sweet" qualities animate innovation, adoption, and the mix of the sublime—the awesome, the ineffable, the uncontrollable, the powerful—with the beautiful—the approachable, the attractive, the pliant, the soothing. In philosophical aesthetics, the sublime and the beautiful are generally regarded as opposites. The unique quality of media technology has been to combine them. This is true at an industrial level as it is at an experiential level; for instance, many of the companies involved in developing and then broadcasting U.S. TV, such as Westinghouse, General Electric (GE), and Du Pont, also participated in the development of nuclear energy and weaponry—and advertised *on* television from the earliest days. The U.S. Advertising Council even sponsored coverage of bomb tests in 1952, under the auspices of the Atomic Energy Commission (Miller, 2010).

In a famous article from half a century ago, the Fairchild Camera and Instrument Corporation chemist and future Intel founder Gordon E. Moore framed what has come to be known as "Moore's Law": that integrated computer circuitry would increase in capacity every two years for the foreseeable future, at minimal additional cost, based on a semi-log graph extrapolating from developments since the integrated circuit's invention in 1958. His estimates have largely been exceeded, and his work is cited approvingly every day even as Intel is criticized for its abusive, avaricious business practices that have led to massive anti-trust cases, including a fine of over a billion euros levied by the European Commission (Moore, 1965; Ceruzzi, 2003, p. 217; Edgerton, 2007, p. 203; "The End of Wintel," 2010).

Moore's renowned paper included a small section that has not been addressed as enthusiastically or as often as his saccharine promise. In a section with the heading "Heat Problem," Moore worried what would happen if computers became so small that they essentially had the same mass as their componentry. This might make them "glow brightly with present power dissipation." Moore ultimately decided the subsequent cost (always his principal concern) would be manageable, thanks to space available for cooling (1965). But the wider implications suggested by Moore can't be so easily dismissed. At current levels, residential energy use by electronic equipment will rise to 30 percent of global demand for power by 2022, and 45 percent by 2030, thanks to server farms (data centers with servers, storage machines, network gadgetry, power supplies, and cooling technology) and the increasing time people around the world spend staring at screens, while those screens themselves are responsible for 70 percent of computer energy use over their lifetimes (Mouawad & Galbraith, 2009; International Energy Agency, 2009, pp. 5, 21; The Climate Group 2008, pp. 18–23; Hancock, 2009; Organisation for Economic Co-Operation and Development, 2010, p. 19).

We must account for the impact of prior inputs from the Earth (extracted via mining and drilling) and subsequent outputs into the Earth (emissions into air, land, and water) in the creation, use, and afterlife of media technologies. The effects of such inputs and outputs outlive a medium's existence, in some cases for generations, through deforestation, carbon dioxide emissions, polychlorinated biphenyls, dioxin, and other assaults. Inputs affect the environment's source functions, some of which are renewable and some not (soils, forests, water, minerals, and so on) (Goodland, 1996, p. 207). Outputs affect the environment's sink functions of absorbing waste from the media's electrical and chemical products and processes (Korten, 1996, p. 23). To discern this reality through the fog of cybertarianism, we need "autonomy from . . . industry and fan logics" (Beaty, 2009, p. 24). And that necessitates transcending the arguments about growth that subtend capitalism itself (R. Smith, 2010).

As environmental economists point out, there is no such thing as sustainable growth: it's "a bad oxymoron—self contradictory as prose and unevocative as poetry." The economy may be "open" but the Earth is "finite, nongrowing, and materially closed" (Daly, 1996, p. 193). Environmental sustainability rests on "non-negotiable planetary preconditions" (Rockstrom et al. 2009, p. 4) that set limits on how much the Earth can give to and absorb from economic, social, and cultural activities.

What is the relation of a sustainable, democratic, and pleasurable life (a healthy Earth, a functioning global democracy, and fun) to the media? What balance could lighten environmental burdens while allowing us to "enjoy, invent and be free in the modern world" (Robins & Webster, 1999, p. 62)?

Conventional economic models omit the environmental and human costs incurred by toxic chemicals, fossil-fuel energy consumption, plastics, and pollution across the supply chains and life cycles of media technologies. Environmental and human "expenses" remain "off-the-books" when net revenues are tallied up to measure growth in media and technology markets, adding to the illusion that these sectors are ecologically benign drivers of economic expansion. Were we to consider ecological and human liabilities as vital financial information, accounting would reveal "fictitious incomes and real costs that haven't been reckoned with yet," demonstrating the need for sustainability and regulated limits to growth (Schor, 2010, p. 18).

This would necessitate a choice between maintaining economic activity while reducing environmental side effects and more radical steps. The problem with the first approach is that it has been tried and its impact is insufficient given the dimensions of the problem. The difficulty with the second approach is that its impact on "the good life" is hard to confront (Jackson, 2009). The OECD exemplifies these dilemmas in its Green Growth Strategy, which relies on heavy use of the media while acknowledging their destructive impact on the environment (Organisation for Economic Co-Operation and Development, 2010).

The ecological context of electronic and electrical equipment, networks, and systems poses unique challenges. Media technology is yesterday's, today's, and tomorrow's news, but rarely in the way that it should be, because the prevailing myth is that the printing press, telegraph, phonograph, photograph, cinema, telephone, wireless radio, television, and Internet changed the world without changing the Earth. Yet their touchstone is environmental destructiveness, tied to the power of the military-industrial-entertainment-academic complex and managerial command over labor. The convergence of chemico-mechanical technology, capitalistic competition, and state collusion made photographic, electric, and electronic media rapacious despoilers. Regardless of its multi-distributional potential, each new media technology is rapidly dominated by centralized and centralizing corporations and depends on a massive contribution from the Earth and labor.

Even in the mildly progressive sphere of media studies, pro-growth ideology dominates. Scholars are dazzled by the aura surrounding media technologies and creative occupations, the so-called aristocracy of talent that comprises the recognized ensemble of workers in production practices. Our aim here has been to throw some shade over that dazzle and develop a more materialist, ecological understanding of the media.

This is a sobering corrective to celebrations of media "freedom." As we track the lives of the commodity signs that fascinate us, we need a complex, nuanced approach that is as broad-minded and expansive as the activists, corporations, unions, and scientists who study labor and environmental processes. That means forming teams with environmental scientists and labor sociologists, reading environmental audits, and learning technical languages—in short, being as nimble as an activist or policymaker.

At the same time, the idea of setting limits to media technologies raises two issues that must be addressed. The first is this: questioning the development, manufacture, and use of consumer electronics reminds us uncomfortably of an Old Testament or Malthusian problematization of pleasure through a pessimistic analysis and rhetoric that places environmentalists on the side of pain versus pleasure and moralism versus markets. The second is that doing so also questions citizenship participation in democracy, given the importance of the media for politics.

These are legitimate gripes. To convey the importance of the environmental peril engendered by the new media, one needs to embrace both pleasure and democracy as counters. There are many alternatives to clickapitalism and clickocracy. Choice can be ethical as well as pleasurable and politics sustainable and participatory (Lewis & Potter, 2011; see also http://culturalstudies.podbean.com/2010/08/06/sarah-banet-weiser). The finger-wagging aspects of environmentalism are easily parodied and criticized, so the style of conveying the message matters. But we are currently in a conjuncture where style has seemed to be everything and the Global North has invested in a laughable yet grotesque economic fantasy of protected agriculture, neglected manufacturing, boosted services, and diminished social security—a debt culture brokered against a former imperial "glory" and achieved under the sign of a supposed ability to trade out of protectionism and deferral through the sale of culture. And the supposed epoch of participatory plenitude that endows all and sundry with the will and capacity to exercise democratic rights coincides with historically pitiful levels of psephological engagement by the popular classes in supposed hubs of democracy such as the U.S. and U.K.

That said, the pleasures of venerable, middle-aged, and newer media are apparent to everyone, including us. We are not immune to the blandishments of Apple's merchandising or satellite television's delivery of *el clásico*. And we acknowledge that clickocracy can encourage some people to engage in activism. But there needs to be a discussion about the costs and benefits of electronic pleasure and participation that is neither anti-fun nor anti-reality.

That means staging a debate that engages prevailing accounts of subjectivity itself as detailed in political theory and public policy. Some philosophers see human beings in absolute instrumentalist terms. For Horkheimer, we are a "rapacious race, more brutal than any previous beasts of prey," preserving ourselves "at the expense of the rest of nature, since [we are] so poorly outfitted by nature in many respects" and must survive through violence (Horkheimer, 1996, p. 32). Hobbes held that as part of "the war of all against all," it was right for people to domesticate or destroy nature (Hobbes, 1998, pp. 105–106). And there are endless examples of captains of industry and techno-science enacting this harsh moral code: Henry Ford argued that "unused forces of nature" must be "put into action . . . to make them mankind's slaves" (Ford, 1929, p. 71); while Vannevar Bush, U.S. director of the Office of Scientific Research and Development during World War II, spoke proudly of the drive to release humanity "from the bondage of bare existence" in an essay that set the tone of national innovation for a generation (Bush, 1945).

Hegel argued that a person can put his or her "will into everything." An object or place thereby "becomes *mine*" since humanity "has the right of absolute proprietorship." Because people are unique in their desire and capacity to conserve objects and represent them, a strange dialectical process affords them a special right to destroy as well. Willpower is independent of simple survival, which sets humanity apart from other living things. Humans' semiotic power confers the right to destructive power, so "[s]acred respect for . . . unused land cannot be guaranteed." The capacity to restrain oneself and master one's "spontaneity and natural constitution" distinguishes people from animals. The necessary relationship between humans and nature asserts itself at the core of consciousness as a site of struggle for people to achieve freedom from risk and want. Nature's "tedious chronicle," where "nothing [is] new under the sun," is rightly disrespected and disobeyed by the progress that comes with human dominion over it (Hegel, 1954, pp. 242–243, 248–250; 1988, pp. 50, 154, 61).

But these boosters of selfishness have also been challenged. Writing against the dominant view of technology as "a means and a human activity," Heidegger argued that technology stages more powerful social struggle. It makes "the unreasonable demand" that nature "supply energy which can be extracted and stored" in a way that challenges seasonal rhythms, bending them to the demands of work, growth, and competition. In this regard, he shares Hegel's view of non-human nature as an instrument of humans. But Heidegger's discomfort opens up the possibility of a mid-green ethical consideration of non-human nature and a critique of instrumentalism (Heidegger, 1977, pp. 288, 296, 299). Similarly, Hume maintained that animals, like people, "learn many things from experience," developing "knowledge of the nature of fire, water, earth, stones, heights, depths, etc." in addition to receiving instruction as part of domestication. Rather than being merely sensate, advanced animals apply reason through inference (Hume, 1955, pp. 112–113). Bentham did not go as far, but appositely asked of our duty of care to animals: "the question is not, Can they *reason?* nor, Can they *talk*? but, Can they *suffer*?" (Bentham, 1970). Here again, the impact of technology is not merely a human problem; it is a problem for other inhabitants of the Earth as well. There is a duty of care to the weak on the part of the strong to preserve their lives as denizens of shared space (Swanton, 2010).

The notion of the media as creatures of garbage sometimes seeps into the public sphere, but often with the utopian yearnings of a world free from institutional constraints. Massive publicity was generated when Kelvin Doe, a 15-year-old Sierra Leonean, visited MIT in 2012. Doe had constructed a functioning radio station from detritus he had found in trash cans. More than two million online viewings of a video about him in the week to November 21 that year testified to the appeal of this tale. But it was, of course, fetishized as a story of an unlikely Third World prodigy and the need to replace aid programs with individual initiative, rather than an impressive moment in centuries of skillful media ragpicking that illustrates the power of creativity, collectivity—and pollution (Lieberman, 2012; Hudson, 2012). New? Here is the great novelist Ralph Ellison's version 80 years earlier:

> There were the accidents through which so much of that world beyond the Negro community became available to me. Ironically, I would have to start with some of the features of American life which it has become quite fashionable to criticize in a most unthinking way: the mass media. Like so many kids of the Twenties, I played around with radio—building crystal sets and circuits consisting of a few tubes, which I found published in radio magazines. At the time we were living in a white middle-class neighborhood, where my mother was a cus-

> todian for some apartments, and it was while searching the trash for cylindrical ice-cream cartons which were used by amateurs for winding tuning coils that I met a white boy who was looking for the same thing. I gave him some of those I'd found and we became friends. . . . I moved back into the Negro community and . . . was never to see him again (quoted in C. H. Smith, 2003, p. 93)

These stories matter because they can draw us into the materiality and inequality at the heart of media innovation and question its utility—if they are analysed in a critical way that focuses on citizenship rights rather than entrepreneurial fictions. That might enable us to think of what a life would look like without media pollution as a core component of rights.

Three zones of citizen rights function within liberal democracies: political citizenship, which confers the right to reside and vote on territorial terms; economic citizenship, which allocates the right to work and prosper; and cultural citizenship, the right to know and speak. These rights correspond to the French Revolutionary cry, *liberté, égalité, fraternité* (liberty, equality, solidarity) and the Argentine left's contemporary version, *ser ciudadano, tener trabajo, y ser alfabetizado* (citizenship, employment, literacy). Each one has normally assumed the capacity to appeal to national jurisdictions, but national boundaries and interests are brought into question by the border-crossing reality of ecosystem welfare and the impact of environmental despoliation. More than an addition to the rights of territorially based citizenship, green citizenship is a critique of them, a corrective that looks to saving infrastructure, ecosystems, and heritage from capitalist growth—a stand taken as early as 1739 when Benjamin Franklin argued that "public rights" over Philadelphia's air and water should supersede private rights of industry. Greening these rights extends green governance over policy, work, and communication channels. Green citizenship also introduces the right to biophysical health—a right to a body free from harmful biotoxins (Martín-Barbero, 2001, p. 9; Miller, 2007; Dean, 2001).

Environmental citizenship changes civil-republican notions of citizen duties too. Examples of such duties could include collective support of ecologically sound regulations that protect rights of workers to enjoy safe working conditions or the right to vote on environmental matters, as opposed to leaving it up to government and corporate "experts" to decide. If an individual were accorded the right to biophysical health, then this would be matched by everyone else's green obligation not to poison ecosystems, food chains, and so on. And bypassing localism and contemporaneity to enter the sphere of universal and future obligations, the responsibilities of green citizenship transcend conventional political economic space and time, extending beyond the here and now toward a globally sustainable ecology. Green citizenship looks generations ahead, refusing to discount the health and value of future ecosystems and opposing elemental risks created by capitalist growth in the present (Dobson, 2003).

Ralph Ellison and Kelvin Doe embody that sense in their able redisposal of media leftovers; capitalist cybertarian scions of privilege at MIT—less so. Those of us who study the media need to be more engaged with critical work on technology and the environment, such that our debates about electronic participation, pleasure, and democracy also speak of phthalates (a poisonous plastic softener), dioxin, and biodiversity (Liu, Shen, Zhang, & Zhang, 2009). When we discuss state assistance to the media, let's insist that such policies guarantee ecologically sound production practices and working conditions. As we download a book or watch a film at home, let's remember that our impact as spectators spills over into our air, water, and soil. To do otherwise would be unsustainable. It would bring an end to democracy, to citizenship—to life as we know it.

References

Anderson, C., & Wolff, M. (2010, August 17). The web is dead: Long live the Internet. *Wired.* http://www.wired.com/magazine/2010/08/ff_webrip/

Basel Action Network and Silicon Valley Toxics Coalition. (2002, February 25). *Exporting harm: The high-tech trashing of Asia.* Seattle, WA: Basel Action Network.

Beaty, B. (2009, January). My media studies: The failure of hype. *Television & New Media, 10*(1), 23–24.

Bentham, J. (1970). *The principles of morals and legislation.* Darien, CT: Hafner.

Boyce, T., & Lewis, J. (Eds.). (2009). *Climate change and the media.* New York, NY: Peter Lang.

Bush, V. (1945, July). As we may think. *Atlantic Monthly,* 101–108.

Carey, J. W. (2005). Historical pragmatism and the Internet. *New Media & Society, 7*(4), 443–455.

Ceruzzi, P. E. (2003). *A history of modern computing* (2nd ed.). Cambridge, MA: MIT Press.

The Climate Group. (2008). *Smart2020: Enabling the low carbon economy in the information age.* London, United Kingdom: Global Sustainability Initiative.

Commission of the European Communities. (2008). *The economics of ecosystems and biodiversity: An interim report.* Brussels, Belgium: European Communities.

Consumer Electronics Association. (2007, January 6). CEA forecasts consumer electronics revenue will surpass $155 billion in 2007. Consumer Electronics Association.

Consumer Electronics Association. (2010). *Digital America 2010.*

Daly, H. E. (1996). Sustainable growth? No, thank you. In J. Mander & E. Goldsmith (Eds.), *The case against the global economy* (pp. 192–196). San Francisco, CA: Sierra Club Books.

de Moraes, L. (2012, November 7). NBC led election night coverage ratings-wise, but ABC's getting all the tweets. *Washington Post.* http://www.washingtonpost.com/blogs-/tv-column/post/nbc-scores-most-viewers-for-election-night-according-to-very-early-stats/2012/11/07/a88b7c3e-2904–11e2-bab2-eda299503684_blog.html

Dean, H. (2001). Green citizenship. *Social Policy & Administration, 35*(5), 490–505.

Dobson, A. (2003). *Citizenship and the environment.* Oxford, United Kingdom: Oxford University Press.

Dyson, E., Gilder, G., Keyworth, G., & Toffler, A. (1994, August). *Cyberspace and the American dream: A magna carta for the knowledge age.* Version 1.2. Progress and Freedom Foundation. http://www.pff.org/issuespubs/futureinsights/fi1.2magnacarta.html

Edgerton, D. (2007). *The shock of the old: Technology and global history since 1900.* Oxford, United Kingdom: Oxford University Press.

Election 2012: How TV networks handled coverage. (2012, November 7). *CBSnews.com.* http://www.cbsnews.com/8301–207_162–57546253/election-2012-how-tv-networks-handled-coverage/?tag=re1.channel

The end of Wintel. (2010, July 31). *Economist,* 53–54.

Environmental Protection Agency. (2007). *Management of electronic waste in the United States.* Washington, DC: Environmental Protection Agency.

Environmental Protection Agency. (2008). *Statistics on the management of used and end-of-life electronics.* Washington, DC: Environmental Protection Agency.

Ford, H. (1929). *My philosophy of industry: An authorized interview by Ray Leone Faurote.* New York, NY: Coward-McCann.

Foucault, M. (2001). Qu'est-ce que les Lumières? In D. Defert & F. Ewald with J. Lagrange, *Dits et Écrits 1954–1988. Volume II: 1976–1988* (pp. 1381–1397). Paris, France: Quarto Gallimard.

Freeman, B., & Chapman, S. (2007). Is YouTube telling or selling you something? Tobacco content on the YouTube video-sharing website. *Tobacco Control, 16*(3), 207–210.

Gibson, W. (2003). *Pattern recognition.* New York, NY: GP Putnam's Sons.

Golumbia, D. (2009). *The cultural logic of computation.* Cambridge, MA: Harvard University Press.

Goodland, R. (1996). Growth has reached its limits. In J. Mander & E. Goldsmith (Eds.), *The case against the global economy* (pp. 207–217). San Francisco, CA: Sierra Club Books.

Grossman, L. (2006, December 13). You—yes, you—are *Time*'s Person of the Year. *Time.* http://www.time.com/time/magazine/article/0,9171,1570810,00.html

Hancock, S. (2009, October 10). Iceland new home of server farms? *BBC News.* http://greencitizenship.blogspot.com/2009/10/iceland-new-home-of-server-farms.html

Hegel, G. W. F. (1954). *The philosophy of Hegel* (C. J. Friedrich, ed. and trans.; P. W. Friedrich, W. H. Johnston, L. G. Struthers, B. Bosanquet, W. M. Bryant, & J. B. Baillie, eds.). New York, NY: Modern Library.

Hegel, G. W. F. (1988). *Lectures on the philosophy of world history. Introduction: Reason in history* (H. B. Nisbet, trans.). Cambridge, United Kingdom: Cambridge University Press.

Heidegger, M. (1977). *Basic writings from "Being and time" (1927) to "The Task of thinking" (1964).* New York, NY: Harper & Row.

Herat, S. (2007). Review: Sustainable management of electronic waste (e-waste). *Clean, 35*(4), 305–310.

Hobbes, T. (1998). *On the citizen* (R. Tuck & M. Silverthorne, ed. and trans.). Cambridge, United Kingdom: Cambridge University Press.

Holpuch, A. (2012, November 7). Obama wins, Fox News (almost) experiences the five stages of grief. *Guardian.* http://www.guardian.co.uk/world/blog/2012/nov/07/barack-obama-fox-news-election?INTCMP=SRCH

Horkheimer, M. (1996). *Critique of instrumental reason: Lectures and essays since the end of World War II* (M. J. O'Connell et al. [unnamed], trans.). New York, NY: Continuum.

Hudson, H. (2012, November 19). Kelvin Doe, self-taught engineering whiz from Sierra Leone, wows MIT. *Huffington Post.* http://www.huffingtonpost.com/2012/11/19-/kelvin-doe-self-taught-en_n_2159735.html

Hume, D. (1955). *An inquiry concerning human understanding with a supplement: An abstract of a treatise of human nature* (C. W. Hendel, ed.). Indianapolis, IN: Bobbs-Merrill.

International Energy Agency. (2009). *Gadgets and gigawatts: Policies for energy-efficient electronics—Executive summary.* Paris, France: Organization for Economic Cooperation and Development.

Jackson, T. (2009). *Prosperity without growth? The transition to a sustainable economy.* London, United Kingdom: Sustainable Development Commission.

Keelan, J., Pavri-Garcia, V., Tomlinson, G., & Wilson, K. (2007). YouTube as a source of information on immunization: A content analysis. *Journal of the American Medical Association, 298*(21), 2482–2483.

Keen, A. (2007). *The cult of the amateur: How today's Internet is killing our culture and assaulting our economy.* London, United Kingdom: Nicholas Brealey.

Korten, D. C. (1996). The failures of Bretton Woods. In J. Mander & E. Goldsmith (Eds.), *The case against the global economy* (pp. 20–30). San Francisco, CA: Sierra Club Books.

Lewis, T., & Potter, E. (Eds.). (2011). *Ethical consumption: A critical introduction.* London, United Kingdom: Routledge.

Lieberman, D. (2012, October 22). Deadline's YouTube channel rankings. *Deadline.com.* http://www.deadline.com/2012/10/deadlines-youtube-channel-rankings/

Liu, W. L., Shen, C. F., Zhang, Z., & Zhang, C. B. (2009). Distribution of phthalate esters in soil of e-waste recycling sites from Taizhou City in China. *Bulletin of Environmental Contamination and Toxicology*, 82(6), 665–667.

Mahapatra, B., Saggurti, N., Halli, S. S., & Jain, A. K. (2012). HIV risk behaviors among female sex workers using cell phone for client solicitation in India. *Journal of AIDS and Clinical Research*, S1, 14. http://dx.doi.org/10.4172/2155–6113.S1–014

Malmodin, J., Moberg, Å., Lundén, D., Finnveden, G., & Lövehagen, N. (2010). Greenhouse gas emissions and operational electricity use in the ICT and entertainment and media sectors. *Journal of Industrial Ecology, 14*(5), 770–790.

Martín-Barbero, J. (2001). Introducción. In J. Martín-Barbero (Ed.), *Imaginarios de Nación: Pensar en Medio de la Tormenta* (pp. 7–10). Bogotá, Colombia: Ministerio de Cultura.

Marx, K. (1987). *Capital: Vol. 1: A critical analysis of capitalist production* (3rd ed., S. Moore & E. Aveling, trans.; F. Engels, ed.). New York, NY: International Publishers.

Mattelart, A., & Constantinou, C. M. (2008). Communications/excommunications: An interview with Armand Mattelart (A. Bled, J. Guot, & C. Constantinou, trans.). *Review of International Studies, 34*(1), 21–42.

McNamara, M. (2012, November 6). Election night 2012: TV coverage for an iPad generation. *Los Angeles Times.* http://www.latimes.com/entertainment/tv/showtracker/la-et-1107-critics-notebook-ipad-20121107,0,2399173.story

Miller, T. (2007). *Cultural citizenship: Cosmopolitanism, consumerism, and television in a neoliberal age.* Philadelphia, PA: Temple University Press.

Miller, T. (2010). *Television studies: The basics.* London, United Kingdom: Routledge.

Moore, G. E. (1965). Cramming more components onto integrated circuits. *Electronics, 38*(8), 114–117. http://www.cs.utexas.edu/~fussell/courses/cs352h/papers/moore.pdf

Mouawad, J., & Galbraith, K. (2009, September 20). Plugged-in age feeds hunger for electricity. *New York Times*, A1.

Organisation for Economic Co-Operation and Development. (2010). *Greener and smarter: ICTs, the environment and climate change.* Paris, France: Organisation for Economic Co-Operation and Development. http://www.oecd.org/site/stitff/45983022.pdf

Pew Research Center. (2012, October 11). One in ten 'dual-screened' the debate. http://www.people-press.org/2012/10/11/one-in-ten-dual-screened-the-presidential-debate/

Robins, K., & Webster, F. (1999). *Times of the technoculture: From the information society to the virtual life.* London, United Kingdom: Routledge.

Robinson, B. H. (2009). E-waste: An assessment of global production and environmental impacts. *Science of the Total Environment, 408*(2), 183–191.

Rockstrom, J. et al. (2009). Planetary boundaries: Exploring the safe operating space for humanity. *Ecology and Society, 14*(2). http://www.ecologyandsociety.org/vol14/iss2/art32

Schor, J. B. (2010). *Plenitude: The new economics of true wealth.* New York: Penguin.

Smith, A. (2010, October 14). *Americans and their gadgets.* Pew Research Center.

Smith, C. H. (2003). "I don't like to dream about getting paid": Representations of social mobility and the emergence of the hip-hop mogul. *Social Text, 77*, 69–97.

Smith, R. (2010). Beyond growth or beyond capitalism? *Real-World Economics Review, 53*, 28–42.

Swanton, C. (2010). Heideggerian environmental virtue ethics. *Journal of Agricultural and Environmental Ethics, 23*(1–2), 145–66.

Twist, J. (2005, January 10). Gadget market 'to grow in 2005.' *BBC News.*

United States Atomic Energy Commission. (1954). *In the matter of J. Robert Oppenheimer. Transcript of hearing before Personnel Security Board.* http://universityhonors.umd.edu/HONR269J/archive/Oppenheimer.htm

Who's afraid of the fiscal cliff? Media companies, and with good reason. (2012, November 19). *Ad Age.* http://adage.com/article/media/media-companies-afraid-fiscal-cliff/238373/

Part Two. Parenting, Schooling, and Socializing: Youth Mediatization Gone Wrong?

4

Life without Markets? Childhood and Consumer Culture

DAVID BUCKINGHAM

To entertain the possibility of a *life without markets* is an interesting thought experiment—perhaps especially now, as market relations appear to have comprehensively permeated almost every imaginable sphere of public and private experience. The position of children—my preoccupation in this chapter—provides an especially pertinent case study, not least because childhood is often seen as something that is, or ideally should be, beyond the reach of markets. In recent years, there has been growing concern in many countries about the potentially harmful influence of commercial forces on children: in the U.K., we have seen several government reports on different aspects of this topic over the past few years (including one for which I was the lead author: Buckingham, 2009a), and there are now some limited moves to restrict marketing to children. Some commentators and campaigners hold out the possibility of a "commercial-free childhood," or at least one that is in key respects held apart from the market.

This discussion inevitably reflects our assumptions about childhood—about what children are, or what they should be. Children, it is assumed, are different from adults in key respects: they possess particular characteristics, needs, or vulnerabilities, which means they should be treated in different ways. These assumptions can in principle be subjected to empirical examination—there is an extensive body of research, for example, about children's understanding of the persuasive intentions of advertising. Yet this debate is also to some extent a normative one:

in making claims about what we want children to be or to become, we are also asserting fundamental values to do with the kind of society we want. Nevertheless, what is desirable may not necessarily be possible. Even if children *should* be protected from the market, it is unlikely that they ever *could* be. Indeed, one might go so far as to say that the notion of a "commercial-free childhood"—a childhood without markets—is, under present circumstances, little more than a fantasy.

Commercial marketing to children is by no means a new phenomenon. Indeed, historical studies show that children have been a key focus of interest at least since the inception of modern mass production (e.g., Cook, 2004; Cross, 1997; Denisoff, 2008; Jacobson, 2004). Nevertheless, in recent years children have become increasingly important both as a market in their own right and as a means to reach adult markets. Marketers are targeting children more directly and at an ever-younger age; and they are using a much wider range of techniques that go well beyond conventional advertising. Marketers often claim that children are becoming "empowered" in this new commercial environment: the market is seen to be responding to needs and desires on the part of children that have hitherto been largely ignored or marginalised, not least because of the social dominance of adults. However, critics have expressed growing concern about the apparent "commercialization" of childhood. Popular publications, press reports, and campaigns have addressed what are seen to be the damaging effects of commercial influences on children's physical and mental health. Far from being "empowered," children are typically seen here as victims of a powerful, highly manipulative form of consumer culture that is almost impossible for them to escape or resist.

In this chapter, I argue that we need to look beyond this rather polarized debate. There are two main reasons for this. First, I suggest that the terms of the debate itself are limited and problematic, in ways that reflect continuing difficulties in our conceptions of childhood. The debate about children's consumption rehearses binary views of childhood and conflates important conceptual distinctions that need to be maintained. Second, I argue that these views of children as consumers fail to address the ways in which consumer culture itself is currently developing and changing. Marketing to children is increasingly being carried out without recourse to "old" media such as television or print: it is using new digital media, but often in ways that replicate much earlier methods relying on "word of mouth." I argue that the more ubiquitous and participatory techniques that are now being used by commercial companies reflect a new construction of the child consumer (and indeed of the consumer more generally). This new construction in turn requires us to rethink the terms of the debate, and some of the basic assumptions of consumer culture theory.

Constructing the Child Consumer: Critics, Marketers, and Academic Theorists

In the wake of Naomi Klein's influential *No Logo* (2001), there has been a flurry of popular critical publications about children and consumer culture: prominent examples include Juliet Schor's *Born to Buy* (2004), Susan Linn's *Consuming Kids* (2004), and Ed Mayo and Agnes Nairn's *Consumer Kids* (2009). Other popular books in this vein include discussions of children's consumption alongside broader arguments about the apparent demise of traditional notions of childhood—as in the case of Sue Palmer's *Toxic Childhood* (2006) or Richard Layard and Judy Dunn's *A Good Childhood* (2009). The arguments in these publications are, by and large, far from new. One can look back to similar arguments being made in the 1970s, for example by groups like Action for Children's Television in the United States (Hendershot, 1998); or to announcements of the "death of childhood" that have regularly recurred throughout the past two centuries (e.g., Postman, 1983). Even so, there now seems to be a renewed sense of urgency in these claims.

Such books typically presume that children used to live in an essentially non-commercial world, or a kind of idyllic "golden age"—an age before markets. Many of them link the issue of consumerism with other well-known concerns about media and childhood: as well as turning children into premature consumers, the media are accused of promoting sex and violence, obesity, drugs and alcohol, gender stereotypes and false values, and taking children away from other activities that are deemed to be more worthwhile. Of course, this is a familiar litany, which tends to conflate very different kinds of effects and influences. It constructs the child as innocent, helpless, and unable to resist the power of the media. These texts describe children as being bombarded, assaulted, barraged, even subjected to "saturation bombing" by the media: they are being seduced, manipulated, exploited, brainwashed, programmed, and branded. And the predictable solution here is for parents to engage in counter-propaganda, to censor their children's use of media, or simply keep them locked away from corrupting commercial influences. These books rarely include the voices of children, or try to take account of their perspectives: this is essentially a discourse generated by parents *on behalf of* children.

Meanwhile, there has been a parallel growth in marketing discourse specifically focused on children. Again, there is a long history of this kind of material. As Dan Cook (2004) and Lisa Jacobson (2004) have shown, the early decades of the 20th century saw marketers increasingly addressing children directly, rather than their parents. In the process, they made efforts to understand the child's perspective, and began to construct the child as a kind of authority, not least by means of market research. In recent years, however, this kind of marketing discourse has proliferated, most notably in relation to the newly identified category of the "tween." More recent examples would include Gene Del Vecchio's *Creating Ever-Cool* (1997) and Anne Sutherland and Beth Thompson's *Kidfluence* (2003); although perhaps the most influential account is Martin Lindstrom's *Brand Child* (2003), which is the basis of a major consultancy business that has effectively become a brand in its own right.

The most striking contrast between these accounts and those of the critics of consumer culture is the very different construction of the child consumer. The child is seen here as sophisticated, demanding, and hard to please. Tweens, we are told, are not easily manipulated: they are an elusive, even fickle market, sceptical about the claims of advertisers, and discerning when it comes to getting value for money—and they need considerable effort to understand and to capture. Of course, given the political pressure that currently surrounds the issue of marketing to children (most notably around so-called junk food), marketers are bound to argue that advertising has very little effect, and that children are "wise consumers." Yet this idea of the child as sovereign consumer often elides with the idea of the child as a citizen, or an autonomous social actor, and with the notion of children's rights; and it is often accompanied by a kind of "anti-adultism"—an approach that is very apparent, for example, in the marketing of the global children's television channel Nickelodeon (Banet-Weiser, 2007; Hendershot, 2004). To use one of Nickelodeon's key marketing slogans, in the new world of children's consumer culture, *kids rule.*

These contrasting views of consumption are also played out in academic theories and debates. On the one hand, we have accounts that see consumption as a kind of betrayal of fundamental human values. From this point of view, the pleasure of consumption is something to be suspected, a matter of inauthentic, short-term gratification—unlike the apparently authentic pleasures of human interaction, true culture, or spontaneous feeling. This argument stands in a long tradition of critical theory, from Adorno and Marcuse (and indeed more conservative critics like F. R. Leavis and Ortega y Gasset) through to contemporary authors such as Zygmunt Bauman (2007) and Benjamin Barber (2007), all of whom posit the possibility of a world without (or before or beyond) markets. For such critics, it is generally *other people's* consumption that is regarded as problematic: the argument is informed by a kind of elitism, whereby largely white, male, middle-class critics have stigmatized the consumption practices of others—women, the working classes, and now children (Seiter, 1993).

On the other hand, there are accounts that emphasise the agency of consumers—that is, their ability to define their own meanings and pleasures, and to exercise power and control. Such accounts were particularly prominent in 'postmodernist' cultural studies at the beginning of the 1990s (e.g., Fiske, 1990, Featherstone, 1991), although they have arguably resurfaced with some more celebratory accounts of fandom and so-called 'participatory culture' (Jenkins, 2006). Far from being passive dupes of the market, consumers are regarded here as active and autonomous; and commodities are seen to have multiple possible meanings, which consumers can select, use, and rework for their own purposes. In appropriating the "symbolic resources" they find in the marketplace, consumers are engaging in a productive and self-conscious process of creating an individual "lifestyle" and constructing or "fashioning" their identities. In the process, they are seen to be evading or resisting the control of what Fiske (1990) calls "the power bloc."

I have sketched these debates in admittedly stark and exaggerated terms here. Nevertheless, there is a clear polarization in accounts of consumer culture—and specifically of children as consumers—that replays a much wider polarization within the human sciences more broadly, between structure and agency. In relation to children, this typically results in a stand-off between two diametrically opposed views of children: the child as innocent victim versus the child as competent social actor. On the one hand, we have the call to protect children from exploitation and manipulation; and on the other, the call to extend their rights to self-determination and autonomy. In relation to children's consumption, this leads to a series of binary oppositions that tend to dominate the debate. Are children active or passive consumers? Are they knowledgeable or innocent, competent or incompetent, powerful or powerless? Does the market destroy or undermine the true needs of children, or does it actually enable them to be realized? And would a life without markets—if indeed it were possible—somehow enable us to rediscover the fundamental human essence of childhood?

Later in this chapter, I will discuss some of the more theoretical problems with this debate, and point to some possible means of moving beyond what has become a kind of conceptual impasse. First of all, however, I want to describe some of the ways in which the children's market itself is changing. In my view, these changes represent a different way of conceiving of, or constructing, the child consumer; and this in turn means that we need to develop different theories and methodologies for research. New developments in the children's market, new techniques and marketing strategies, and new discourses about the child consumer seem to make redundant the binary oppositions I have outlined above, and require us to ask some new questions.

Children: A Growing but Uncertain Market

Estimates of the size of the children's market are somewhat variable, and occasionally seem quite hyperbolic. Child marketing guru Martin Lindstrom (2003), for instance, suggests that children aged 8–14 in the United States spend around $150 billion annually, "control" another $150 billion of their parents' money, and influence family spending of up to $600 billion a year. He asserts that children may be responsible for almost two *trillion* dollars of annual global expenditure. Figures for Europe tend to be more modest. In the U.K., one annual survey of children's pocket money suggests that children aged 7–16 receive an average of ¤35 per month, making a total of almost ¤80 million—a figure that has increased by 600 percent over the past 20 years (HBOS, 2007). The cost of bringing up a child from birth to the age of 21 is estimated to be in excess of ¤220,000, a figure that is rising significantly faster than inflation (Liverpool Victoria Friendly Society, 2010).

From a marketing perspective, children are generally seen to play three main roles. They are an increasingly significant market in their own right, through spending their own disposable income, gained from gifts and part-time work as well as regular allowances. However, they are also an important means of reaching adults: the influence that children exert on adults' purchases is more economically significant than what they buy themselves, and can include choices of holidays, cars, new technology, and other expensive goods. Third, they are seen as a future market—a "market potential"—with whom companies wish to establish relationships and loyalties that they hope will be carried through into adulthood (McNeal, 1999).

Nevertheless, the children's market is significantly more volatile and uncertain than adult markets. The failure rate for new products is much higher here than in the adult market (McNeal, 1999); and while enormous amounts of money can undoubtedly be made from successful brands and product ranges, there is also a high degree of risk. The history of children's "crazes" (such as Pokémon or Ninja Turtles) shows recurring patterns of rise and fall, which companies have significant difficulties in predicting or managing (Tobin, 2004). At the peak of a craze, desperate parents may queue for hours in toy shops to buy scarce merchandise; while a few months down the line, vast quantities of the same goods may be on their way to a landfill. Even very well-established brands are not immune from competitive challenge, as the "doll wars" between Barbie and the Bratz range have recently shown (Clark, 2007).

One approach that marketers have used in attempting to manage risk in the children's market is segmentation, although it is an approach that has some ambivalent consequences. On the one hand, segmentation provides a means for marketers to manage risk—to know and perhaps exercise greater control over potential markets; but the more segmented markets are, the smaller they become. The logic then points towards globalization: smaller national markets can be amassed into much larger markets if they are targeted on a global scale—although this in turn requires products to be produced for global rather than national consumption, which itself requires difficult calculations about cultural specificity (Buckingham, 2007).

Thus, gender differentiation is a key factor, particularly for younger children, where the market is heavily polarized into "pink and blue." There are significant risks for marketers here in trying to cross the line, in order to appeal to both groups. It used to be the received wisdom among marketers that the way to succeed was to appeal to boys first—girls were quite likely to buy boy-oriented products, although boys were less comfortable with products they perceived as too "girly" (Schneider, 1987). More recent analyses of contemporary toy advertising would suggest that this polarization has been maintained (Griffiths, 2002); and some products (and indeed entire television channels) are sometimes developed in distinct "boy" and "girl" versions. Yet while critics argue that the market actively produces or at least reinforces these gender distinctions and identities, it would clearly be in the commercial interest of marketers to minimize such differences (and hence to maximize the size of the market) rather than to accentuate them.

Likewise, age differences are also highly significant, but complex to manage. Dividing children into a series of niche markets defined by age means that new products can be sold at different stages, while others are cast off or "outgrown"; and the history of children's marketing has seen the ongoing construction of new age-defined categories such as "toddlers," "teenagers," and most recently "tweens" (Cook, 2004). Yet children do not always "act their age." While younger children may well aspire to consume products that appear to be designed for those who are older than they, older children are unlikely to wish to be associated with items that are seen as too "childish." Commercial goods serve as powerful but often very ambivalent markers of "age identities"—although here again, it is often very difficult for marketers to manage and control the meanings that children produce.

New Marketing Techniques

Another way in which marketers have sought to manage risk in the children's market is through the use of new media and new techniques. Pre-eminent amongst these has been the rise of integrated, cross-media marketing—sometimes variously termed "360-degree marketing" or "synergistic marketing." This practice has been especially apparent in most of the leading children's "crazes" and product ranges of the past 30 years: examples of current successes would include Disney's *High School Musical* and *Hannah Montana* and Warner Brothers' *Harry Potter*, as well as franchised characters aimed at younger children such as Bob the Builder and Thomas the Tank Engine. In each case, the core text or product provides the basis for an ever-expanding range of ancillary products and merchandise.

Of course, this is far from being a recent development. Disney is the best-known example of this phenomenon: right from the early days of the Mickey Mouse Club (which began in cinemas in the 1930s, and came to television in the mid-1950s), merchandising has been an indispensible aspect of the enterprise, and has even sometimes served to keep the media production operation afloat (see Bryman, 1995; de Cordova, 1994; Wasko, 2001). Yet following the advent of so-called program-length commercials on U.S. television in the late 1970s—cartoons produced or commissioned by toy companies as "shop windows" for their products—media and merchandising have become inextricably connected. The presence of such branded merchandise in so many media and market sectors—including not just toys, but also clothing, food, gifts, and other paraphernalia—effectively makes them impossible to avoid, generating a "virtuous circle" of ubiquitous mutual promotion.

In this context, traditional advertising (for example on television or in print media) is gradually becoming redundant—and indeed goods such as Pokémon products were never advertised as such. Traditional advertising is now in decline, and an increasing proportion of marketing budgets is now spent on other forms of promotion, public relations, and branding. To some extent, we can be seen to be entering an age of "marketing without media," or at least "old" media. Marketers are developing a range of new techniques, many of which are particularly prevalent in the children's and youth markets (see Montgomery, 2007). These include the following:

- Product placement: not in itself a new strategy, but nevertheless a practice that is becoming more widespread in a range of media, and has recently been legalized at a European level (albeit not in children's programmes);
- Other methods of embedding commercial messages, for example through the use of advertising in computer sports games or online social worlds;
- Advergaming, whereby players are involved in games (most obviously on company websites) using commercial or branded imagery or content;
- Viral marketing, whereby commercial messages (in the form of e-mails or SMS texts or images) are forwarded from one user to another;

- "Immersive" marketing and the gathering of personal data in online social worlds, both subscription sites and "free" branded ones;
- Social networking—in particular, the use of "applications" that involve users in competitions featuring branded products and services, the use of branded materials (such as "skins" or backgrounds), and the ways in which users are invited to define and construct their personal profiles in terms of preferences for consumer goods;
- Sponsorship: again, a well-established strategy but one that appears to be becoming more widespread, not least as part of the wider privatization of public institutions, events, and services (for instance in education);
- Peer-to-peer marketing, whereby opinion leaders are recruited and paid as "brand champions" or "ambassadors" who will actively display and advocate the use of particular products within their contact group (the ubiquitous display of logos on branded clothing might be seen as a "softer" form of this practice);
- The commercial cultivation of forms of "fan culture" that involve collecting commodities (often those with a market-induced "rarity" value), or creating forms of fan "art" (for example, creating and circulating re-edited video material);
- So-called user-generated content, in which companies recruit consumers to create blogs or online videos (or alternatively masquerade as ordinary consumers to do so) promoting particular brands or products.

These new techniques are fairly diverse, and some may ultimately prove much more successful than others, although the expenditure on such approaches is undoubtedly increasing quite significantly at present. However, they have certain qualities in common. For the most part, they are about *branding*—creating a set of values or emotions associated with the brand—rather than the marketing of specific products. Many of them depend to a large extent on the use of digital media, with its immediacy of access, its networking capacity, and its apparent "youth" appeal, as well as its capacity for surveillance of consumer behaviour. Many are personalised, in the sense that they seem to appeal and respond to the individual's wants and needs, rather than addressing them as a member of a mass market. They are often deceptive or "stealthy," in the sense that their persuasive intentions are not made apparent—for example through commercial messages being embedded in other content, rather than clearly identifiable, as is the case with television commercials or banner advertising online. Finally, many of them are "participatory" or "interactive," in that they require the positive engagement of the consumer, who may be called upon to engage actively with the communication, to pass it on to others, or even to help create the message.

In all these respects, these new techniques reflect much broader trends in contemporary consumer culture, which apply to adults as well as children. Rather than adopting aggressive, hard-sell techniques, marketers increasingly have to take account of consumers' scepticism and potential resistance. The consumer is defined and addressed, not as vulnerable and open to manipulation, but as savvy, sophisticated, and discriminating. Again, there is a long history of this approach, dating back at least to the late 1950s (see Frank, 1997), but it has become increasingly de rigueur in the business. The aim here is not so much to sell specific products but rather to engage with consumers' sense of personal agency, and to create more intense forms of intimacy and "bonding" in the relations between consumers and brands (Arvidsson, 2006).

Knowing Consumers?

The increasing risks and uncertainties of the children's market also place a new premium on knowledge. Marketers can never be sure that they can fully "know" children or predict their behaviour. As a result, a thriving research business has grown up around the children's market, which now seeks to access children's perspectives directly, rather than merely those of their parents. These "commercial epistemologies" (Cook, 2000) often draw on the creative and ethnographic tools for accessing children's "voice" developed within academic disciplines such as anthropology and cultural studies. For instance, researchers may visit children repeatedly in their homes, spending extended periods with them in their most private spaces, such as bedrooms and bathrooms. They film children playing with toys and engaged in other mundane tasks such as eating, using these methods because interviews do not always reveal behaviour that children are reluctant to admit (such as playing with toys they claim to have grown out of). In this way, researchers access new information that can be used commercially: for instance, seeing children playing with empty bubble-bath containers inspired the redesign of packaging (Schor, 2004).

Likewise, in the practice known as "cool hunting," young people may be recruited as "consultants" to supply their own views on products and advertisements, or employed to track trends among their peer groups. For example, Dubit, a U.K.-based youth research company, has a website aimed at young people that pays them to answer surveys about new ad campaigns, technologies, or products, alongside chat and games. Digital media also provide new means of gathering and accessing data about consumer behaviour. The practice of "data mining" involves the gathering, aggregation, and analysis of data about consumers, either based on their responses to online requests or questionnaires or (more covertly) through the use of "cookies" that track their movements online. Such practices are widely used in social networking sites and online worlds, not only in online shopping or commercially branded sites. In these ways, the media that are often celebrated for their ability to "empower" consumers also provide powerful means of surveillance.

Companies operating in this market typically claim to offer privileged insights into the views and perspectives of young people. Their research is often aligned with the rhetoric of "empowerment" identified above: young people are frequently described as self-determining, autonomous and innately "savvy" in their dealings with the commercial world. Children, we are told, want to be in control, to be "listened to, heard, respected and understood": they must not be patronized. They can recognise when advertisers are trying to manipulate them; and while they are quick to adopt new trends, they are also quick to move on. As such, they are extremely powerful and influential consumers: "they get what they want when they want it" (Sutherland & Thompson, 2003). This new rhetoric of the competent child consumer is also aligned with a familiar discourse about young people and technology. Children are represented as "digital natives," who are "born with a mouse in their hands," as Lindstrom (2003) puts it. As such, they can best be reached through the kinds of "participatory" techniques I have identified above. While campaigners frequently express alarm about the deceptive and invasive nature of such approaches, for marketers they are a means to empowerment: they provide children with the means to register their needs, find their voices, build their self-esteem, define their own values, and develop independence and autonomy.

Yet while their methods and discourses might appear relatively innovative, the theories on which such companies draw to explain young people are often much more traditional: Maslow's "hierarchy of needs" and Piagetian developmental psychology are frequently cited, along with pop psychology and simplistic theories of generational change. For all the emphasis on novelty, marketers are also advised to address needs that are seen as somehow timeless and innate—needs for mastery, stability, fantasy, romance, rebellion, and so on. Children at different ages are seen to be "looking for an identity," seeking "to identify with a role model," beginning "to develop and understand their personal power in the world" or seeking "power, freedom, fun and belonging"—assertions that seem to do little more than rehearse common-sense truisms about childhood (see also Siegel, Coffey, & Livingston, 2001).

Ethics and Theories: Beyond the Binaries

These new practices undoubtedly raise new ethical questions. Regulations that apply to conventional media advertising (for example on television) do not yet apply online, or to these more pervasive forms of marketing. Many new marketing techniques blur the boundaries between promotional messages and other content, making it possible to embed advertising in contexts where it is less likely to be recognised as such. They often entail the gathering, aggregation, and use of personal data about consumers without them necessarily being aware that this is taking place; and children may also be encouraged or required to provide personal information about others, for example parents or friends, without their knowledge, raising significant concerns about privacy (see Buckingham, Whiteman, Willett, & Burn, 2007; Livingstone, 2006; Nairn & Monkgol, 2007). "Peer-to-peer" and viral marketing represent a modern form of "word of mouth," although they also depend on a degree of deception, whereby users (rather than companies) are seen as the authors or at least the distributors of commercial messages. There are also justified concerns that children are being recruited for market research at an ever younger age, and that the aims of such research are not always clearly explained. There may be further violations of privacy here, as such researchers are increasingly keen on studying children in their "natural habitat" of the home or the peer group.

These issues in turn raise new questions about children's understanding of commercial motivations and practices, and more broadly about their competence as consumers. Research has recently begun to explore how children engage with these new practices (e.g., Nairn & Dew, 2007)—although there may be little reason to expect that children are any less knowledgeable about them, or indeed more vulnerable to deception, than adults. There are justified concerns here; yet the issues raised also go beyond questions about children's competence, or lack of it. Children (or indeed adults) may be more or less knowledgeable about such techniques, but that knowledge in itself does not necessarily confer the power to resist them. Furthermore, the fact that children are now increasingly addressed and engaged as "active" participants does not necessarily mean that they have greater agency or power.

As I have suggested, these developments can be seen to represent a much more general paradigm shift in the nature of consumer culture, away from a "mass-media" model towards one that is significantly more pervasive, more personalized, and more participatory. In this context, consumers' agency itself is being produced and engaged in new ways. Easy oppositions of the kind with which we began—between active and passive, knowledgeable and innocent, competent and incompetent, powerful and powerless—no longer apply. We need to look beyond such binary thinking, towards a more complex understanding of children's consumer practices.

Ultimately, the limitations of much of the debate in this area derive from the broader assumptions about childhood on which it is based. It seems to be assumed that there is a natural state of childhood that has been destroyed or corrupted by marketers—or alternatively, that children's "real" innate needs are somehow being acknowledged and addressed, even for the first time. It is also believed that there is something particular to the condition of childhood that makes children necessarily more vulnerable—or indeed spontaneously more wise and sophisticated—for example in their dealings with technology; and that adults are somehow exempted from these arguments.

Aside from the sentimentality of these assumptions, this kind of polarization fails to acknowledge some of the paradoxes here. For example, it is entirely possible that children (or indeed adults) might be active and sophisticated readers of media, but might nevertheless still be influenced—or indeed that an *illusion* of autonomy and choice might be one of the pre-requisites of contemporary consumer culture. *Activity* is not necessarily the same thing as *agency*. At the same time, we need to acknowledge the genuine difficulties, risks, and uncertainties that are entailed for marketers in actually targeting children—and that the power of the marketers may also be more limited than is often assumed.

Theoretically, the question here is typically posed in terms of the relationship between structure and agency (Buckingham & Sefton-Green, 2003). On the side of structure, the market clearly does attempt to construct and define the child consumer: it offers children powerful definitions of their own wants and needs, while purporting to satisfy them. Yet on the side of agency, children also construct and define their own needs and identities, not least by how they appropriate and use consumer goods. The paradox of contemporary marketing is that it is bound to construct children as active, desiring, and autonomous, and in some respects as resisting the imperatives of adults, while simultaneously seeking to make them behave in particular ways. As such, it is positively misleading to see this in terms of a simple *opposition* between structure and agency, or as a kind of zero-sum game in which more of one automatically means less of the other. Structure requires agency, but agency only works through structure: each, in this sense, actively produces the other.

Consumption Out of Context

The other recurring problem with this polarized debate is its tendency to displace attention away from other possible causes of the phenomena that are at stake. This arises largely because children's consumption is removed from the social contexts in which it occurs—and indeed which it helps to produce. Much of the research in this area focuses on children's responses to advertising—especially television advertising—rather than on other aspects of marketing or of consumption. A great deal of it is also concerned with purchasing behaviour (or aspects of "pre-purchasing" such as information-seeking, preference, and choice); and relatively little with how children appropriate and use products in their everyday lives. As such, this work focuses on a relatively narrow aspect of the broader nexus of production, distribution, circulation, and consumption.

Much of the research in this field has been conducted by psychologists, working within two main traditions: media effects and consumer socialization. Both approaches have been widely challenged on methodological grounds, which do not need to be rehearsed here. More significant in this context are the theoretical and political problems of these approaches. Effects research is self-evidently premised on a view of children's relationship with media as a matter of cause and effect. A classic behaviourist perspective (which is sometimes misleadingly termed "social learning theory") conceives of this process in terms of stimulus and response, of which the most obvious example would be imitation. From this perspective, television advertising would be seen to produce direct effects on viewers, not only in terms of purchasing behaviour, but also in terms of attitudes and values. More sophisticated exponents of this approach posit the existence of "intervening variables" (both individual differences and social factors) that come between the stimulus and the response, and thereby mediate any potential effects; although the basic cause-and-effect model continues to apply. This kind of research implicitly conceives of the child consumer as a tabula rasa, a blank slate on which marketers inscribe their harmful messages. (For reviews of this kind of work, see Gunter, Oates, & Blades, 2005; and Gunter & Furnham, 1998.)

By contrast, consumer socialization research tends to draw on frameworks from developmental psychology in proposing a sequence of "ages and stages" in maturation (John, 1999; McNeal, 2007). From this perspective, children's development as consumers is related to the development of more general cognitive skills and capacities, such as the ability to process information, to understand others' perspectives, to think and reflect in more abstract ways, and to take account of multiple factors that might be in play in decision making. Influenced by parents and peers, as well as media and marketing, children's consumer behaviour is seen to become gradually more autonomous, consistent, and rational. This approach inevitably leads to a "deficit model" of the ways in which children understand, interpret, and act upon their world: they are seen simply in terms of what they lack. The view of socialisation here is fundamentally teleological: it regards development as a linear progression towards the final achievement of adult rationality. In common with developmental psychology more broadly, this approach also neglects the emotional and symbolic aspects of consumer behaviour, in favour of cognitive or intellectual ones.

Critics of this approach argue that a more socio-cultural account of consumer socialisation is required. Karin Ekstrom (2006), for example, proposes that consumer socialisation is an ongoing, lifelong process, rather than something that is effectively concluded at the point of entry to adulthood; that it varies among different social and cultural groups, and over time; and that it involves different life experiences and contexts of consumption. As such, there can be no single definition of what counts as a "competent" consumer. Ekstrom also argues that children should be seen as active participants in the process of socialisation, not as passive recipients of external influences. Likewise, Dan Cook (2010) proposes that the notion of socialisation should be replaced by the notion of "enculturation," which he suggests would help to move beyond the normative, monolithic approach of consumer socialisation research. He argues that children are already implicated in consumer culture from before the point of birth; and that rather than seeking to assess children's knowledge in the abstract, we need to consider how that knowledge is used (or not used) in everyday social practice. Learning to consume is seen here not as a matter of one-way transmission from parent to child, but on the contrary as a process of negotiation involving diverse social agents, in which multiple meanings are in play.

As objects of psychological inquiry, children tend to be perceived and defined in particular ways. The primary interest is in *internal* mental processes of cognition or emotion: the "social context" is predominantly understood as an external variable or influence. Children are also conceptualised principally in terms of development; that is, in terms of their progression towards the goal of adult maturity. And methodologically, much of the focus is on what children *think*—or say they think, often in response to psychometric tests—rather than on what they *do*, or even on how their knowledge is used in everyday life. By and large, children are not seen here as independent social actors: as sociologists of childhood would have it, they are seen not as *beings*, but only as *becomings* (cf. Lee, 2001).

Politically, this kind of approach also feeds into a familiar game of "blaming the media." For example, there is a growing tendency in many countries to blame marketers and advertisers for the rise in childhood obesity; and this is an issue that is also becoming an increasing preoccupation for researchers (see Buckingham, 2009b, 2009c). Yet there may be many other complex reasons for this phenomenon. In fact, poor people are most at risk of obesity—and this clearly has something to do with the availability and price of fresh food, and the time that is available to people to shop and prepare their own meals. The rise of obesity might also be related to the rise of "car culture," the fact that children (at least in some countries) are now much less independently mobile, and the increasing privatisation of public leisure facilities. As with debates about media violence, blaming the media allows politicians to displace attention away from other potential causes, while also being seen to be "doing something" about the problem.

Consumption in Context

The key point here is that it makes little sense to abstract children's relationship with advertising, or their consumer behaviour, from the broader social and historical context. Indeed, the distinction between consumption and the "context" in which it occurs may itself be misleading: it might be more appropriate to regard consumption as a form of social practice, and as a dimension of other social practices, which collectively *construct* "contexts." In a capitalist society, almost all our social activities and relationships are embedded within economic relations: childhood—and indeed adulthood—are inevitably constructed in and through market relations. The children's market works through and with the family, the peer group, and—increasingly—the school. We need to address how consumption practices are carried out in these different settings, how they help to define the settings themselves, and how they are implicated in the management of power, time, and space. In the process, we need to move beyond the notion of the consumer as a self-contained individual, and beyond individualistic notions of desire, identity, and lifestyle, to focus instead on relationships and reciprocity.

Johansson (2010) points to actor network theory as an alternative to this individualistic view, by virtue of its emphasis on connections, networks, and flows. Agency is seen here, not as a possession of the individual, but rather as something that is exercised in specific situations and events, and via "assemblages" of human and non-human actors (including objects, artefacts, and texts, as well as people). In my view, this approach has much in common with the "circuit of culture" that is characteristic of cultural studies (see du Gay, Hall, Janes, & Mackay, 1997;

Buckingham, 2008), not least in that it moves beyond the dichotomy of structure and agency: power is not seen to lie either with consumers or with producers, but precisely in the interrelationships between them.

Anthropological and sociological studies of childhood have begun to address these dynamics in other areas of children's lives (see Qvortrup, Corsaro, & Sebastian-Honig, 2009); and in some recent studies, this approach has begun to be applied to children and parents' everyday consumption practices as well (see Martens, Southerton, & Scott, 2004). This work addresses central questions to do with the construction of childhood identities and the wider "generational order," drawing on the sociology of childhood as well as on cultural studies and on anthropological studies of "material culture" (see Buckingham & Tingstad, 2010; Buckingham, 2011).

One particular focus of interest here is how consumption produces and sustains hierarchies of status and authority in children's peer groups. Thus, some research shows how children's clothing purchases can be a site of anxiety about status and belonging as well as of play and creativity (Boden, Pole, Pilcher, & Edwards, 2004). To what extent does knowledge of consumer culture function as a kind of cultural (or subcultural) capital for children? How do the hierarchies of taste and "cool" within the peer group relate to the hierarchies within adult culture (for example, of class, ethnicity, or gender)? How might such hierarchies work with or against the imperatives of consumer culture (for example, by rendering the "cool" uncool overnight)? How do we interpret the anti-consumerist rhetoric of some forms of youth culture—and the ways in which it has been appropriated for so-called ethical consumption?

Another focus here is the changing role of parenting, and the social expectations that surround it. Gary Cross (2004) has identified the symbolic tension here between parents' desire to shelter the child, to use childhood as a place for pedagogic nurturing, and their desire to allow the child a space for expression, to indulge the freedom they themselves have lost. As parents spend less and less time with their children, they may be more inclined to compensate by providing them with consumer goods. As such, contemporary parenting is now increasingly implicated with the operations of the market—and yet parents often regard this with considerable ambivalence (Pugh, 2009).

Other studies have addressed the experience of young people who are excluded from peer-group culture because of their lack of access to consumer goods (e.g., Chin, 2001; Croghan, Griffin, Hunter, & Phoenix, 2006). Not all consumers are equally able to participate, since participation depends not just on one's creativity but also on one's access to material resources: the market is not a neutral mechanism, and the marketised provision of goods and services (not least in the media and in education) may exacerbate existing inequalities. In this context, it is particularly important to understand the consumption practices of children in disadvantaged communities, for whom "consumer choice" may be a fraught and complex matter. While many children may be able to access some aspects of the goods that become the lingua franca of children's culture—for instance, by being part of the audience for the advertising that surrounds them—their experience of the actual products is likely to vary widely with material purchasing power. Elizabeth Chin's work (2001) on poor African American children usefully challenges the idea that less wealthy children are somehow more at risk from the seductions of consumer culture, exploring how their strikingly altruistic consumption practices—during a shopping trip she arranged as part of the research—are embedded within their social and familial relationships.

Conclusion

Children's relationship with the commercial market is thus a profoundly ambivalent phenomenon. Of course, there is always an economic "bottom line": the global child market is a significant source of commercial profit—although, as I have argued, profit is by no means easy or straightforward to secure. On the other hand, the meanings and pleasures that consumer culture affords children—and the roles it can play in the formation of childhood identities—are significantly more difficult to predict. The market clearly does have a considerable power to determine the meanings and pleasures that are available to children; but children themselves also play a key role in creating those meanings and pleasures, and they may define and appropriate them in very diverse ways. Seeing this in terms of a simple opposition between structure and agency is inadequate, especially in the changing context of contemporary consumer culture. As I have argued, new forms of marketing—which operate to a large extent without or beyond "old" media—construct and define the child consumer in new ways; and we need to develop new theories and paradigms if we are to fully understand what is taking place here.

Is it possible then to conceive of a childhood without markets? While it might be challenging to entertain such an idea, we need to acknowledge that contemporary childhoods are always already commercial childhoods. Childhood is not, and cannot be, a pure space that can somehow be held apart from the market relations that surround and help to define it, any more than adulthood can. As Ellen Seiter (1993) has argued, the idea that children can be somehow sheltered from consumption is a peculiarly middle-class delusion, one which fuels its own specialised consumer markets in "quality" toys and "educational" services. Those who imagine they can provide children with a life without markets may well be one of the most profitable markets of all.

The real problem here, I would suggest, is not primarily to do with the "commercialization" of some imaginary pre-commercial or non-commercial "essence" of childhood. Rather, it is to do with the much broader processes of marketisation and privatisaton. Commercial forces now play an increasingly important role, not just in children's leisure and play, but also in education, in the provision of welfare and social services, and in resources and support for parenting. Despite the often melodramatic claims of campaigners and the generalised optimism of the marketeers, the outcomes of children's increasing immersion in consumer culture are by no means the same for all. The logic of the market is such that it is bound to serve those who offer the most lucrative means of generating profit: and as such, it must inevitably contribute to growing inequalities. Advertising and marketing to children may provide convenient and even therapeutic targets for campaigners; but the marketisation and privatisation of public services have much more far-reaching consequences for children's lives. The more significant problem here is not so much that markets produce "commercialism" or "materialism," but rather that they inevitably accentuate inequality.

References

Arvidsson, A. (2006). *Brands: Meaning and value in media culture.* London, United Kingdom: Routledge.

Banet-Weiser, S. (2007). *Kids rule! Nickelodeon and consumer-citizenship.* Durham, NC: Duke University Press.

Barber, B. (2007). *Consumed: How markets corrupt children, infantilize adults, and swallow citizens whole.* New York, NY: Norton.

Bauman, Z. (2007). *Consuming life.* Cambridge, United Kingdom: Polity.

Boden, S., Pole, C., Pilcher, J., & Edwards, T. (2004). New consumers: The social and cultural significance of children's fashion consumption. *Working Papers: Cultures of Consumption Series*, 16.

Bryman, A. (1995). *Disney and his worlds.* London, United Kingdom: Routledge.

Buckingham, D. (2007). Childhood in the age of global media. *Children's Geographies, 5*(1–2), 43–54.

Buckingham, D. (2008). Children and media: A cultural studies approach. In K. Drotner & S. Livingstone (Eds.), *Handbook of children, media and culture.* London, United Kingdom: Sage.

Buckingham, D. (2009a). *The impact of the commercial world on children's wellbeing: Report of an independent assessment.* London, United Kingdom: Department of Children, Schools and Families and Department of Culture, Media and Sport. http://www.academia.edu/679743/The_Impact_of_the_Commercial_World_on_Childrens_Wellbeing

Buckingham, D. (2009b). The appliance of science: The role of research in the making of regulatory policy on children and food advertising in the U.K. *International Journal of Cultural Policy, 15*(2), 201–215.

Buckingham, D. (2009c). Beyond the competent consumer: The role of media literacy in the making of regulatory policy on children and food advertising in the U.K. *International Journal of Cultural Policy, 15*(2), 217–230.

Buckingham, D. (2011). *The material child: Growing up in consumer culture.* Cambridge, United Kingdom: Polity.

Buckingham, D., & Sefton-Green, J. (2003). Gotta catch 'em all: Structure, agency and pedagogy in children's media culture. *Media, Culture & Society, 25*(3), 379–399.

Buckingham, D., & Tingstad, V. (Eds.). (2010). *Childhood and consumer culture.* London, United Kingdom: Palgrave Macmillan

Buckingham, D., with Whiteman, N., Willett, R., & Burn, A. (2007). *The impact of media on children and young people with a particular focus on computer games and the Internet.* Prepared for the Byron Review on Children and New Technology. Commissioned by the Department of Children, Schools and Families. London, United Kingdom: Institute of Education, University of London. http://dera.ioe.ac.uk/7363/1/Buckingham%20Impact%20of%20Media%20Literature%20Review%20for%20the%20Byron%20Review.pdf

Chin, E. (2001). *Purchasing power: Black kids and American consumer culture.* Minneapolis: University of Minnesota Press.

Clark, E. (2007). *The real toy story: Inside the ruthless battle for Britain's youngest consumers.* London, United Kingdom: Black Swan.

Cook, D. T. (2000). The other "child study": Figuring children as consumers in market research, 1910s–1990s. *Sociological Quarterly, 41*(3), 487–507.

Cook, D. T. (2004). *The commodification of childhood: The children's clothing industry and the rise of the child consumer.* Durham, NC: Duke University Press.

Cook, D. T. (2010). Commercial enculturation: Moving beyond consumer socialization. In D. Buckingham & V. Tingstad (Eds.), *Childhood and consumer culture.* London, United Kingdom: Palgrave Macmillan.

Croghan, R., Griffin, C., Hunter, J., & Phoenix, A. (2006). Style failure: Consumption, identity and social exclusion. *Journal of Youth Studies, 9*(4), 463–478.

Cross, G. (1997). *Kids' stuff: Toys and the changing world of American childhood.* Cambridge, MA: Harvard University Press.

Cross, G. (2004). *The cute and the cool.* New York, NY: Oxford University Press.

de Cordova, R. (1994). The Mickey in Macy's window: Childhood, consumerism and Disney. In E. Smoodin (ed.), *Disney discourse.* London, United Kingdom: British Film Institute.

Del Vecchio, G. (1997). *Creating ever-cool.* Gretna, LA: Pelican.

Denisoff, C. (Ed.). (2008). *The nineteenth-century child and consumer culture.* Aldershot, United Kingdom: Ashgate.

du Gay, P., Hall, S., Janes. L. Mackay, H. (1997). *Doing cultural studies: The story of the Sony Walkman.* London, United Kingdom: Sage.

Ekstrom, K. (2006). Consumer socialization revisited. In R. W. Belk (Ed.), *Research in consumer behavior* (Vol.10, pp. 71–98). Oxford, United Kingdom: Elsevier.

Featherstone, M. (1991). *Consumer culture and postmodernism.* London, United Kingdom: Sage.

Fiske, J. (1990). *Understanding popular culture.* London, United Kingdom: Unwin Hyman.

Frank, T. (1997). *The conquest of cool.* Chicago, IL: University of Chicago Press.

Griffiths, M. (2002). Pink worlds and blue worlds: A portrait of infinite polarity. In D. Buckingham (Ed.), *Small screens: Television for children.* London, United Kingdom: Leicester University Press.

Gunter, B., & Furnham, A. (1998). *Children as consumers.* London, United Kingdom: Routledge.

Gunter, B., Oates, C., & Blades, M. (2005). *Advertising to children on TV: Context, impact and regulation.* London, United Kingdom: Routledge.

HBOS. (2007). Pocket money rises 600% in 20 years [Press release]. http://www.hbosplc.com/media/pressreleases/articles/halifax/2007–07–21-Pocketmone.asp?section=halifax, accessed April 2009,

Hendershot, H. (1998). *Saturday morning censors: Television regulation before the V-chip.* Durham, NC: Duke University Press.

Hendershot, H. (Ed.). (2004). *Nickelodeon nation: The history, politics, and economics of America's only TV channel for kids.* New York, NY: New York University Press.

Jacobson, L. (2004). *Raising consumers: Children and the American mass market in the early twentieth century.* New York, NY: Columbia University Press.

Jenkins. H. (2006). *Convergence culture.* New York, NY: New York University.

Johansson, B. (2010). Subjectivities of the child consumer: Beings and becomings. In D. Buckingham & V. Tingstad (Eds.), *Childhood and consumer culture.* London, United Kingdom: Palgrave Macmillan.

John, D. R. (1999). Consumer socialization of children: A retrospective look at twenty-five years of research. *Journal of Consumer Research, 26*(3), 183–213.

Klein, N. (2001). *No logo.* London, United Kingdom: Flamingo.

Layard, R., & Dunn, J. (2009). *A good childhood: Searching for values in a competitive age.* London, United Kingdom: Penguin.

Lee, N. (2001). *Childhood and society: Growing up in an age of uncertainty.* Buckingham, United Kingdom: Open University Press.

Lindstrom, M., with Seybould, E. (2003). *Brand Child.* London, United Kingdom: Kogan Page.

Linn, S. (2004). *Consuming kids.* New York, NY: Anchor Books.

Liverpool Victoria Friendly Society. (2010, February 23). The cost of raising a child tops £200,000 [Press release]. http://www.lv.com/media_centre/press_releases/, accessed August 2010.

Livingstone, S. (2006). Children's privacy online. In R. Kraut, M. Brynin, & S. Kiesler (Eds.), *Computers, phones and the Internet.* New York, NY: Oxford University Press.

Martens, L, Southerton, D., & Scott, S. (2004). Bringing children (and parents) into the sociology of consumption. *Journal of Consumer Culture, 4*(2), 155–182.

Mayo, E., & Nairn, A. (2009). *Consumer kids: How big business is grooming our children for profit.* London, United Kingdom: Constable.

McNeal, J. U. (1999). *The kids' market: Myths and realities.* New York, NY: Paramount.

McNeal, J. U. (2007). *On becoming a consumer: Development of consumer behavior patterns in childhood.* Burlington, MA: Butterworth-Heinemann.

Montgomery, K. (2007). *Generation digital.* Cambridge, MA: MIT Press.

Nairn, A., & Dew, A. (2007). Pop-ups, pop-unders, banners and buttons: The ethics of online advertising to primary school children. *Journal of Direct, Data, and Digital Marketing Practice, 9*(1).

Nairn, A, & Monkgol, D. (2007). Children and privacy online. *Journal of Direct, Data, and Digital Marketing Practice, 8,* 294–308.

Palmer, S. (2006). *Toxic childhood.* London, United Kingdom: Orion.

Postman, N. (1983). *The disappearance of childhood.* London, United Kingdom: W. H. Allen.

Pugh, G. (2009). *Longing and belonging: Parents, children and consumer culture.* Berkeley: University of California Press.

Qvortrup, J., Corsaro, W., & Sebastian-Honig, M. (Eds.). (2009). *The Palgrave handbook of childhood studies.* London, United Kingdom: Palgrave.

Schneider, C. (1987). *Children's television: The art, the business and how it works.* Lincolnwood, IL: NTC Business Books.

Schor, J. (2004). *Born to buy: The commercialized child and the new consumer culture.* New York, NY: Scribner.

Seiter, E. (1993). *Sold separately: Children and parents in consumer culture.* New Brunswick, NJ: Rutgers University Press.

Siegel, D. L., Coffey, T. J., & Livingston, G. (2001). *The great tween buying machine: Marketing to today's tweens.* Ithaca, NY: Paramount Market.

Sutherland, A., & Thompson, B. (2003). *Kidfluence: The marketer's guide to understanding and reaching Generation Y.* New York, NY: McGraw Hill.

Tobin, J. (ed.) (2004). *Pikachu's global adventure; The rise and fall of Pokémon.* Durham, NC: Duke University Press.

Wasko, J. (2001). *Understanding Disney.* Cambridge, United Kingdom: Polity.

5

The Use of Information and Communication Technologies (ICTs) and the Digital Divide Among Adults and Teenagers[1]:
Initial Theoretical Considerations Around a Supposed Generational Conflict

JORDI BUSQUET AND ANA CINTHYA URIBE

Introduction

The discussion on whether the Internet is creating a new kind of divide among teenagers and adults (parents and teachers) has been booming in the last few years. It is not a new argument, since it sounds very similar to the argument that made radio, TV, and other types of mass media a different kind of threat to the relations of power and knowledge among the previous generation. However, beyond the notions of the dangers of mass media, it seems like the Internet poses a unique challenge to creating and maintaining healthy relationships at home and in school.

To further our understanding of media and how children and teenagers visualize and understand violence on TV and other media, in 2010 the research group CONINCOM started a project called AUSTICA, which focused on the so-called digital divide among teenagers, parents, and teachers, the cultural distance between generations, and how this distance might involve conflicts at school and at home. From different theoretical perspectives such as sociology, communication theory, and other disciplines, our research network wants to address the issue of the digital divide that supposedly exists between parents and children and/or teachers and students. This intergenerational conflict occurs in a very specific moment and should be seen within the general context of new cultural paradigms and a process of deep cultural transformation.

In this chapter, we will first explain the theoretical approach to the subject and also (re)formulate some of the initial work hypotheses. The main objectives of the text are to present the initial premises of the project, to initiate a discussion on definitions now being questioned such as the term "digital divide," explain the research methodology used so far, and give some preliminary conclusions.

Technology as an Agent of Social Change

In the last 20 years, far-reaching socio-cultural transformations that involve a profound transformation of social life have occurred. By the second half of the 19th century, Marx said that while economic and technological changes were (or could be) relatively fast, cultural changes were much slower and always part of other "infrastructural" and "structural" modifications. Today, this notion seems quite inaccurate. The historical changes that we have been witnessing in the last few years are intense, fast, and deep; in the time of just one generation (around 15 years), we've experienced changes of huge historical significance.

We live in a time of crisis marked by turbulent and contradictory processes of globalization. This globalization has brought with it an acceleration of social relations across the globe, enhancing cultural exchanges and at the same time significantly changing lifestyles and acquisition of experience in all areas of life (Giddens, 2000). Perhaps one of the most important changes we have witnessed is the unprecedented transformation of the cultural and communication paradigm in which we live. Alessandro Baricco (2008), in his essay *The Barbarians* (*Los bárbaros*), explains the "mutations" that are profoundly altering the world of culture, now invaded and ruled by what he calls the "new barbarians." From the point of view of the Turinese author, we are experiencing a new cultural order based on speed, immediacy, and superficiality—a deep cultural paradigm change. In recent decades, for example, there has been an increase in reading proficiency and an extension of the reading public, but paradoxically, the dominant cultural paradigm is no longer based on the culture of the book:

> With the introduction of new communications technologies, systems and methods of human communication, the production and processing of information and knowledge have changed substantially. As a result, there has been [a] shift on the gravity center of culture: from writing matters to audiovisual content. This mediated culture has a privileged space for consumption at home and gradually slides,

> through microelectronics and mobility, to locate its anchor point at the user himself. (Ariño, 2010, p. 223) (Translation by Uribe)

While it is undeniable that technological development applied to communication processes has contributed to the intensification of human relationships, the changes that are occurring do not belong exclusively to the technological level, but also to the socio-cultural one. It is important to cast away the technological determinism that underlies most of ideas generated around the so-called information society. As pointed out by Manuel Castells, it is not technology that determines society, but an element that reflects it (Castells, 1997–1998). In other words, technology does not transform the social world in a mechanical way, but different social groups choose the innovations that are best suited to their purposes.

Castells (2006, 2009) also mentions the emergence of a new form of culture: the culture of "real virtuality." In that culture, the participation at social and cultural spheres is based more than ever in the articulation of the physical spaces with the environments of virtual communication—now a reality available to (almost) all (Cardoso, 2008).[2] For new generations, the separation between those "two realities" (the real-reality and the virtual-reality) is completely diluted and empty of meaning.

In this new world order characterized by a dynamic of constant change and a situation of growing uncertainty, new risks are added to others already present in the history of mankind. Both the scientific development and the application of technology—which in theory should allow greater control over the environment by human beings—are the source of the deep challenges in the digital era (Beck, 1994; Bauman, 2003).

We are now seeing an unprecedented process of acceleration of historical processes. However, social behaviors facing this tide of changes follow familiar patterns. Sonia Livingstone (2002) notes that, with the rise of the Internet, ancestral fears that beset mankind every time a new technological artifact is invented are (re)-produced.

Attitudes of fear and distrust towards new inventions in the field of social media do not represent anything new. The discovery and application of new technological means of cultural diffusion have always led to expressions of fear and mistrust, while at the same time they generate fascination caused by innovation (Busquet, 2008). Information and communication technologies might also represent a dark side. For example, ICTs emphasize parental anxiety issues related to violence, stereotypes, commercial exploitation, and pornographic content. This is a fairly widespread fear in society that, according to Livingstone, presents again and again each time a new technology developed and directed towards the younger population is introduced. Clear examples of these fears are videogames. As noted by the British author, this "apocalyptic trend" has a huge weight in the fears or "moral panics" that adults have about the use that the young generation is giving to certain technology and also about the technology itself.

This more traditional outlook—based on fear—prevents those adults from seeing the positive aspects offered by the new technologies, which is not to imply that all reasonable precautions around the new environments should be disposed. Livingstone asserts that ICTs are a great opportunity to rethink the relationships within the family and in the context of everyday life in order to challenge some cultural aspects such as education, identity, community, and so on (Livingstone, 2002).

ICTs are understood as possible tools to create new relations and social communication networks.[3] It is suspected that this kind of use, which is more social, is more important to young people. Hence, it's easier to see why some adults may be concerned or confused by children's use of ICTs. At times, the older generation may not comprehend the possibilities that new technological developments could bring to the communicative process; consequently, they find it more difficult to understand and/or support the use of such technologies by the younger generation.

A Reversal in the Educational Process

As noted above, the fundamental change that we want to highlight in this study is the alteration that is occurring in one of the basic assumptions of all educational processes. The transfer of knowledge, values, habits, and behavioral patterns used to go *from* the adults (who by their life experience "know better") *to* the young ones. This knowledge transfer circuit has allowed and still allows some social stability and historical continuity of models and cultural forms.

However, from the second half of the 20th century, it is possible to see that in certain circumstances there is a complete change of these "ancient principles"—which previously assured the continuity of power roles with an alleged effective control over the younger generation (Rascovsky, 1975). With the emergence of youth culture in the 60s and 70s, young people started openly rebelling against the existing cultural models. Youth emancipated from such models and developed their own lifestyles—directly in contrast to the values and behavior of their immediate social environment. Thus, "youth culture" is not so much understood as something related to a certain developmental stage but as an alternative culture or a counterculture (Roszak, 1968; Maffesoli, 1990; Feixa, 2006). Perhaps this generational cultural gap is one of the precedents to what's now called the digital divide.

However, after reviewing the state of the art on the subject, within this research project we question the pertinence of using the controversial notion of a "digital divide." In the first stage, the notion of first digital divide (based on economic and technological factors) was a significant step forward. But today, when access to ICTs is almost universal, this notion is beginning to be questioned.

In this new cultural environment, the terms of the conventional educational process both at school and home have been at least partially reversed. Since the middle of the last decade, various initiatives aimed at inter-generational interaction in the learning of ICTs have been launched. The introduction of these technologies in the classroom is also common. In this sense, the younger population seems to be called to play an important role in the social and educational spheres. For example, in Finland, teenagers play the role of volunteer teachers, helping senior citizens with Internet issues. In a similar way, among other projects in the European context, the Ómnia project—supported by the Fundació Catalana de l'Esplai and the Generalitat de Catalunya—has a similar proposal of integration among generations. It is important to note that these kinds of practices, far from being anecdotal, have begun to be replicated locally (albeit with fewer resources) in many Spanish towns.

But beyond these integration proposals, young people perceive themselves (and, more importantly, are perceived) as owners of skills and even "knowledge" exclusive to them and completely alien to adults. However, the image of young people that the media portray is not necessarily the image young people have of themselves. According to a study of INJUVE (Rodriguez & Megías, 2007), young people feel that media images of them are "simple, stereotyped, and exaggerated." In general, young people complain about their portrayal in the media and ask to be represented with images that are closer to their real problems, like their difficulties in the labor and housing markets.

Research on education and new technologies presents a field in constant evolution, in which some technological applications question certain axioms in the model and suppose a first-level challenge for specialized research. In some cases, the integration of ICTs in traditional education involves a complete reformulation of the educational system. However, in most of the observable examples, what is happening is that traditional patterns of teaching and knowledge transference are reproduced, simply adding technology for aesthetic purposes.

Traditional education, understood as a process of one-sided transmission of knowledge, tends to be diluted towards a growing recognition that education is, in essence, a communicative process characterized by collaboration and negotiation of meaning.

In the field of communication theory, the concept of *prosumer* (producer + consumer) is getting stronger every day. This supports the belief that the so-called receptor is, in essence, a creator of new meanings and contents with strong abilities and capabilities to spread messages on a massive scale (Castells, 2009). At the same time, in the field of education theory, for decades now the concept of "competence" defends the ability of young people to assume a participative and active role in their own learning process. In this context, the concept of literacy itself—closely linked to the culture of books and to the school as the main institution—is being transformed as never before.

Under the denomination "new literacies" it is more than evident that reading, writing, and knowing the basics of math are not (and will not be) enough to participate actively in the information society. While school is dominated by conventional literacies, new literacies are exercised in the new digital cultural practices that students use outside of the classroom: mostly in a fun, informal context, without any adult supervision (Lankshear & Knobel, 2008, p. 50).

It is then very significant that young people themselves start to explore and work—generally in an intuitive way—these new forms of digital literacy. They test and create new spaces and areas of collaborative learning that are far away from the linearity, single direction, and formality of the traditional learning institution. In this way, they generate new ways of learning through play, creativity, socialization, and peer communication (Jenkins, 2006).

Through digital technologies, most of the young people maintain a constant contact with what Henry Jenkins calls a "participative culture": "a culture with relatively low barriers to artistic expression and civic engagement, strong support for creating and and sharing one's creations, and some type of informal mentorship whereby what is known by the most experienced is passed along to novices. A participatory culture is also one in which members believe their contributions matter, and feel some degree of social connection with one another" (Jenkins, 2006, p. 3).

The "Digital Gap": An Evolving Concept

The idea of digital gap is a relatively new definition with some controversy around it already. We understand the digital gap as describing the inequality experienced by individuals in the so-called information society who do not have access to ICTs. Also, there's another "gap" among those who, even if they have access to ICTs, don't have the knowledge or skills to take full advantage of them.

The digital gap is a key element of inequality in the access or quality of use for electronic services and it could be caused by technological, geographical, economic, social, cultural, or educational reasons. In 1970, Tichenor, Donohue, and Olien wrote about the *knowledge divide*, according to which every new ICT or new media increased the separation in the social system by creating those who were either "rich" or "poor" in information. Against the general opinion—that usually is more "kind-minded" with all new technologies—these authors sustained that a society that is more complex and rich in opportunities will create more differences and inequalities among its members.[4]

It is not surprising then that the "digital revolution" generates new conflicts and social tensions. It is important to state that the digital gap represents a mirror image of the social inequalities that can be seen in our societies.[5] For these reasons, the digital gap cannot be fought just with investment in technologies and digital access, but also with policies that fight against the causes of inequalities and poverty. Summarizing, the kind of policies needed are those that could deactivate the cast-away mechanisms that are part of the new socio-communicative structures, characterized by a network configuration (Castells, 2009).

When trying to research further around the idea of a digital gap, it is possible to find at least two fundamental historical moments with two completely different notions. At the beginning, the concept of "digital gap" or "digital divide" was more technological and economic. This "first gap" was detected at the moment when ICTs were initially implanted and the main problem was to ensure that the connections could be extended and guaranteed in all regions of the planet (this was also the moment when the term "informational highways" was created). This divide, accordingly, can be (re)produced basically in a geographical level, among regions or settlements that could be "connected" or "disconnected."

The second digital divide is produced at the moment when infrastructures already allow a connection in the whole territory and can theoretically guarantee universal access to the so-called information society.[6] However, it is possible to still see important differences in the availability and use of ICTs. This generates a general consensus according to which the main digital divide nowadays is related to the *conditions of access* and the *quality of use* of the ICTs.

The most appealing factor to explain this difference is age, but as we will discuss further on, there are many other cultural and economic factors that also contribute to the divide. The second divide has a highly generational component and includes what is called *digital literacy*—the ability to use such technology. In this sense, there is a clear difference among adults and young people, which sometimes can be explained by the availability of technology and the attractions it holds for people of different generations.

Digital Divide and a Generational Divide

The "Net Generation" is explained by Don Tapscott in his book *Growing Up Digital* (*Creciendo en un Entorno Digital*, 1998). According to Tapscott, the children of the baby boomers (those born between 1946 and 1964) are characterized by being the first generation in history that would grow up surrounded by digital media in an everyday basis. Offices, factories, homes, and schools have computers and usually other kinds of technologies like photo and video cameras, video games, DVD players, etc. All these media can also be interconnected as well as connected to the web, which is constantly growing in users and content. The members of this new generation are surrounded by various screens since their earliest days. As a consequence, to them ICTs are parts of their usual (natural) context: "To them, digital technology is as intimidating as a VCR or a toaster. . . . For the first time in history, the young generation knows more than their parents about an essential innovation for society, and also feels more comfortable about it than all their elders" (Tapscott, 1998, p. 1).

The members of the Net Generation, or Generation N, are already a force for social transformation, since they are learning, playing, communicating, working, and creating communities in a completely different way than their parents did. Tapscott offers data that show every day, the Millennials become more submerged in their digital world, alongside their "real" life.

Marc Prensky, in his article "Digital Natives, Digital Immigrants" (2001a, 2001b), clarifies what he considers to be a digital native as opposed to a digital immigrant. He maintains that students have already changed radically and those in the classrooms today are nothing like the previous generation who shaped the existing educational system. He's not only talking about superficial changes that might affect their clothes, their way of expressing themselves, or their accessories, as has happened in previous generations. The digital natives are those who—being born after 1990—form the first generation in a fully digitalized environment, are greatly familiar with the use of technological tools, and show an intuitive ability for such technologies

In this context, that group of young people—the digital natives as opposed to the digital immigrants—is considered to have a supposed new ability: the one to "understand" the use of the technology much better than those born to previous generations. This is because they consider their "virtual" life to be a natural and logical extension of their "real" life.

Growing up with audiovisual media, several screens, and technologies that are used synchronically gives them, according to Prensky, a "singularity" that makes them different from previous generations (2001a). The same author later notes this difference—although somewhat softens the radical dichotomy—and discusses how to produce a rapprochement between the two generations in the school and family relations through the use of ICTs (2006).

However, the concepts of digital natives and immigrants, as well as a digital divide, are labels that generalize and simplify a social change with many different nuances. The same authors who created those concepts are refining their initial positions towards them. The great merit in creating such new concepts is that at a certain moment in time they could explain essential issues related to new inequalities in advanced societies. However, they were not explained enough at that point, not by theoretical research, much less by observation or field work.

At this point, the research and approach between generations at school as well as at home through the use of ICTs can be clarifying and, at the same time, create new problems New intermediate scales are being created according to which it is possible to state that in a digital context, *digital native* is not a synonym for expert, nor is *digital immigrant* a synonym for ignorant.

The concept of the digital divide brings little information into this discussion since its—two key variables—knowledge of technology and economic growth around it—do not consider that it could be simply one more part of the generational difference. In order for it to be valid, this concept must add a new parameter of "quality of use" that can separate and clearly explain such gaps. Even if it is true that a young person can be more skillful in the technical use of a device (training), his/her parents and teachers have the possibility of using it with more sophistication, more critically, and involving richer contents and knowledge.

Therefore, the concept of digital divide, understood in terms of a generational divide, lacks depth. It is necessary to take into account new dimensions in the analysis in order to understand better a reality that is so complex.

Researching on the Digital Divide: A Methodological Proposal

Starting from the conflict and the generational divide that is given as a fact between parents and children (as well as teachers and students), the AUSTICA project aims to analyze the cultural distance among the generations and how such distance grows—or not—related to the degree of knowledge and use of ICTs. It aims to observe the most important differences in the use of these tools among teenagers, parents, and teachers. There is a whole system of beliefs, values, and attitudes developed by each of these groups relating to technology. It is also interesting to know what ideas are supported around these uses, in order to understand how the different generations complement or oppose each other.

We can at this point mention the three main objectives of the study: initially, we aim to confirm or prove false the hypothesis of a digital divide between generations; second, we want to study how such digital divide could influence the conflicts between teenagers and adults; and, finally, we would like to determine any conflicts related to this phenomenon, both at home and at school.

When embarking on a project of this nature and with the aim of getting the most comprehensive findings, the AUSTICA research group has searched for an interdisciplinary approach that combines sociology with communication theory, education, and other related disciplines. We have proposed a triangular process in the methodology combining qualitative and quantitative techniques in order to get results that are more interesting to different areas of knowledge.

Starting from here, the research being done is divided in three phases: an exploratory phase, a qualitative research, and a quantitative research. During the exploratory phase, interviews were conducted and a "state of the art" of research on the subject was collected and produced. This phase was fundamental to the development of our study, since it created the bases for the next two phases.

The qualitative study, which corresponds to the second phase, took place during the 2011–2012 school year with 30 focus groups in secondary and high schools in five Spanish cities: Madrid, Barcelona, Seville, Zaragoza, and Santiago de Compostela. There, students, parents, and teachers were interviewed. The third phase, an analysis of quantitative data, is already in preparation, taking into account information and databases lent by other entities that will allow a more complex overview on the subject.

Key Elements for Discussion

While it's a bit too early to offer conclusive findings, we have advanced on a series of important elements for discussion. As a result of the first exploratory phase of the study, we can pose these preliminary conclusions:

- The review of the studies conducted so far on the subject show a clear dominance of an "apocalyptic" imagery, based on a series of "negative fables" and the use of many negative terms (for example, references to "addictions" of "abductions") that seem to give ICTs a certain endogenous capacity to override the will of their users. As an answer to this, we think it is necessary to include other perspectives in the analysis (socio-cultural, socio-political and on media and communication education), going from appropriation to familiarization and vice versa.

- Even if *digital divide* is a concept largely used and accepted, doubts frequently arise regarding it. There is not a clear agreement on the ages where this divide appears, and who could be called digital natives or immigrants. According to authors like Prensky, this is not about a generational distance but about a social transformation where the ideas of the traditional educational cycle are changed. This matches with the ideas explained at the beginning of this chapter.
- When we talk about the digital gap and digital natives versus immigrants, it seems unavoidable to establish which are the abilities and competences that we are comparing: those that are strictly technological (use related), or the ones related to information management. Beyond the sophistication of the tool and its technical complexity, it is necessary to know what kind of interactions can be made with it.
- With respect to the generation of competence and the value of such new technologies, new concepts will be included in the discussion as *social network capital/value.*
- Young people and teenagers value the web as a continuation of their real world, while for most of their parents these are completely different environments.
- If for the young people the web is a continuation of the real world, parents and teachers should then also understand it as a continuum in the social fabric where they could also exert authority and create teaching opportunities that hitherto existed in the traditional classroom or the private living room.
- There is a clear concern inside the families regarding the amount of hours devoted to the use of ICTs. Again, the argument behind the so-called divides on the use of new technologies has been seen before—with television, for example. It is built upon a series of fears related with the fracture in the classic mechanisms of control that are not adopted in the family (or even the school).
- In the educational area, notwithstanding the possible gap or difference in the technical abilities that teenagers, parents, and teachers could have as users, these last ones have to face a new educational paradigm that asks for a greater disposition to learn from everyone.
- At the same time, it is important to reflect on aspects as the very much needed renovation of teaching methodologies, searching—as the society does in many other areas—new ways of participation and more flex-

ible roles for teachers and students, making education less a transmission and more a collaboration, negotiated, communicative, and creative.

- Finally, there is an important paradox according to which, despite the fact that we are constantly talking about digital literacy (the ability to use technology), ICTs are not taken into account in home and school habits. While teachers are using technological tools to teach and learn in the same way it was done since the 18th century (teacher using tools, in front of a classroom, not being confronted by students, not collaborating and receiving feedback), young people use technology in order to find new areas for social relationships and managing emotions.

Even if "digital gap" is a term with a lot of controversy in our field of research at this point, the results of the first phase of the AUSTICA group show, with several nuances, the explanatory value of the concept to illustrate differences in attitudes, knowledge, and practices involving ICTs among families, teachers, and teenagers, both in the home and in the classroom.

Our study suggests the need to move toward normalizing the discourse on ICT practices and uses—to give value while avoiding ontological or essentialist concepts of a digital divide. This discourse needs to play down the objective difficulties for efficient use by parents and educators, to promote a more active attitude on their part and to step away from the demonization of new technologies. At this point, we assume that teenagers, although they may show a high level of technical, creative, and instrumental competence in the use of technology and in the development of new digital practices, also need support and training that can only be provided by adults to achieve a true digital literacy that is more sophisticated and richer in content.

As a general conclusion, it can be said that there is a quest for control through new technologies. Hence, it is also necessary to strive for normalization within regulated environments and family life. This is not necessarily new, since the fight for control of new technologies—understood as media or not—has been a constant during the introduction of every one of them. So, with or without media as we traditionally know them, the quest for control is still there, now focused and transformed into the new possibilities that the Internet has to offer.

Endnotes

1. The AUSTICA project—"Use of ICTs and the Digital Gap Among Adults and Teenagers: Together and Far Away at School and Home" (AUSTICA) (National Research Program for Social, Economical and Law Sciences-National R+D+I program

2010–2012)—aims mainly to analyze the cultural distance between different generations. The team of the AUSTICA projected, directed by Jordi Busquet, PhD (Universitat Ramón Llull [URL]-Blanquerna School of Communication), is formed by Sue Arán (URL), Daniel Aranda (UOC), Sonia Ballano (URL), José Antonio Gabelas (UOC), Manuel Garrido (Universidad de Sevilla), Alfons Medina (URL), Silvia Morón (URL), Rosa Auriá Munté (URL), Alejandro Perales (URJC), Ismael Perecaula (URL), Pedro Reinares (URJC), Laura Ruano (URL-UOC), and Ana Cinthya Uribe (URL).

2. We maintain that communication research is now the cutting-edge research in social sciences, especially since its main subject of study is one of the most dynamic aspects of social interaction: the changes in the world associated with technological-communicational innovations.
3. It should be clarified that there have always been "new technologies" that, in one way or another, affect users' education and have generated public debate questioning the nature of the education itself. Since the creation of mass-circulation press in the late 19th century until the arrival of television, researchers have seen the mass media as a "parallel school" (Porcher, 1976; Goodman, 1976; Reimer, 1974; Illich, 1976). In fact, in the mid, 60s and early 1970s, the technological advances applied to the communication processes emphasized that education is ongoing and extends throughout one's lifetime, taking place in formal as well as informal settings (Ballano, 2009).
4. A similar vision was explained by P. Bourdieu and J. C. Passeron when in The Reproduction (1970/1977), they confirmed that during that time in France, the school system attempted to reproduce the same social and cultural models as the pupils lived at home, instead of creating greater equality among them.
5. When we talk about inequalities, we seldom think only of economic inequalities. However, there are also educational and cultural inequalities that have deep repercussions in complex societies.
6. At this point, the concept of gap/divide is mostly associated to the inequalities among the different potential users to access and use ICTs.

References

Aranda, D., Sánchez-Navarro, J., Tabernero, C. (2009). *Jóvenes y ocio digital. Informe sobre el uso de herramientas digitales por parte de adolescentes en España.* Barcelona, Spain: Editorial UOC.

Ariño, A. (2010). *Prácticas culturales en España: desde los años sesenta hasta la actualidad.* Barcelona, Spain: Ariel.

Asociación para la Investigación de Medios de Comunicación (AIMC). (2007). *Audiencia Infantil/Juvenil de medios en España 2007–2008* (En línea). http://www.aimc.es/-Audiencia-Infantil-.html

Ballano, S. (2009). *Educación, medios de comunicación y sociedad: Consideraciones sobre la educación mediática en el curriculum escolar* (Research work). Barcelona, Spain: Universitat Ramon Llull, Facultat de Comunicació Blanquerna.

Baricco, A. (2008). *Los bárbaros. Ensayo sobre la mutación.* Barcelona, Spain: Anagrama.

Bauman, Z. (2003) *Comunidad. En busca de seguridad en un mundo hostil.* Madrid, Spain: Siglo XXI.

Beck, U. (1994). *La sociedad de riesgo. Hacia una nueva modernidad.* Madrid, Spain: Siglo XXI.

Bourdieu, P., & Passeron, J. C. (1970/1977). *La reproducción. Elementos para una teoría del sistema de enseñanza.* Barcelona, Spain: Laia.

Busquet, J. (2008). *Lo sublime y lo vulgar. La "cultura de masas" o la perspectiva de un mito.* Barcelona, Spain: UOC.

Cardoso, G. (2008). *Los medios de comunicación en la Sociedad en Red. Filtros, escaparates y noticias.* Barcelona, Spain: UOC.

Castells, M. (1997–1998). *La era de la Información: La sociedad red.* Madrid, Spain: Alianza Editorial.

Castells, M. (2006). *La sociedad red: Una visión global.* Madrid, Spain: Alianza.

Castells, M. (2009). *Comunicación y poder.* Madrid, Spain: Alianza.

Feixa, C. (2006). *De jóvenes, bandas y tribus.* Barcelona, Spain: Ariel.

Gabelas, J. A., & Marta Lazo, C. (2008). *Consumos y mediaciones de familias y pantallas: Nuevos modelos y propuestas de convivencia.* Zaragoza, Spain: Gobierno de Aragón.

Giddens, A. (2000). *Un mundo desbocado. Los efectos de la globalización en nuestras vidas.* Madrid, Spain: Taurus.

Goodman, P. (1976). *La des-educación obligatoria.* Barcelona, Spain: Fontanella.

Illich, I. (1976). *La sociedad desescolarizada.* Barcelona, Spain: Barral.

Jenkins, H. (2006). *Convergence culture: Where old and new media collide.* New York, NY: New York University Press.

Jenkins, H., Purushotma, R., Clinton, K., Weigel, M., & Robison, A. J. (2008). *Confronting the challenges of participatory culture: Media education for the 21st century.* Chicago, IL: MacArthur Foundation.

Lankshear, M., & Knobel, M. (2008). *Nuevos alfabetismos. Su práctica cotidiana y el aprendizaje en el aula.* Madrid, Spain: Morata.

Livingstone, S. (2002). *Young people and new media: Childhood and the changing media environment.* London, United Kingdom: Sage.

Maffesoli, M. (1990). *El tiempo de las tribus.* Barcelona, Spain: Icaria.

Porcher, L. (1976). *La escuela paralela.* Buenos Aires, Argentina: Kapelusz.

Prensky, M. (2001a, October). Digital natives, digital immigrants. *On the Horizon, 9*(5). http://www.marcprensky.com/writing/prensky%20-%20digital%20natives,%20digital%20immigrants%20-%20part1.pdf

Prensky, M. (2001b, December). Digital natives, digital immigrants, Part II: Do they really *think* differently? *On the Horizon, 9*(6). http://www.marcprensky.com/writing/prensky%20-%20digital%20natives,%20digital%20immigrants%20-%20part2.pdf

Prensky, M. (2006) *"Don't bother me, Mom—I'm learning!":How computer and video games are preparing for 21st-century success and how you can help!* St. Paul, MN: Paragon House.

Rascovsky, A. (1975) *Filicidio, violencia y guerra.* Buenos Aires, Argentina: Shapire Editor.

Reimer, E. (1974). *La escuela ha muerto. Alternativas en materia de educación.* Barcelona, Spain: Barral.

Rodriguez, E., & Megías, I. (2007). *Jóvenes en los medios: La imagen mediática de la juventud, desde su propia mirada.* Madrid, Spain: FAD, INJUVE.

Roszak, T. (1968/1973). *El nacimiento de una contracultura.* Barcelona, Spain: Kairós.

Tapscott, D. (1998). *Creciendo en un entorno digital: La generación net.* Bogotá, Colombia: McGraw-Hill.

Tichenor, P. J., Donohue, G. A., & Olien C. N. (1970) Mass media flow and differential growth in knowledge. *Public Opinion Quarterly, 34*(2), 159–170.

6

Connecting and Protectecing?
Adolescents, Social Network Sites, and Privacy

MICHEL WALRAVE, WANNES HEIRMAN, AND ELLEN VAN GOOL

Introduction

The evolution of social media into a mainstream phenomenon constitutes one of the most important shifts on the Internet landscape to date. Social network sites (SNS) such as Facebook and MySpace have developed rapidly as a preferred communication medium. Along with the increasing amount of SNS, the number of people using these applications has sky-rocketed, with teenagers numbering amongst the most avid users. Notwithstanding considerable cross-national differences in this regard, eight out of ten online U.S. teenagers (80 percent of 12- to 17-year-olds) and European adolescents (77 percent of ages 13- to 16-year-olds) have personalized pages on at least one SNS (Lenhart et al., 2011; Livingstone, Olafsson, & Staksrud, 2011). These online platforms offer unprecedented opportunities for identity exploration and interaction with other social media users (Brown & Bobkowski, 2011). On the one hand, some studies highlight that young people's need for connectedness is compatible with their use of some "mainstream" media: media multitasking offers them the opportunity to use several media simultaneously, such as using a personal computer while watching TV (Roberts & Foehr, 2008). On the other hand, some studies report that young people, growing up in a media-saturated world, are turning more to digital platforms and take a step away from so-called mass media. For instance, in one study, adolescents, young adults, and older adults were asked what they had done during the past 24 hours. A majority of the adolescents and young adults were more likely to have watched a video online, to have posted a message on their SNS page, or to have played a video game. However, in the same study, the majority of older adults reported that they had watched TV or read a newspaper (Taylor & Keeter, 2010). Other studies report a steady decline of newspaper readership, especially among adolescents (Casero-Ripollés, 2012; Huang, 2009; Patterson, 2007; Raeymaeckers, 2002). Although adolescents' news consumption is influenced by socioeconomic status and other family-related context variables (Roberts & Foehr, 2008; Roe, 2000), this decrease can partially be attributed to an age and cohort effect. As they age, young people acquire the need for news and competencies to consume it. The cohort effect refers to the fact that the current cohort of adolescents would be less inclined to turn to traditional news sources (Vandebosch, Dhoest, & Van den Bulck, 2009). In sum, mainstream media are under pressure, especially among youth. Conversely, social media have permeated adolescents' lives not only for connecting with peers and entertainment, but seemingly also as a preferred news source (Casaro-Ripollés, 2012). Major media companies are therefore embracing social media, in order to spread news messages through online social networks. By doing so, they also gain access to the personal data of social media users, which can inspire marketing campaigns. Consequently, "Instead of interpersonal media becoming divorced from centrally produced media flows and offering an alternative social 'centre' to that offered by the media, it is more likely that 'social' media and centrally produced media become ever more closely linked" (Couldry, 2009, pp. 444–445).

As young people are enthusiastically integrating social media into their lives, one could question what motivates young people to engage in using social media in general and SNS in particular. Therefore, this chapter first highlights how SNS affordances match with the developmental processes that adolescents experience. Although SNS offer tremendous opportunities to share online content and socialize with peers, questions are increasingly raised on possible privacy threats. These concerns have inspired the two central research questions of a study that was conducted among teenage respondents: To what extent are teenagers disclosing personal data and using privacy settings in SNS? Which factors help predict personal data disclosure and the use of privacy settings? This chapter's central aim is therefore to investigate adolescents' motives for using SNS and which factors fuel their online data disclosure and privacy settings use. Finally, implications of the study's findings for awareness raising and education on SNS related risks are summarized.

Adolescents' Life Through Social Media

Adolescence is a life phase characterized by important and rapid physical, social, and emotional changes. The major psychosocial developments adolescents experience can be centred on five areas that take a special turn during adolescence: autonomy, identity, intimacy, sexuality, and achievement (Steinberg, 2011). Adolescents strive for more autonomy, independence of feeling, thinking, and acting, most notably from their parents (McElhaney, Allen, Stephenson, & Hare, 2009). Further, they develop a greater sense of who they are and develop their identity, including gender, sexual, moral, and other cultural components. In this, peers become increasingly important as adolescents develop a broader range of relationships with friends and romantic partners. Therefore, adolescents develop intimacy, close and caring relationships with others, and generally also become sexually active (e.g., Côté, 2009; Kroger, 2005; Steinberg, 2011). Finally, important decisions are made during adolescence with possibly long-lasting consequences, with regard to education and their expectations for the future. Many of the future plans and directions depend on educational achievements and other competencies youngsters develop during adolescence (Steinberg, 2011).

In this crucial life phase, social network sites and other social media can take an important role. They provide adolescents several affordances that help them develop and refine competencies that are crucial for their development (Livingstone, 2008; Peter & Valkenburg, 2011). First, profile and other content-sharing sites offer them opportunities to present themselves. They can easily develop their online profile page, by adding pictures and more personal information on tastes and hobbies, and engage in self-narratives. Adolescents can also compare how they present themselves in order to possibly validate their selves (Schouten, 2007). Youngsters can pre-test opinions and looks in the privacy of a selected group of other SNS users. They can decide which facets of their personality they want to highlight, but also aspects they want to explore or even aspire to assume (Subrahmanyam & Smahel, 2011). These try-outs can lead to feedback from which youngsters can learn.

Moreover, young SNS users can share important life events with a narrow or broad group and gain encouragements or support. By self-disclosing, reciprocity can be stimulated that can lead to closer relationships (Buhrmester & Prager, 1995). In fact, computer-mediated communication (CMC) has been found to stimulate more self-disclosure in comparison to face-to-face communication (Schouten, Valkenburg, & Peter, 2009). The reduced nonverbal and contextual cues in CMC could reduce people's inhibitions (Walther, 1996). This disinhibition effect can lead to more intimate conversations and mutual support (or "benign disinhibition") but can also lead to harsh or rude comments (or "toxic disinhibition") (Suler, 2004, p. 321). Next to other characteristics, one peculiar aspect of SNS can stimulate disinhibition, namely the asynchronicity of most SNS communication. On the one hand, asynchronous communication could augment adolescents' perception of control over the information they wish to disclose (Schouten, Valkenburg, & Peter, 2007). On the other hand, as users do not have to cope immediately with other users' reactions, they feel less inhibited (Suler, 2004). Therefore youngsters could engage in a broader range of topics and discuss more in-depth personal issues, than in face-to-face contact (Peter & Valkenburg, 2006). The same holds for other social media, where youngsters can share pictures, videos, or other content that depicts their hobbies or talents. With all of these venues for self-expression, young people can disclose and test several facets of their personality. Moreover, these conversations and information seeking and sharing can often slip under the parental radar.

In sum, social media offer youngsters peculiar opportunities to explore their identity, engage in intimate conversations, and more easily find advice and support, beyond the confines of face-to-face conversations (Subrahmanyan & Greenfield, 2008).

Research has also highlighted the positive outcomes of teenagers' SNS use. The inherent social function of these communication platforms allows users not only to engage in contacts established offline, but also to make connections with people who do not yet belong to their social circles (D'hanens, Courtois, Mechant, & Paulussen, 2010). These online social networks have been found useful both for consolidating ties in networks of close friends and families, or in the terms of Putnam (2000), the *bonding social capital*, and for strengthening weaker ties or *bridging social capital* (Burke, Marlow, & Lento, 2010; Ellison, Steinfield, & Lampe, 2007; Putnam, 2000; Steinfield, Ellison, & Lampe, 2008).

These expanded contact opportunities have been associated with elevated levels of self-esteem, thereby enhancing experienced well-being (Pelling & White, 2009). Self-esteem is particularly likely to be fostered as teenagers provide each other with positive feedback (Valkenburg, Peter, & Schouten, 2006). In this way, SNS can fulfill a very important function during adolescence, a period during which young people are developing their own identities (Calvert, 2002).

Privacy at Stake

Despite the tremendous success with which SNS providers have convinced Internet users to make profile pages, and to add to the sites' vibrancy by disclosing and updating personal information and opening up their profile page, concerns have risen about potential privacy-related risks for adults but more particularly for adolescents, ranging from inadvertently disclosing personal data to online aggression such as harassment and cyberbullying (Livingstone, 2008; Livingstone, Haddon, Görzig, & Olafsson, 2011; Palfrey, 2008; Vandoninck, d'Haenens, De Cock, & Donoso, 2011). Privacy issues also emerge from the SNS business models, which include the processing of personal data from users and subsequently exposing them to micro-targeted online advertising, in addition to the use of applications or other enhanced features and micro-payments for gift exchanges (Thelwall, 2009). Moreover, the policies of some SNS providers stipulate that particular pieces of personal information can be shared with third parties. The communication strategies in which advertisers use the personal information disclosed on profiles as a way to deliver highly personalized advertisements, however, imply that the usage of personal information extends beyond the original wishes of the SNS user (Hoy & Milne, 2010). In sum, while users willingly decide which information they will release, they may not consider that their information will be shared with third parties.

Although sharing personal information with other users is necessary to reap the benefits of SNS, the need to control the amount, nature, and audience of personal data is key in the present privacy debate. This concept of personal data control is central in Westin's (1967, p. 7) often cited conceptualization of (informational) privacy as "the claim of individuals, groups, or institutions to determine for themselves when, how, and to what extent information about them is communicated to others." In the context of SNS, Ziegele and Quiring (2011) expand this definition by explicitly referring to the *addressees* of the personal information and the *nature* of personal data disclosed, as both audience of information and type of data can be segmented in SNS and other social media. In short, they define privacy as an individual's ability to determine "what information will be made available in which way, to whom, when, and to what extent" (Ziegele & Quiring, 2011, p. 180). These definitions echo Altman's (1975, p. 24) conception of privacy as "selective control of access to the self."

As privacy is seen as an inherently social and dynamic process of optimization between disclosure and withdrawal (Tufekci, 2008), the relationship between Internet users' concerns with privacy and their actual privacy protective behaviours is rather complex (Ellison, Vitak, Steinfield, Gray, & Lampe, 2011). Previous research about data disclosure suggests that, although individuals report being concerned about their privacy, they disclose a great deal of personal information on SNS (Acquisti & Gross, 2006; Utz & Krämer, 2009). This apparent conflict between users' attitudes towards privacy and their actual data disclosure is known as the *privacy paradox* (Barnes, 2006; boyd & Hargittai, 2010; Norberg, 2007). This ambiguity can be partially explained by the level of *trust* that individuals share in other SNS users and operators, as well as by the level of *perceived control* over the access to their personal data on SNS (Acquisti & Gross, 2006; Dwyer, 2007; Krasnova & Veltri, 2010). In fact, users can implement two strategies to control their disclosures on SNS to a certain extend: (1) limiting the amount of personal information disclosed online, and (2) restricting access to this information to specific groups or individuals using privacy settings. In the following sections, we elaborate on both of these privacy-management strategies, as they constitute the focal variables of the present study.

Privacy-Management Strategies

Self-disclosure in the context of SNS is defined as "the amount of information shared on a user's profile as well as in the process of communication with others" (Krasnova & Veltri, 2010, p. 1). When users open SNS accounts or update their profiles, they can choose whether they are willing to enter some types of personal information in the entry fields provided.

Early research has found that SNS users apply a *privacy calculus* affecting the decision-making process concerning whether to disclose particular personal information on their profiles. More specifically, SNS users assess whether the benefits of data disclosure outweigh the possible risks (Hann, Hui, Sang-Yong, & Png, 2007; Krasnova, Günther, Spiekermann, & Koroleva, 2009).

In addition to decisions about data-disclosure, SNS users can also use fine-grained privacy settings to determine who will have access to these data, ranging from a broad group (e.g., all site users) to a narrower group of users (e.g., friends, friends of friends, or specific individuals). A study by Lenhart and Madden (2007) revealed that almost seven of ten teenagers restrict access to their profile pages in one way or another. More recently, Livingstone and colleagues (Livingstone, Haddon, Görzig, & Olafsson, 2011) found that 43 percent of 9- to 16-year-olds make their profiles private, so that only friends can access them. Almost three out of ten (28 percent) open their profiles to friends of friends and their networks, and a similar proportion (26 percent) make their profiles public.

Although privacy settings allow users to manage their accessibility, ignorance may prevent many users from using them to their full advantage. For example, not all young people know how to change the privacy settings. In Europe, slightly more than half (56 percent) of children ages 11–12, and three-fourths (78 percent) of 15- to 16-year-olds claim to be able to change these settings (Livingstone, Olafsson,

& Staksrud, 2011). Tufekci (2008) suggests another reason why teenagers do not increase their privacy settings: because teenagers' need to be seen is greater than their fear of experiencing negative privacy consequences, they choose not to conceal all of their personal information on their SNS profiles from larger audiences.

Research Purpose

The importance of SNS in the lives of young people and the numerous marketing campaigns targeting minors in the social media and on other websites, have inspired an increasing number of academic studies investigating teenagers' disclosure of personal data on SNS or other commercially driven sites (De Souza & Dick, 2009; Fogel & Nehmad, 2009; Hinduja & Patchin, 2008; Lenhart & Madden, 2007; Livingstone, 2008; Moscardelli & Divine, 2007; Walrave & Heirman, 2011; Youn, 2005). The previous paragraph addressed two strategies that allow users to protect their privacy on SNS. In this study, we examine factors that predict teenagers' willingness to disclose personal information and their use of privacy settings to conceal the information disclosed on their profiles.

Hypotheses Development

A literature review concerning the online privacy experiences of teenagers was conducted to identify which variables to include in the questionnaire and subsequent analyses. The search yielded the following variables: demographics (age, gender), level of privacy concern, socialization variables (peer influence, parental mediation strategies), and perceived importance of SNS. The hypothesized effects of these variables on teenagers' willingness to disclose personal information and their application of privacy settings were inspired by previous research results, as summarized below.

Demographic Factors

Previous research strongly suggests that the ways in which teenagers decide to use the Internet are partially determined by demographic factors (e.g., age, gender).

Age

During adolescence, young people increasingly disclose personal information to peers. In a review of 50 studies addressing self-disclosure among children and teenagers, Buhrmester and Prager (1995) found an overall age-related increase in self-disclosure to peers. Adolescence is a period of identity exploration, culminating in what Arnett (2000, p. 469) called "emerging adulthood." In the areas of love, work, and worldviews, adolescents try out various possibilities, gradually moving towards enduring choices. Self-disclosure can help adolescents to develop their identities by clarifying their own self-image and through external feedback from peers. Self-disclosure also serves other functions, including the development of intimacy (Buhrmester & Prager, 1995). Given that teenagers' use of SNS for self-presentation and peer communication increases with age (Lenhart & Madden, 2007; Livingstone, Haddon, Görzig, & Olafsson, 2011), self-disclosure on SNS could be expected to increase with age. Lenhart and Madden (2007) observed that older teenagers disclosed more pictures and school names than younger teenagers did, although there were no significant differences with other types of data. In their sample of adolescents, Christofides and colleagues (2012a) observed an increase in information disclosure with age. Livingstone and colleagues (2011b) found that older teens were more prone than younger teens to display their telephone number, school, or address on their SNS profile. Given that teenagers disclose more, however, they could become more inclined to use the SNS privacy settings to manage access to personal information. Interestingly, the same study found that adolescents' competence at changing privacy settings on SNS increases strongly with age (Livingstone, Olafsson, & Staksrud, 2011). Teenagers actually put this knowledge into practice, as children and younger teens (9–12 years) were slightly more likely than older teens (ages 13–16) to have a public profile (Livingstone, Olafsson, & Staksrud, 2011). This insight corroborates the finding by Christofides and colleagues (2012a) that adolescents' age predicts an increase in the use of privacy settings. In contrast, Tufekci (2008) found that adolescents tend to open their profiles to a broader audience as they grow older. Findings are thus mixed regarding the relationship between age and the use of privacy settings. Most studies, however, indicate that older teenagers use privacy settings more than young teenagers do. In this study, we hypothesize that:

H1a: Age is positively associated with the amount of personal information disclosed on SNS.

H1b: Age is positively associated with the extent to which teenagers restrict access to their profile data.

Gender

Early research suggests that females are generally more prudent and concerned with regard to online privacy (Fogel & Nehmad, 2009; Hoy & Milne, 2010; Lenhart & Madden, 2007; Turow & Nir, 2000; Youn, 2005). Women are more likely than men are to be concerned about third-party usage of personal information divulged on the Internet (Hoy & Milne, 2010).

Other research suggests that differences in the motives of men and women affect the type of personal information they prefer to disclose on SNS (Tufekci, 2008). Consistent with studies by Lenhart and Madden (2007) and by Fogel and Nehmad (2009), men were more eager than women to provide their telephone numbers and home addresses and to have public profile pages. In explanation, Tufekci states that men are more inclined to use SNS to meet new people and engage in new romantic relationships. In contrast, the women in this study revealed more than men did about their favourite music, books, and religion on their profiles. This could suggest that women use SNS primarily to consolidate existing relationships with friends instead of to meet new people (Tufekci, 2008).

With regard to profile accessibility, girls are significantly more likely than boys are to have private profiles, restricting access to their accepted friend lists (Hoy & Milne, 2010; Lewis, Kaufman, & Christakis, 2008; Livingstone, Haddon, Görzig, & Olafsson, 2011; Raacke & Bonds-Raacke, 2008). These findings suggest the two following hypotheses:

H2a: Girls tend to disclose less personal information on their profile pages than boys do.

H2b: Girls apply more access restrictions to their profile data than boys do.

Level of Privacy Concern

Numerous studies have explored the relationship between privacy concerns and online self-disclosure in marketing situations (Castaneda & Montoro, 2007; Diney & Hart, 2006; Moscardelli & Divine, 2007; Sheehan & Gleason, 2001; Sheehan & Hoy, 1999; Youn, 2005). More specific to SNS usage, several studies have found a negative correlation between privacy concerns and personal data disclosure (De Souza & Dick, 2009; Dwyer, 2007; Krasnova & Veltri, 2010; Nov & Wattal, 2009; Stutzman, Capra, & Thompson, 2011).

Utz and Krämer (2009) and Nov and Wattal (2009) found an association between higher levels of privacy concern and stricter privacy settings. More particularly, Stutzman et al. (2011) found that concern about information leakage increased privacy customization, namely restricting SNS-users' access to the profile content. Based on these findings, we expect:

H3a: Privacy concern is negatively associated with personal data disclosure on SNS.

H3b: Privacy concern is positively associated with teenagers' inclination to restrict access to their profile data.

Perceived Importance of SNS in Adolescents' Lives

SNS use is amongst the top five online activities of European adolescents (Livingstone & Brake, 2010). As these websites gain importance in teenagers' lives, intensive use could affect online self-disclosure and data protective strategies. As SNS users are more intensively discovering the benefits of online social networking, they could be inclined to disclose more about themselves. Self-disclosure has been found to beneficially affect befriending and bonding in several forms of computer-mediated communication (Trepte & Reinecke, 2011). As self-disclosure often leads to reciprocity, a process in which communication partners disclose more about themselves, this could further stimulate and intensify social interactions and again more self-disclosure (Buhrmester & Prager, 1995). Therefore, as SNS gain importance in an individual's social life, the tendency to self-disclose could be augmented to increasingly enjoy the benefits of SNS use. This is echoed by a longitudinal study, finding that not only individuals with a disposition to self-disclose use SNS more frequently. In turn, SNS use also influences the disposition for self-disclosure (Trepte & Reinecke, 2011). These effects are moderated by the amount of social rewards users receive, in terms of bonding with other users. Therefore, to investigate the possible impact of SNS use on self-disclosure and privacy settings use, the present study developed a scale for measuring respondents' perceived importance of SNS in their daily lives to assess their dependence upon SNS for communication with peers. Based on the above, we expect that as youngsters perceive SNS use to be more important for their daily contacts with peers, they will be more inclined to self-disclose, possibly to further augment their social rewards. Moreover, we expect that as youngsters find SNS use more important, they will open up their profile to a broader audience, to lower the thresholds to initial contact and the formation of common ground. Based on the aforementioned, we therefore expect:

H4a: The perceived importance of SNS in adolescents' lives is positively associated with the amount of personal data they are willing to disclose.

H4b: As respondents perceive more importance of SNS in their lives, they are less inclined to restrict the access to their personal data.

Socialization Variables: Parental Mediation and Peer Influence

Social factors also mediate children's and adolescents' online and offline experiences. In addition to parents, peers are amongst the most important socialization agents for teenagers. In the following sections, we explain our expectations regarding the potential influence of both agents on teenagers' privacy-management behaviour on SNS.

Parental Mediation

Parental mediation strategies involve "any strategy used to control, supervise, or interpret [media] content" (Warren, 2001, p. 212). An extensive body of literature has demonstrated that different parental-intervention approaches cause different outcomes in children's media consumption (Livingstone & Helsper, 2008; Sook-Jung & Young-Gil, 2007; Valkenburg, Krcmar, Peeters, & Nies, 1999). Research on parental mediation of media consumption amongst children and adolescents, however, has concentrated more on television viewing than Internet use (Kirwil, 2009; Livingstone & Helsper, 2008; Lwin, Stanaland, & Miyazaki, 2008; Mendoza, 2009; Sook-Jung & Young-Gil, 2007; Valcke, Bonte, De Wever, & Rots, 2010). Specific to the focus of this study, research on the possible influence of parental mediation on teenagers' online data disclosure is scarce, and the results are mixed. Studies by Livingstone and Helsper (2008) and by Walrave and Heirman (2011) report that parental mediation is a very weak predictor of the online disclosure behaviour of teenagers. Conversely, Youn (2008) found that parental efforts to use the Internet jointly and to discuss online content are related to the level of privacy concerns among teenaged Internet users. Similarly, Lwin and colleagues (2008) found that instructive mediation was more likely than restrictions to affect adolescents' online disclosure of personal data.

Parental mediation is generally regarded as a three-dimensional construct: *active* (or instructive) mediation, *restrictive* mediation (or rule-making), and *co-*

viewing (or parental monitoring) (Austin, 1993; Mendoza, 2009; Nathanson, 2001; Nikken & Jansz, 2006; Valkenburg et al., 1999).

Active mediation encompasses discussion about media content while the child is engaging with the medium (Nathanson, 2002). Various studies link active mediation to positive outcomes, such as increased levels of scepticism toward media content (Austin, 1993), reduced effects of advertising (Buijzen & Valkenburg, 2003) or violent programmes (Corder-Bolz, 1980).

Restrictive mediation involves establishing restrictions and/or rules for media usage (e.g., time or content restrictions). Meta-analysis has linked restrictions on television to slight reductions in television viewing amongst children (Allen, Burrell, & Timmerman, 2006). Pasquier (2001) found that restrictions could be inefficient, as children regard them as challenging, stimulating them to engage in forbidden behaviour to show their parents that they are growing up. Nathanson (1999) links very high and very low levels of restrictions to increased aggression amongst youths, associating a moderate level of restriction with reduced aggression. Mesch (2010) found that parental restrictions are effective protective measures against cyberbullying.

Co-viewing (or more broadly, *co-surfing*, which encompasses the joint use of media), involves parental presence while the child is using the medium. Several studies indicate that co-viewing increases the belief that television content is real (Corder-Bolz, 1980; Nathanson, 2002). Other findings indicate that this mediation strategy improves the learning level of children (Nathanson, 1999). Within the context of children's online activities, Sook-Jung and Young-Gil (2007) found a positive association between co-surfing the Internet and children's engagement in online educational activities. Cho and Cheon (2005) related parental engagement in shared online activities with their children to parents' perceptions of control over their children's Internet usage, thereby decreasing children's exposure to inappropriate Internet content.

In addition to the negative outcomes discussed above, studies largely show that parental mediation strategies improve children's understanding of television content and minimize some negative consequences associated television use by children. Research on the effects of parental mediation strategies on children's online activities remains limited. Based on findings mentioned above, we expect that mediation strategies for adolescents' online activities will improve children's ability to assess risks associated with online data disclosure. Equipped with this better understanding, teenagers whose parents apply these mediation strategies are likely to demonstrate lower levels of online disclosure and higher levels of privacy-setting use. We therefore hypothesize:

H5a: Higher levels of parental mediation are negatively associated with adolescents' disclosure of personal information.

H5b: Higher levels of parental mediation strategies are positively associated with teenagers' use of privacy settings to restrict access to profile data.

Peer Influence

An extensive body of literature addresses how peer influence affects adolescents' decision making in daily life (for a review, see Rubin, Bukowski, & Laursen, 2011). In the field of consumer socialization, peers are considered important agents of consumer socialization, especially during adolescence, influencing many adolescent behaviours (Ekström, 2010).

Previous research shows that young people are especially likely to use social networks to communicate with peers (Lenhart & Madden, 2007; Subrahmanyam, Reich, Waechter, & Espinoza, 2008; Valkenburg & Peter, 2007). These online interactions potentially foster the development of individual identity, the quality of peer relationships and self-esteem in young people (Valkenburg, Peter, & Schouten, 2006). Adolescents' use of SNS may provide a venue for receiving peer feedback about the self. This is especially useful for teenagers, who are highly susceptible to peer influence. Although empirical research on the relationship between peer influence and SNS disclosure is scarce, previous studies have suggested peer influence as a possible venue for future investigations on the amount of data disclosed by young people disclose on SNS (Acquisti & Gross, 2006). More specifically, teenagers who are more susceptible to peer influence and who feel more need for popularity among peers are presumed to be more inclined to provoke peer feedback by disclosing more and subsequently applying fewer restrictions to the disclosed information (Christofides, Muise, & Desmarais, 2009). We therefore hypothesize:

H6a: Adolescents who are more susceptible to peer influence will disclose more personal data.

H6b: Adolescents who are more susceptible to peer influence are more likely to open their profile data to a large audience.

Methods

Sample and procedure

In collaboration with MSN, an online survey was conducted in Belgium. A total of 343 young people ages 10 to 19 completed the questionnaire (55 percent girls; Mean age = 16; *SD* = 2). All respondents indicated having at least one profile page. To avoid priming the respondents, the survey was presented on the MSN starting page as a study on SNS use, and no allusions were made to privacy issues or concerns.

Measures

Importance of SNS: To measure the perceived importance of SNS in adolescents' daily lives, we developed a specific multi-item scale (e.g., "Being active on SNS is important in my life"; "When I cannot go online, I really miss my SNS"; "My SNS use sometimes causes me to neglect my homework"). Factor analysis identified one latent construct. Comrey and Lee (1992) specify the following standards for loadings: .32 = "poor," .45 = "fair," .55 = "good," .63 = "very good," and .71 = "excellent." According to these standards, two items had very good loadings (>.63) and four had excellent loadings (>.71). Factor-analysis results support a single-factor model, comprising six items. Cronbach's alpha (α) for this single-factor solution (.85) indicated good reliability in the current sample.

Privacy concern: To assess respondents' level of privacy concern, nine statements were presented (e.g., "I am concerned about what websites do with my personal data"). Responses were measured along a five-point Likert scale anchored by 1 (totally disagree) and 5 (totally agree). A single factor was identified with seven items loading as fair or good on the factor (>.45). The remaining items loaded poorly (<.32) and were excluded from further analyses. The reliability coefficient (α) for this seven-item scale was .77. Raw scores were summed, with higher values indicating a higher level of privacy concern.

Data disclosure: Respondents were asked whether they included various types of personal information on their online profiles (if respondents had several online profiles, they were asked to focus on the SNS profile they most frequently use). The 18 types of personal data included identity data (e.g., name, age, gender, hobbies, studies), contact data (e.g., email, mobile phone) and more sensitive data (e.g., relationship status, political orientation). The reliability coefficient for this 18-item scale was .86. For further analysis, raw scores were aggregated, with higher values indicating more disclosure.

Privacy settings use: Respondents were asked about the access that they granted for all items of personal data they reported revealing on their profiles. Four answer categories were presented: "only myself" (personal information provided on an online profile form but not accessible to anyone other than the user), "only friends," "friends of friends," and "everybody." The reliability coefficient (α) for this 18-item privacy-settings scale was .87. For further analysis, raw scores were aggregated, with higher values indicating broader access to personal data.

Peer influence: To assess the possible influence of peers, respondents were presented with seven statements based on Mangleburg and Bristol's *Peer Influence Scale* (1998). A single-factor solution was found, with two items loading as very good (>.63) and five loading as excellent (>.71) ($\alpha = .85$).

Parental Mediation: Parental Internet-mediation strategies were investigated using 23 items derived from Livingstone and Helsper (2008) and Youn (2008). A composite scale was constructed for the various parental mediation strategies ($\alpha = .75$); factor analysis discerned three sub-scales, with most items loading high on a single factor. Three mediation strategies were discerned. The first factor, *active co-surfing*, groups four variables depicting several aspects of parent-child interaction while using the Internet (e.g., "I sometimes surf together with my parent(s)"). The second strategy groups five restrictions that parents can place on their child's Internet use (e.g., "My parent(s) restrict me from visiting some websites"). The final strategy encompasses monitoring activities that involve checking children's online behaviour and using specific software (e.g., "My parent(s) check which websites I have visited"; "My parents have installed a program that registers which websites I visit").

Analysis

To investigate the hypothesized relationships among the focal variables, sequential regression was conducted with following dependent variables: personal-data disclosure on the SNS and use of privacy settings to restrict or broaden access to personal information. The literature review identified these as two possible strategies teenagers can use to guarantee their privacy on SNS.

Results

Descriptive Findings

Most Belgian youth active on SNS use Facebook (83 percent) and/or Netlog (79 percent). We found that teenagers often behave passively by checking updates of other SNS member profiles rather than actively posting messages themselves. A majority (54 percent) of teenagers consult the SNS at least once a day, while only one of six (17 percent) posts comments daily. Respondents were also asked about why they use SNS. Their answers suggest that teenagers use their profiles primarily to stay in touch with friends they rarely see (90 percent), those they often see (78 percent) and their schoolmates after class hours (68 percent). Most communicate also with family members (57 percent). About 46 percent explicitly reported using SNS as a venue for making contact with new people.

A large majority of the teenagers in this study disclosed general identity data, including forename, gender, and age (99 percent) and surname (89 percent), and most (96 percent) uploaded profile pictures. Slightly fewer users entered their hometowns (80 percent) and hobbies (81 percent), group memberships (82 percent) and schools (72 percent). Seven out of ten respondents provided the site with contact information, including email address (76 percent) or instant messaging (IM) contact details (67 percent), while fewer than half (48 percent) entered their mobile phone numbers. Other personal details were provided less frequently, including favourite brands (51 percent), political orientation (29 percent), or philosophy/faith (33 percent). Nonetheless, more than half (69 percent) noted their sexual orientation, and even more (77 percent) provided their relationship status.

Teenagers' Application of Privacy Settings

As Table 1 shows, teenagers readily share some types of personal data with a larger audience, while restricting access to specific other data to their friends. General identity data that make users searchable by other users (e.g., forename, gender, age and, to a lesser extent, surname) are particularly likely to be shared with all SNS users. Conversely, contact details (e.g., email, IM account, mobile phone) are often restricted to friends only. Moreover, many teenagers did not include (or restricted access to) contact details in their profiles, although one in six did make mobile phone numbers accessible to their friends. Although some data involving identity and personal life could be considered more personal in nature (e.g., relationship, sexual orientation), one in three respondents reported sharing these data with all SNS users.

To identify the variables with the highest predictive value for SNS disclosure and privacy-setting use, the formulated hypotheses were tested using hierarchical multiple regression.

Table 1. Personal data disclosure and privacy settings use (in order of disclosure)

Data disclosure and privacy settings / Personal data	Not disclosed	Not accessible	Only friends	Friends and their friends	All SNS users
Forename	1%	4%	18%	11%	66%
Gender	1%	3%	17%	11%	68%
Age	1%	4%	24%	15%	56%
Picture	4%	2%	34%	18%	42%
Family name	11%	12%	21%	12%	44%
Group member	18%	4%	24%	11%	43%
Hobbies	19%	5%	30%	11%	35%
City	20%	10%	35%	12%	23%
Relationship status	23%	5%	24%	11%	37%
e-Mail	24%	28%	33%	7%	8%
Studies	26%	7%	26%	13%	28%
School	28%	9%	27%	11%	25%
Sexual orientation	31%	8%	23%	7%	31%
IM	33%	26%	28%	7%	6%
Favourite brands	49%	6%	19%	8%	18%
Mobile phone	52%	27%	16%	4%	1%
Philosophy/faith	67%	12%	8%	4%	9%
Political orientation	71%	13%	8%	2%	6%

Predicting Teenagers' Data Disclosure

The initial sequential regression assessed possible predictors of personal data disclosure. The regression equation accounted for about 16 percent of the overall variance in SNS disclosure. The final model is summarized in Table 2.

Our analyses indicate that peer influence is the most important predictor of teenagers' disclosure of personal information on SNS. Teenagers with high susceptibility to peer influence disclose significantly more data. The second most important factor was gender. Girls disclose significantly less information about themselves than boys do. The third highest predictor was the perceived importance of SNS, indicating that teenagers who attribute a crucial role in their lives to SNS are more likely to disclose vast amounts of personal information.

Of the parental mediation strategies addressed in this study, only active co-surfing was found negatively related to the extent of personal information that teenagers disclose on SNS. No significant relationship was found between the other parental mediation strategies and SNS disclosure, or between respondents' level of privacy concern and SNS disclosure. In short, our analyses offer statistical support for H2a, H4a, H6a, with partial support for H5a. Conversely, H1a and H3a must be rejected.

Predicting Teenagers' Use of Privacy Settings

Sequential regression was conducted to determine which variables significantly improved the prediction of privacy-setting use. The regression equation accounted for 19 percent of the variance in the dependent variable measuring the use of privacy settings (see Table 2). The use of privacy settings was measured by a summation index, with higher values indicating a broader access to personal data.

Our analyses indicate that the application of privacy settings as another way for teenagers to manage their online privacy is best predicted by level of privacy concern. Teenagers with high levels of privacy concern are far more likely to restrict access to their profile information. This is remarkable, as we found no significant relationship between the level of privacy concern and SNS disclosure. Consistent with the results on SNS disclosure, gender was the second most important predictor of the application of privacy settings, with girls placing more restrictions on access to their online profiles than boys. Another similarity with SNS disclosure is that the perceived importance of SNS in teenagers' lives was the third highest predictor of the application of privacy settings. Teenagers attaching more importance to SNS in their daily lives reported placing fewer restrictions through privacy settings.

Other significant predictors of the application of privacy settings were age and peer influence. Contrary to H1b, we found that as teenagers grow older, they are more likely to provide a broad access to their profile data. Teenagers with higher susceptibility to peer influence placed fewer restrictions on access to their profile data. Parental mediation strategies did not significantly predict privacy-setting use.

In short, our analyses provide support for H2b, H3b, H4b and H6b, while H1b and H5b must be rejected.

Table 2. Multiple regression predicting personal data disclosure and privacy settings use

Disclosure of personal data		
		Final β
Demographics	Gender (1)	-.184***
	Age	.079
Privacy concern		-.063
Importance of SNS		.168**
Peer influence		.265***
Parental Mediation	Active Co-surfing	-.124*
	Restrictive Mediation	-.027
	Parental Monitoring	-.077
Adjusted R^2		.16***

Privacy settings use		
		Final β
Demographics	Gender (1)	-.213***
	Age	.185**
Privacy concern		-.255***
Importance of SNS		.196**
Peer influence		.167**
Parental Mediation	Active Co-surfing	-.046
	Restrictive Mediation	-.027
	Parental Monitoring	-.033
Adjusted R^2		.19***

(1) Coded as 0= boy 1=girl
*p < .05; **p< .01; ***p < .001

Discussion

Teenagers eagerly use SNS for self-expression and sociability, and these exchanges are based on personal data disclosure. Although profile sites offer important opportunities for strengthening existing relationships and expanding peer networks, disclosing information and giving broad access to this information could endanger the privacy of young people online. In this regard, early research has found a relation between SNS use, personal data disclosure behaviour, and teenagers' involvement in cyberbullying or other online risks (Livingstone, Haddon, Görzig, & Olafsson, 2011; Ybarra & Mitchell, 2008). Previous research suggests that, compared with adults, teenagers do disclose more personal information on SNS as well as other commercial websites (e.g., Christofides et al., 2012a; Earp & Baumer, 2003; Turow & Nir, 2000). Other more general studies of adolescents' behavioural decision making have found that this age group has a higher tendency to engage in risky behaviour (Furby & Beyth-Marom, 1992).

The explicit aim of this study was therefore to examine the predictive value of the selected variables with regard to the dependent variables: two privacy-management strategies for teenagers on SNS. We first investigated factors that predict teenagers' willingness to disclose personal information on SNS. We then studied factors that could help explain how teenagers use privacy settings to manage access to their personal data.

We found that the most important predictor of SNS disclosure was peer influence. Teenagers, who are more susceptible to their peers, tend to disclose more information on their profile pages. This echoes the results of another study (Christofides et al., 2009), which determined that the need for popularity among peers significantly influenced adolescents' SNS disclosure. Greater information disclosure augments the signals given to others about the self, thus possibly helping to establish common ground with potential friends and provoking additional peer feedback (Ellison, Lampe, Steinfield, & Vitak, 2010).

The second most important predictor of SNS disclosure was gender, with girls disclosing significantly less information on SNS than boys. These findings align with the outcomes of previous research (Youn, 2005; Hoy & Milne, 2010). This gender difference could be explained partially by differences in the motivations of boys and girls for using SNS: girls use SNS explicitly to consolidate existing relationships, while boys are more eager to meet new people through SNS (Tufekci, 2008). Disclosing more detailed personal information could pave the way for soliciting friendship requests from new people on SNS.

The third most important predictor of SNS disclosure was the perceived importance of SNS in teenagers' lives. This echoes results of a longitudinal study by Trepte and Reinecke (2011): users' predisposition to self-disclose has a positive influence on SNS use, subsequently affecting the disposition of self-disclosure. This process is reinforced by the social rewards users receive. In summary, the more users receive what they perceive as social rewards (in terms of bonding with other users), the more personal information they tend to disclose. Users who consider SNS important in their daily lives could therefore be intensive users, enjoying the social rewards associated with self-disclosure.

The most important predictor of teenagers' use of privacy settings, as a second-order SNS privacy-management strategy, was privacy concern. Teenage respondents with high levels of privacy concern were far less likely to provide broad access to their profile data than were respondents with low privacy concern. Interestingly, privacy concern did not significantly predict personal data disclosure. A potential explanation is offered by Livingstone (2008) who, based on qualitative interviews with teenagers, suggests that adolescents' definitions of privacy do not refer to the disclosure of specific types of personal information, centring instead on having control over who has access to which information. In other words, teenagers disclose personal information in order to sustain intimacy, although they wish to control this disclosure (Livingstone, 2008). This could explain why many of our respondents readily disclose sensitive information (e.g., relationship status, sexual orientation) while simultaneously trying to limit access to this information. It is thus possible that privacy concerns do not affect the mere disclosure of information, playing a role only when teenagers must decide to whom they will grant access to their profile data.

Moreover, as Peter and Valkenburg (2011) state, the affordances of SNS as highlighted by boyd & Hargittai (2010), namely the persistence, replicability, scalability, and searchability, while being potentially privacy-threatening, could be interpreted by adolescents as giving them opportunities to achieve their developmental goals. These goals of autonomy, identity formation, intimacy, and the exploration of the sexual self (Lerner & Steinberg, 2009; Steinberg, 2011) can be pursued also by adolescents' activities in SNS: especially the opportunities given to select and adapt information to present themselves online, to control the public to which they present this information, to search for other users, to engage in new relations, and intensify existing ones. This *perception of control* may partially explain adolescents' engagement in SNS and more particularly their inclination to disclose (sensitive) information.

Besides, research among adolescents observed that respondents who had a bad experience on Facebook (e.g., bullying, unwanted contact) were more likely to narrow the access to their profile using privacy settings (Christofides et al., 2012b). Moreover, the study demonstrated that the relation between bad experiences on SNS and controlling information access to the SNS profile was fully mediated by the respondents' knowledge of privacy settings. In other words, when confronted with a negative experience, youngsters would be more likely to seek out information on privacy settings to possibly prevent future negative experiences (Christofides et al., 2012b). Therefore, awareness raising and educational initiatives could focus on real-life negative experiences of young people, in the form of testimonials for instance, which could subsequently sensitize young people for possible risks and increase their motivation to use privacy settings.

Gender was the second most important predictor of the use of privacy settings. Again, we suggest that this difference could be explained partly by gender-based differences in motivation for using SNS (Tufekci, 2008). Moreover, Thelwall's Social Web Gendered Privacy Model states that concerns about physical security and harassment, but also social communication skills and needs, influence privacy concern and privacy-related behaviour. He argues that women have more concerns about their physical integrity and are more at risk of harassment while at the same time they have communication needs that are well met by SNS. Moreover, the remote access of SNS use provides them some kind of protection from physical harm. Therefore, women will be more motivated to use SNS while using the social web in a more privacy-conscious way (Thelwall, 2011).

Furthermore, our study found that teenagers attributing high value to SNS in their lives were far less likely to use privacy settings. As suggested above, heavy SNS users could partially depend on their visibility in order to find the gratification they need. This implies, however, that they must disclose more information and apply fewer privacy settings in order to remain visible.

Moreover, the present study found that as teenagers grow older, they open up their profile data to a larger audience. This is in line with Tufekci's (2008) finding that adolescents tend to open their profiles to a broader audience as they grow older. Conversely, Christofides and colleagues (2012a) found that adolescents' age predicted an increase in the use of privacy settings. Given that teenagers' use of SNS for self-presentation and peer communication increases with age (Lenhart & Madden, 2007; Livingstone, Haddon, Görzig, & Olafsson, 2011), relaxing their privacy settings could offer them more opportunities to broaden their online network, by being searchable and reachable by users outside their actual friend network.

As one of the main purposes of the present study consisted in comparing the influence of peers and parents, the role of both socialization agents is further underscored.

In contrast to the strong predictive power of peer influence, only one of the three parental mediation strategies (active co-surfing) was even weakly related to SNS disclosure. This could indicate that, when co-surfing with their children, parents try to sensitize them to possible risks of online self-disclosure. No significant relationships were found between any of the parental mediation strategies and the use of privacy settings. The socialization literature suggests a possible explanation: as children grow older, they perceive less severe consequences for not complying with their parents' wishes (Grolnick & Farkas, 2002). During adolescence, teenagers increasingly question the social norms and moral behaviours advised by their parents. Parental restrictions or monitoring could therefore be less effective than co-surfing (which shows interest in children's activities) and discussing specific issues. Another possible explanation for the lack of parental influence on privacy-setting use could be that the mediation efforts of parents are counteracted by their lack of knowledge and technical expertise (Livingstone & Helsper, 2008). Parents could therefore benefit if SNS providers were to assist them with more information and suggestions about using privacy settings and addressing this issue with their children. Still, parental mediation may become increasingly difficult, as an important number of teenagers (27 percent in the U.S., according to Lenhart, Ling, Campbell, & Purcell, 2010) go online using mobile phones. The rapid growth of mobile devices such as smartphones, game consoles, and tablets may render parental restrictions and monitoring more difficult, therefore increasing the importance of an open dialogue on ICT-related risks.

Our findings also indicate that adolescents stimulate their peers to disclose more information and to open their profiles to a larger audience. Relaxing their privacy settings allows teenagers to be more reachable by persons outside their direct networks, thus augmenting the number of weak ties (Krasnova & Veltri, 2010).

This study has several important limitations. First, it is based on a self-selected convenience sample of respondents who agreed to participate in an online survey. The data are thus derived from a purposive sample, thus limiting the generalizability of the results. Second, the cross-sectional nature of the data does not allow causal assertions. Despite these limitations, our study reveals important predictors of two privacy-management strategies that teenagers can adopt in order to warrant their online privacy.

The finding that teenagers' level of privacy concern is the most important predictor of their use of privacy settings could be particularly inspiring for future policy initiatives, as it implies that helping teenagers become aware of online privacy could help to optimize the use of privacy settings among adolescents. As observed in the second assessment of the European Safer Social Networking Principles, major SNS are already assisting young users by grouping e-safety hints in security centres or other dedicated websites. In half of all SNS, however, this guidance is difficult to find and understand. Moreover, despite their commitment to doing so, most SNS do not set minors' profiles to private by default (Donoso, 2011). Providers and other stakeholders should therefore concentrate on providing more adapted information to youngsters to empower them to manage online-profile information and access.

References

Acquisti, A., & Gross, R. (2006). *Imagined communities: Awareness, information sharing, and privacy on the Facebook.* Proceedings from Privacy Enhancing Technologies Workshop, Cambridge, United Kingdom, 36–58.http://www.heinz.cmu.edu/~acquisti/papers-/acquisti-gross-facebook-privacy-PET-final.pdf

Allen, M., Burrell, & Timmerman, L. (2006). *Impact of parental mediation on children: A meta-analysis.* Paper presented at the National Communication Association annual conference, San Antonio, TX.

Altman, I. (1975). *The environment and social behavior: Privacy, personal space, territory, crowding.* Monterey, CA: Brooks/Cole.

Arnett, J. J. (2000). Emerging adulthood: A theory of development from the late teens through the twenties. *American Psychologist, 55*(5), 469–480.

Austin, E. W. (1993). Exploring the effects of active parental mediation of television content. *Journal of Broadcasting & Electronic Media*, 147–158.

Barnes, S. B. (2006). A privacy paradox: Social networking in the Unites States. *First Monday: Peer-Reviewed Journal on the Internet, 11*(9). http://firstmonday.org/htbin/cgiwrap/bin/ojs/index.php/fm/article/view/1394/1312

boyd, d., & Hargittai, E. (2010). Facebook privacy settings: Who cares? *First Monday: Peer-Reviewed Journal on the Internet, 15*(8).

Brown, J. D., & Bobkowski, P. S. (2011). Older and newer media: Patterns of use and effects on adolescents' health and well-being. *Journal of Research on Adolescence, 21*(1), 95–113.

Buhrmester, D., & Prager, K. (1995). Patterns and functions of self-disclosure during childhood and adolescence. In K. J. Rotenberg (Ed.), *Disclosure processes in children and adolescents* (pp. 10–57). Cambridge, United Kingdom: Cambridge University Press.

Buijzen, M., & Valkenburg, P. M. (2003). The effects of television advertising on materialism, parent–child conflict, and unhappiness: A review of research. *Journal of Applied Developmental Psychology, 24*(4), 437–456.

Burke, M., Marlow, C., & Lento, T. (2010). *Social network activity and social well-being.* Paper presented at the ACM CHI 2010: Conference on Human Factors in Computing Systems, New York.

Calvert, S. L. (2002). Identity construction on the Internet. In S. L. Calvert, A. B. Jordan, & R. R. Cocking (Eds.), *Children in the digital age: Influences of electronic media on development.* Westport, CT: Praeger.

Casero-Ripollés, A. (2012). Beyond newspapers: News consumption among young people in the digital era. *Comunicar, 20*(39), 151–158.

Castaneda, J., & Montoro, F. (2007). The effect of Internet general privacy concern on customer behaviour. *Electron Commerce Research, 7*(2), 117–141.

Cho, C.-H., & Cheon, H. J. (2005). Children's exposure to negative Internet content: Effects of family context. *Journal of Broadcasting & Electronic Media, 49*, 488–509.

Christofides, E., Muise, A., & Desmarais, S. (2009). Information disclosure and control on Facebook: Are they two sides of the same coin or two different processes? *CyberPscyhology & Behavior, 12*(3), 341–345.

Christofides, E., Muise, A., & Desmarais, S. (2012a). Hey, Mom, what's on your Facebook? Comparing Facebook disclosure and privacy in adolescents and adults. *Social Psychological and Personality Science, 3*(1), 48–54.

Christofides, E., Muise, A., & Desmarais, S. (2012b). Risky disclosures on Facebook: The effect of having a bad experience on online behavior. *Journal of Adolescent Research, 27*(6), 714–731.

Comrey, A. L., & Lee, H. B. (1992). *A first course in factor analysis.* Hillsdale, NJ: Lawrence Erlbaum Associates.

Corder-Bolz, C. R. (1980). Mediation: The role of significant others. *Journal of Communication, 30*(3), 106–118.

Côté, J. E. (2009). Identity formation and self-development in adolescence. In R. M. Lerner & L. Steinberg, *Handbook of adolescent psychology,* (3rd ed.) *Vol. I: Individual bases of adolescent development* (pp. 266–304). Hoboken, NJ: Wiley.

Couldry, N. (2009). Does "the media" have a future? *European Journal of Communication, 24*(4), 437–449.

De Souza, Z., & Dick, G. N. (2009). Disclosure of information by children in social networking: Not just a case of "You show me yours and I'll show you mine." *International Journal of Information Management, 29*, 255–261.

D'hanens, K., Courtois, C., Mechant, P., & Paulussen, S. (2010). Apestaartjaren 3. Onderzoeksrapport. http://www.apestaartjaren.be

Diney, T., & Hart, P. (2006). Privacy concerns and levels of information exchange: An empirical investigation of intended e-services. *E-Services Journal*, 25–59.

Donoso, V. (2011). *Assessment of the implementation of safer social networking principles for the EU on 14 websites: Summary report.* Luxemburg: European Commission, Safer Internet Programme.

Dwyer, C. (2007). *Digital relationships in the "My Space" Generation: Results from a qualitative study.* Paper presented at the 40th International Conference on System Sciences, Hawaii. http://support.csis.pace.edu/CSISWeb/docs/techReports/techReport235.pdf

Earp, J. B., & Baumer, D. (2003). Innovative web use to learn about consumer behavior and online privacy. *Commun ACM, 46,* 81–83.

Ekström, K. M. (2010). Consumer socialization in families. In D. Marshall (Ed.), *Understanding children as consumers* (pp. 42–60). London, United Kingdom: Sage.

Ellison N. B., Lampe, C., Steinfield, C., & Vitak, J. (2010). With a little help from my friends: how social network sites affect social capital processes. In Z. Papacharissi (Ed.), *The networked self: Identity, community, and culture on social network sites* (pp. 124–145). New York: Routledge.

Ellison, N. B., Steinfield, C., & Lampe, C. (2007). The benefits of Facebook "friends": Social capital and college students' use of online social network sites. *Journal of Computer-Mediated Communication,* 12, 1143–1168.

Ellison, N. B., Vitak, J., Steinfield, C., Gray, R., & Lampe, C. (2011). Negotiating privacy concerns and social capital needs in a social media environment. In S. Trepte & L. Reinecke (Eds.), *Perspectives on privacy and self-disclosure in the social web.* (pp. 19–32). Heidelberg, Germany: Springer.

Fogel, J., & Nehmad, E. (2009). Internet social network communities: Risk taking, trust and privacy concerns. *Computers in Human Behaviour, 19,* 153–160.

Furby, L., & Beyth-Marom, R. (1992). Risk taking in adolescence: A decision-making perspective. *Developmental Review, 12*(1), 1–44.

Grolnick, W. S., & Farkas, M. (2002). Parenting and the development of children's self-regulation. In B. Webber (Ed.), *Handbook of parenting: Practical issues in parenting* (Vol. 5, pp. 89–111). Mahwah, NJ: Lawrence Erlbaum Associates.

Hann, I.-H., Hui, K.-L., Sang-Yong, T. L., & Png, I. (2007). Overcoming online information privacy concerns: An information-processing theory approach. *Journal of Management Information Systems, 24*(2), 13–42.

Hinduja, S., & Patchin, J. W. (2008). Personal information of adolescents on the Internet: A quantitative content analysis of MySpace. *Journal of Adolescence, 31,* 125–146.

Hoy, M. G., & Milne, G. (2010). Gender differences in privacy-related measures for young adult Facebook users. *Journal of Interactive Advertising, 10*(2), 28–45.

Huang, E. (2009). The causes of youths' low news consumption and strategies for making youths happy news consumers. *Convergence, 15*(1), 105–122.

Kirwil, L. (2009). Parental mediation of children's Internet use in different European countries. *Journal of Children and Media, 3*(4), 394–409.

Krasnova, H., Günther, O., Spiekermann, S., & Koroleva, K. (2009). Privacy concerns and identity in social networks. *IDIS, 2*(1), 1–25.

Krasnova, H., & Veltri, F. N. (2010). *Privacy calculus on social networking sites: Explorative evidence from Germany and USA.* Paper presented at the 43rd Hawaii International Conference on System Sciences, Hawaii.

Kroger, J. (2005). *Identity in adolescence: The balance between self and other.* London, United Kingdom: Routledge.

Lenhart, A., Ling, R. Campbell, S. & Purcell, K. (2010, April 20). *Teens and mobile phones.* Washington, DC: Pew Internet & American Life Project. http://www.pewinternet.org/Reports/2010/Teens-and-Mobile-Phones/Summary-of-findings.aspx

Lenhart, A., & Madden, M. (2007). *Teens, privacy and social networks.* Washington, DC: Pew Internet & American Life Project. http://www.pewinternet.org/Reports/2007-/Teens-Privacy-and-Online-Social-Networks.aspx

Lenhart, A., Madden, M., Smith, A., Purcell, K., Zickuhr, K., & Rainie, L. (2011). *Teens, kindness and cruelty on social network sites.* Washington, DC: Pew Internet & American Life Project. http://pewinternet.org/Reports/2011/Teens-and-social-media.aspx

Lerner, R. M., & Steinberg, L. (2009). *Handbook of adolescent psychology,* (3rd ed.) *Vol. I: Individual bases of adolescent development.* Hoboken, NJ: Wiley.

Lewis, K., Kaufman, J., & Christakis, N. (2008). The taste for privacy: An analysis of college student privacy setttings in an online social network. *Journal of Computer-Mediated Communication, 14,* 79–100.

Livingstone, S. (2008). Taking risky opportunities in youthful content creation: Teenagers' use of social networking sites for intimacy, privacy and self-expression. *New Media & Society, 10,* 393–411.

Livingstone, S., & Brake, D. R. (2010). On the rapid rise of social networking sites: New findings and policy implications. *Children & Society, 24*(1), 75–83.

Livingstone, S., Haddon, L., Görzig, A., & Olafsson, K. (2011). *Risks and safety on the Internet: The perspective of European children. Full findings.* London, United Kingdom: LSE, EU Kids Online. http://www.eukidsonline.net

Livingstone, S., & Helsper, E. J. (2008). Parental mediation of children's Internet use. *Journal of Broadcasting & Electronic Media, 52*(4), 581–599.

Livingstone, S., Olafsson, K., & Staksrud, E. (2011). *Social networking, age and privacy.* London, United Kingdom: LSE, EU Kids Online. http://www.eukidsonline.net

Lwin, M. O., Stanaland, A. J. S., & Miyazaki, A. D. (2008). Protecting children's privacy online: How parental mediation strategies affect website safeguard effectiveness. *Journal of Retailing, 84*(2), 205–217.

Mangleburg, T. F., & Bristol, T. (1998). Socialization and adolescents' skepticism toward advertising. *Journal of Advertising, 27*(3), 11–21.

McElhaney, K. B., Allen, J. P., Stephenson, J. C., & Hare, A. L. (2009). Attachment and autonomy during adolescence. In R. M. Lerner & L. Steinberg, *Handbook of adolescent psychology,* (3rd ed.) *Vol. I: Individual bases of adolescent development* (pp. 358–403). Hoboken, NJ: Wiley.

Mendoza, K. (2009). Surveying parental mediation: Connections, challenges and questions for media literacy. *Journal of Media Literacy Education, 1,* 28–41.

Mesch, G. S. (2010). Parental mediation, online activities, and cyberbullying. *Cyberpsychology & Behavior, 12*(4), 387–393.

Moscardelli, D., & Divine, R. (2007). Adolescent's concern for privacy when using the Internet: An empirical analysis of predictors and relationships with privacy-protecting behaviours. *Family and Consumer Sciences Research Journal, 35*(3), 232–252.

Nathanson, A. (1999). Identifying and explaining the relationship between parental mediation and children's aggression. *Communication Research, 26*(2), 124–143.

Nathanson, A. (2001). Parent and child perspectives on the presence and meaning of parental television mediation. *Journal of Broadcasting & Electronic Media, 45*(2), 201–220.

Nathanson, A. (2002). The unintended effects of parental mediation of television on adolescents. *Media Psychology, 4*(3), 207–230.

Nikken, P., & Jansz, J. (2006). Parental mediation of children's videogame playing: A comparison of the reports by parents and children. *Learning, Media and Technology, 31*(2), 181–202.

Norberg, P. A. (2007). The privacy paradox: Personal information disclosure intentions versus behaviours. *The Journal of Consumer Affairs, 41*(1), 100–126.

Nov, O., & Wattal, S. (2009). *Social computing privacy concerns: Antecedents and effects.* Paper presented at the Proceedings of the 27th International Conference on Human Factors in Computing Systems, Boston, MA.

Palfrey, J. (2008). *Enhancing child safety and online technologies. Final report of the Internet Safety Technical Task Force to the Multi-State Working Group of State Attorneys General of the United States.* Cambridge, MA: Berkman Center for Internet & Society at Harvard University. http://cyber.law.harvard.edu/pubrelease/isttf/

Pasquier, D. (2001). Media at home: Domestic interactions and regulation. In S. Livingstone & M. Bovill (Eds.), *Children and their changing media environment* (pp. 161–178). Mahwah, NJ: Lawrence Erlbaum Associates.

Patterson, T. E. (2007). *Young people and news.* Cambridge, MA: Joan Shorenstein Center on the Press, Politics and Public Policy, John F. Kennedy School of Government, Harvard University.

Pelling, E. L., & White, K. M. (2009). The theory of planned behaviour applied to young people's use of social networking web sites. *Cyberpsychology & Behaviour, 12*(6), 755–758.

Peter, J., & Valkenburg, P. M. (2006). Research note: Individual differences in perceptions of Internet communication. *European Journal of Communication, 21*(2), 213–226.

Peter, J., & Valkenburg, P. M. (2011). Adolescents' online privacy: Toward a developmental Perspective. In S. Trepte & L. Reinecke (Eds.), *Perspectives on privacy and self-disclosure in the social web* (pp. 221–234). Heidelberg, Germany: Springer.

Putnam, R. (2000). *Bowling alone: The collapse and revival of American community.* New York, NY: Simon & Schuster.

Raacke, J., & Bonds-Raacke, J. (2008, April). MySpace and Facebook: Applying the uses and gratifications theory to exploring friend networking sites. *CyberPsychology & Behavior, 11*(2), 169–174.

Raeymaeckers, K. (2002). Young people and patterns of time consumption in relation to print media. *European Journal of Communication, 17*, 369–383.

Roberts, D. F., & Foehr, U.G. (2008). Trends in media use. *The future of children, 18*(1), 11–37.

Roe, K. (2000). Adolescents' media use: A European view. *Journal of Adolescent Health, 27*(2), 15–21.

Rubin, K. H., Bukowski, W. M., & Laursen, B. (2011). *Handbook of peer interactions, relationships and groups* (p. 654). New York, NY: Guilford Press.

Schouten, A. P. (2007). *Adolescents' online self-disclosure and self-presentation.* (PhD dissertation). Amsterdam School of Communication Research (ASCoR), Amsterdam, Netherlands.

Schouten, A. P., Valkenburg, P. M., & Peter, J. (2007). Precursors and underlying processes of adolescents' online self-disclosure: Developing and testing an "Internet-attribute-perception" model. *Media Psychology, 10*(2), 292–315.

Schouten, A., Valkenburg, P. M., & Peter, J. (2009). An experimental test of processes underlying self-disclosure in computer-mediated communication. *Cyberpsychology, 3*, article 3. http://www.cyberpsychology.eu/view.php?cisloclanku=2009111601&article=3

Sheehan, K. B., & Gleason, T. W. (2001). Online privacy: Internet advertising practitioner's knowledge and practices. *Journal of Current Issues and Research in Advertising, 23*(1), 31–41.

Sheehan, K. B., & Hoy, M. G. (1999). Flaming, complaining, abstaining: How online users respond to privacy concerns. *Journal of Advertising, 28*, 37–51.

Sook-Jung, L., & Young-Gil, C. (2007). Children's Internet use in a family context: Influence on family relationships and parental mediation. *CyberPsychology & Behavior, 10*(5), 640–644.

Steinberg, L. (2011). *Adolescence, 9th ed.* New York, NY: McGraw-Hill.

Steinfield, C., Ellison, N. B., & Lampe, C. (2008). Social capital, self-esteem, and the use of online social network sites: A longitudinal analysis. *Journal of Applied Developmental Psychology, 29*, 434–445. https://www.msu.edu/~nellison/Steinfield_Ellison_Lampe(2008).pdf

Stutzman, F., Capra, R., & Thompson, J. (2011). Factors mediating disclosure in social network sites. *Computers in Human Behaviour, 27*, 590–598.

Subrahmanyam, K., & Greenfield, P. M. (2008). Communicating online: Adolescent relationships and the media. *The Future of Children, 18*, 119–146.

Subrahmanyam, K., Reich, S. M., Waechter, N., & Espinoza, G. (2008). Online and offline social networks: Use of social networking sites by emerging adults. *Journal of Applied Developmental Psychology, 29*, 420–433.

Subrahmanyam, K., & Smahel, D. (2011). *Digital youth: The role of media in development.* New York, NY: Springer.

Suler, J. (2004). The online disinhibition effect. *CyberPsychology & Behavior, 7*(3), 321–326.

Taylor, P., & Keeter, S. (Eds.) (2010). *The millennials: Confident. Connected. Open to change.* Pew Research Center. http://www.pewresearch.org/millennials

Thelwall, M. (2009). Social network sites: Users and uses. In M. Zelkowitz (Ed.), *Advances in computers* (Vol. 76, pp. 19–73). Amsterdam, Netherlands: Elsevier.

Thelwall, M. (2011). Privacy and gender in the social web. In S. Trepte & L. Reinecke (Eds.), *Perspectives on privacy and self-disclosure in the social web* (pp. 251–265). Heidelberg, Germany: Springer.

Trepte, S., & Reinecke, L. (2011). *Social network site use and self-disclosure online: A model of reciprocal influences.* Paper presented at the 61th Annual Conference of the International Communication Association (ICA), Boston, MA.

Tufekci, Z. (2008). Can you see me now? Audience and disclosure regulation in online social network sites. *Bulletin of Science, Technology & Society, 28*(1), 20–36.

Turow, J., & Nir, L. (2000). *The Internet and the family 2000: The view from parents, the view from kids.* Philadelphia, PA: Annenberg Public Policy Center.

Utz, S., & Krämer, N. (2009). The privacy paradox on social network sites revisited: The role of individual characteristics and group norms. *CyberPsychology, 3*(2).

Valcke, M., Bonte, S., De Wever, B., & Rots, I. (2010). Internet parenting styles and the impact on Internet use of primary school children. *Computers & Education, 55,* 454–464.

Valkenburg, P. M., Krcmar, M., Peeters, A. L., & Nies, M. M. (1999). Developing a scale to assess three styles of television mediation: "Instructive mediation," "restrictive mediation," and "social coviewing." *Journal of Broadcasting & Electronic Media, 43*(1), 52–66.

Valkenburg, P. M., & Peter, J. (2007). Preadolescents' and adolescents' online communication and their closeness to friends. *Developmental Psychology, 43,* 267–277.

Valkenburg, P. M., Peter, J., & Schouten, A. P. (2006). Friend networking sites and their relationship to adolescents' well-being and social self-esteem. *CyberPsychology & Behaviour, 9*(5), 584–590.

Vandebosch, H., Dhoest, A., & Van den Bulck, H. (2009). News for adolescents: Mission impossible? An evaluation of Flemish television news aimed at teenagers. *Communications, 34,* 125–148.

Vandoninck, S., d'Haenens, L., De Cock, R., & Donoso, V. (2011). Social networking sites and contact risks among Flemish youth. *Childhood: A Global Journal of Child Research,* 1–17.

Walrave, M., & Heirman, W. (2011). Disclosing or protecting? Teenagers' online self-disclosure. In S. Gutwirth, Y. Poullet, P. De Hert, & R. Leenes (Eds.), *Computers, privacy and data protection: An element of choice* (pp. 285–307). Dordrecht, Netherlands: Springer.

Walther, J. B. (1996). Computer-mediated communication: Impersonal, interpersonal, and hyperpersonal interaction. *Communication Research, 23*(1), 3–43.

Warren, R. (2001). In word and deeds: Parental involvement and mediation of children's television viewing. *Journal of Family Communication, 1*(4), 211–231.

Westin, A. F. (1967). *Privacy and freedom.* New York, NY: Atheneum.

Ybarra, M. L., & Mitchell, K. J. (2008). How risky are social networking sites? A comparison of places online where youth sexual solicitation and harassment occurs. *Pediatrics, 121,* e350–e357.

Youn, S. (2005). Teenagers' perception of online privacy and coping behaviors: A risk-benefit appraisal approach. *Journal of Broadcasting & Electronic Media, 49*(1), 86–110.

Youn, S. (2008). Parental influences and teens' attitude toward online privacy protection. *Journal of Consumer Affairs, 42*(3), 362–388.

Ziegele, M., & Quiring, O. (2011). Privacy in social network sites. In S. Trepte & L. Reinecke (Eds.), *Perspectives on privacy and self-disclosure in the social web* (pp. 175–189). Heidelberg, Germany: Springer.

7 Hyperreal Higher Education

JAMES MOIR

Introduction

Tara Brabazon (2007) in her book, *The University of Google*, argues that being a student in today's world of higher education is like living in someone else's iPod given the need for permanent reskilling. This is deemed necessary in order to mirror market flexibility and produce graduates whose programmes of study are being packaged as such. It is claimed content has become a means to procure more or less elaborate competencies, and as a result, graduates are considered as aggregates of attributes. She argues that:

> The transference from a manufacturing to an information-driven economy necessitates permanent reskilling. The cost of labour market flexibility is educational standards and scholarly excellence. (p. 163)

If we are to avoid reducing student learning to solely being an index of employability, then we must harness the capabilities of digital media in such a way that we ensure that scholarship is the engine of its usage in higher education rather than simply developing the student into a "future worker."

This chapter argues that such a diminution of critical independent learning is not an inevitability in an age of life without traditional media, and that we should grasp the new rhetoric of democratisation afforded by the process of cultural and knowledge digitization at face value. In other words, it is suggested that far from letting this process move beyond students' ability to analyse it, higher education should instead work from within digital culture in terms of engaging with the changing relations between audience and author, expert and amateur, and creator and consumer. If, as Baudrillard suggests, we consume signs, then consumers have to be capable of reading the system of consumption in order to gain the knowledge of what to consume. This indeed is Baudrillard's hyperreality, where in sociological terms production and consumption have been transformed and where "we no longer partake in the drama of alienation, but are in the ecstasy of communication." (1988, p. 22).

Beyond Books, Beyond Reading?

Lamenting the rise of the e-book and the e-book reader, Klinkenborg (2010) writes:

> I already have a personal library. But most of the books I've ever read have come from lending libraries. Barnes & Noble has released an e-reader that allows short-term borrowing of some books. The entire impulse behind Amazon's Kindle and Apple's iBooks assumes that you cannot read a book unless you own it first—and only you can read it unless you want to pass on your device. That goes against the social value of reading, the collective knowledge and collaborative discourse that come from access to shared libraries. That is not a good thing for readers, authors, publishers or our culture.

However, is the rise of e-books, and in particular e-books in higher education, a sign of the times that students are switching to electronic media as a key information sources in their studies? As the great American author Mark Twain said on hearing that his obituary had been published in the *New York Journal*: "Reports of my death have been greatly exaggerated." Is this the case with printed books? The rise of the e-book has often been regarded as something of an inevitability in higher education, as in the world of popular literature. However, matters are not so clear-cut; as a recent study has highlighted, only 12 percent of students were found to use e-textbooks, and when those who were required to do so as part of their studies were removed, the actual figure choosing to use them was 4 percent (Marques de Oliveira, 2012). Despite the rise of digital resources and e-textbooks, it is still the case that the majority of students are not engaging with these resources.

However, while students may be less inclined to use e-books due to such factors as lack of awareness, cost, and eyestrain, it is also the case that they value portability and instant access, and that the library is not their main point of entry for search for e-books. Indeed taking this further by applying Brabazon's arguments above, it is perhaps more of a case of students simply not reading books per se. Slow learning through reading has given way to instant access, to snippets of "information" that are downloaded for specific instrumental purposes such as assessments that test for specific and sometimes narrowly defined learning outcomes. This can be thought of as analogous to the way in which popular music is now downloadable in terms of specific songs. It is now easy to personalize your own choice of songs and download them at relatively little cost. Meanwhile, the idea of buying an album as a coherent body of work by an artist has been largely lost. Likewise, students now download academic material to garner specific bits of "information" rather than to gain depth of understanding through extended reading. Such is higher education in the information age, where the agency of the student in terms of choice and selection of downloadable material overrides broader educational ends.

Higher Education and the Knowledge Economy

In presenting these arguments, I want to turn to the work of Watts (2008, 2010) in his examination of higher education as a form of hyperreality. Watts asks the question: Does higher education "really" take place? In particular, does it take place for those students targeted by government policy for better access to higher education? The crux of his arguments is that higher education policy is akin to Jean Baudrillard's notion of the simulacrum—the model of something that does not exist (1983, 1993, 2004). He goes on to use this social theory to argue that educationalisation—the framing of social problems as educational problems—contributes to the perpetuation of the very problems it sets out to remedy; in this case, the policy of widening access to higher education in the United Kingdom.

In the U.K., as in other countries, higher education is held up as a means of addressing problems of social and economic inequality. Widening participation strategies are therefore intended to tackle these problems in order to increase the level of social capital, and in so doing, enhance employability. Yet as Bourdieu (1977, 1996; Bourdieu & Passeron, 1977) argues, educational systems are complicit in the reproduction of inequalities. Watts therefore blends this argument with the notion of higher education policy as a hyperreality of widening participation to suggest that the problems of access diverts attention away from what he argues is the real issue: that higher education policy in the United Kingdom is failing a significant proportion of the population. In other words, it is considered as a simulacrum in that it has taken on a life of its own such that even educational researchers are caught up in the discourse of improving participation in and of itself with respect to preparation for the knowledge-based economy. The assumption is that we need greater numbers of graduates who are able to operate in such an economy and who have the information literacy and technology skills to be able to adapt and future-proof their employability prospects.

This is particularly the case with respect to newer universities in the U.K., which present their course offerings as building employability skills as a means of preparing the knowledge workers of the future. However, from Bourdieu's sociology of education perspective, students with lower reserves of cultural capital progress through universities that typically provide them with less capital but often use the rhetoric of employability found among more prestigious institutions (Bourdieu, 1977, 1996; Bourdieu & Passeron, 1977). Watts uses this argument to suggest that this policy is in the realm of the hyperreal because it has become its own "reality" regardless of the economic and social justice arguments that originally framed it. Thus although more students may be entering higher education, they are not necessarily coming out of it with the economic and social benefits that are still used to justify the current policies, and this is particularly acute in light of the current economic climate.

Extending the Argument: From Higher Education as Hyperreality to Higher Education as Authentic Self-Realisation

In presenting Watts' argument above, my aim has been to demonstrate that higher education policy can be characterised as in the realm of the hyperreal. However, it is also possible to extend his argument into the world of higher education practice down at the level of individual student engagement. In doing so, my aim is to show how an associated focus on the personalisation of higher education can also be characterised as a simulacrum.

Personalisation and the personal have rapidly risen up the agenda within the pedagogical discourse of higher education. This is perhaps unsurprising in a mass higher education system in which questions of diversity, difference, and widening participation have taken centre stage. It is also arguable that this focus on the personal is an effective counter to the notion that mass higher education has brought with it mass teaching. However, it is also acknowledged that the notion of personalisation has been imported from the United States and has also been associated with changes in a variety of sectors and services to include the notion of customisation. In this regard, the users or customers are considered as of utmost importance in the way that products and services can be tailored to their requirements. It was in *Future Perfect* by Davis (1987) that the notion of "mass customisation" was elaborated in terms of the same large number of customers being reached in the mass markets of the industrial economy, and yet simultaneously being treated individually. However, whilst the rhetoric of customisation is couched in terms of meeting individual customer needs, there is also an underlying business drive to ensure that this serves to build up a lasting individual relationship with each customer, and thus increase customer loyalty and their purchasing power. The application of this commercial model to the new world of market-like public services has meant a similar tailoring of services to meet individual users' needs.

However, in the world of education there has also been the application of a psychological perspective on personalisation that equates this with improved learning and motivation. The major pedagogical implication of such an approach is the adoption of measures designed to encourage students to be self-learning, self-actualising, and self-initiating. As with customisation, there is an assumption that a homogeneous offering is not sufficient in meeting students' needs. The goal is therefore to employ pedagogies that meet these with an efficiency that is deliverable for a mass higher education system. Yet, despite the emphasis on meeting needs, there is also a major driver behind the move towards personalisation: the explicit recognition that mass higher education has led to increased drop-out rates because some students fail to engage sufficiently with their programmes of study. The reasons for this are complex, but it is clear that the drive to widen participation has been accompanied by a drop corresponding retention rates. This in turn has led to a focus on the extent to which students can maintain a sustained effort over the course of their studies, their ability to persevere.

Influential writers such as Barnett (2007, 2009) suggest that the "will to learn" is a key aspect of the student experience that needs to be encouraged and nurtured. According to this view, it is not the subject of study or the acquisition of skills that educators need to focus on, but rather personal aspects such as authenticity, dispositions, inspiration, passion, and spirit. Of course, this is not a new idea but what perhaps Barnett has drawn attention to more than others is how this process is related to an increasingly uncertain age. As he puts it:

> The fundamental educational problem of a changing world is neither one of knowledge nor of skills but is one of *being*. To put it more formally, the educational challenge of a world of uncertainty is ontological in nature. (Barnett, 2007, p. 51)

In this regard, his work chimes to some extent with the zeitgeist of the times (Beck, 1992; Sennett 2006; Elliot & Lemert, 2006): an age of insecurity and risk, of individualism set in relation to appeals to the market-like structures and globalisation that are valued in and of themselves as an ethic for guiding human action, of constant self-reinvention capable of producing greater freedom but also anxiety. This has been exacerbated by the current worldwide economic downturn and the requirement for higher education to be seen as "delivering" in terms of employability in an increasingly insecure economic and organisational environment. The requirement for graduates to be adaptable and entrepreneurial has therefore never been greater, and it exists within a world of instability and uncertainty.

However, whilst this age may well be one of uncertainty, Barnett calls upon educators in higher education to consider how they can develop curricula and pedagogies that provide students with the qualities to persist, adapt, and thrive in this environment. Much of his focus is therefore directed towards how such qualities or attributes can be developed, and in doing so this connects with related concepts such as personal development planning (PDP) and graduate attributes (GAs). One of the most influential researchers on GAs is Simon Barrie, and his work has had a significant impact on thinking about the nature of generic GAs in higher education (Barrie, 2004, 2006, 2007). For, example, in developing a conceptual framework for the development of GAs, Barrie (2007) notes a series of factors including, under the heading of participation, "generic attributes are learnt by the way students participate and engage with all the experiences of university life" (pp. 444–449).

This move away from the almost exclusive focus on higher education as involving the transmission of knowledge to a growing focus of the learner and the transformational nature of the experience is very much in alignment with the focus on GAs. The ability to adapt to changing circumstances, to work across knowledge boundaries, and to become active and engaged citizens are therefore crucial outcomes for this approach. Examples of such work include: inquiry-based learning as a route to the development of graduate attributes, critical thinking skills modules, changes in assessment practices that involve self and peer assessment, and work-based learning. The eventual aim is to consider a more holistic and unified approach to the development of GAs as a defining aspect of student identity.

However, this approach to higher education reform is not without a number of challenges and tensions with respect to how students consider their identities as being the subject of a process of engineering and re-engineering in terms of graduate attributes. Indeed this begs the question about the attribution of graduate attributes themselves. Are these attributes part of the hyperreality of higher education or are they a genuine means to shaping particular kinds of personal identity? And if the latter is the case, a further question arises as to how students themselves regard this overt focus on "engineering the personal" and the notion that they should be engaged in a continual process of re-engineering in light of current economic and even perhaps ideological conditions? In other words, the view that students themselves should internalize a view of personal and individual responsibility with regards to issues of employability and citizenship is one that is profoundly ideological in terms of attribution for actions and accountability. This is all the more acute when considering the discourses that surround the causes, consequences, and solutions of the current economic recession.

If GAs are considered as a means of developing social capital, then a question that follows is how they are related to notions of self-development. It is at this point that I wish to draw upon the contemporary writing of Petersen (2011), who draws attention to the way in which authentic self-realisation has become *the* guiding normative demand in modern society. His focus is very different from mine in that he is concerned with how this is related to the pathology of depression when people fail to maintain a sense of self-development. However, I want to focus on the flip side of this in terms of the drive to develop graduate attributes as a form of self-realisation. Therefore, although I do not share his focus on the sociological roots of pathology, I am nonetheless interested in the manifestation of authentic self-realisation through the vehicle of GAs.

Petersen begins by aligning himself with Boltanski and Chiapello's (2005) insight in *The New Spirit of Capitalism*, with regard to the emergence of a new ideological commitment to capitalism based on self-realisation. They argue that this commitment is premised on a different normative foundation than previously adhered to, one based on people's engagement with the capitalist system in terms of the project of self-realisation. Boltanski and Chiapello argue that capitalism has thrived on critique in order to mutate and adapt to changing socio-historical circumstances. That critique of capitalism has taken two broad forms: social and artistic. The social critique has involved exposing the exploitative nature of capitalism in terms of such aspects as poverty, social injustice, and rampant individualism. The artistic critique has focused on the ways in which capitalism reduces people to being cogs in an economic machine and thereby delivers a technocratic and dehumanized society. In other words, they point out that the artistic critique is concerned with the oppression of individual creativity, autonomy, spontaneity, and authenticity through the relentless pursuit of standardisation (Boltanski & Chiapello, 2005, p. 37). However, this latter form of critique has taken hold to such an extent that capitalism has had to move with the times and has in large measure absorbed it into its own ideological basis by stressing the need for individuals to seek self-realisation through the various inter-connecting spheres of an individual's life (in work, through education, at home, etc.).

This new form of ideology requires that the individual considers him or herself as an ongoing "project" of authentic self-realisation. This is attained through activities that allow this aspect of self to be developed in the workplace, private life, and leisure. Given this logic, and the rapidly changing world of the knowledge economy and society, individuals must learn to develop and deploy a range of attributes that allow them to be flexible, mobile, enterprising, creative, adaptable, and malleable. As Petersen notes in direct reference to the work of Chiapello and Fairclough:

> What is relevant is to be always pursuing some sort of activity, never to be without a project, without ideas, to be always looking forward to, and preparing for, something along with other persons, who are brought together by the same drive for activity. (Chiapello & Fairclough, 2002, p. 192)

It is but a short step from this characterisation of modern subjectivity to consider the common stock of GAs such as "flexible collaborators," "active enquirers," and "creative handlers of complexity" as nothing less than an attempt to specify the normative content of self-realisation. And yet, there is a clear tension here for some between what they regard as the academic nature of personal development leading to personal growth and the concomitant contribution to an educated citizenry, and the underlying national imperative that requires knowledge linked to economic wealth creation. However, in an era of mass higher education, it is often the latter that is a priority for governments, and no more so than in the current economic climate. In other words, the project of authentic self-realisation has also been assimilated into the hyperreality that is higher education policy.

It is also the case that with the concept of GAs, the purpose and meaning of higher education qualifications now extends to that of individual behaviour. An individual's personal and social patterns of behaviour have become normalized as part of his or her portfolio of GAs related to "graduateness" and "employability skills." This new vocationalist emphasis has been conceptualized as part of a neoliberal discourse in which "the market" has come to dictate how we view the "outputs" of higher education. This new rhetoric represents a fundamental change in how higher education is legitimated; one in which it is less in terms of subject-specific qualifications and more towards the possession of attributes that equip graduates to respond to the changing nature of the labour market. In this sense, the personal is made public and in effect codifies desired individual behaviour resulting from the educational process.

The whole notion of GAs is one that involves PDP and the idea of the self. Thus, at one and the same time it can appear that such a focus on the individual represents "empowerment" whilst also normalizing the notion that it is the student who is required to measure up to GAs in order to acquire the human capital necessary to meet the demands of a rapidly changing world, and with particular reference to "the market." And given that this is now a world of rapid change and uncertainty, these attributes are related to self-competencies that enable strategic "coping mechanism" for gaining employment, keeping it, constant re-skilling, and the use of entrepreneurial skills to create new employment. The graduate of the 21st century is therefore one who is autonomous, self-organizing, self-motivated, self-controlled, and able to generate his or her own opportunities. In other words, today's graduates are expected to engage in higher education as a pathway towards a career of authentic self-realisation through the internalization of PDP. More often than not, this is now conducted through platforms for virtual learning environments within higher education institutions. Such an instrumental approach all but confirms higher education's role as being in the service of the economy, and of course it is difficult to argue otherwise given the worldwide economic situation.

Beyond Engineered Authenticity: A Life Within Digital Media

Perhaps an ideal goal for some would be for students to step into the world of digital web-based learning as they step back from the more engineered modes of learning associated with GAs as authentic self-realisation. Within higher education, there may be many who wish to promote the ideal of graduate attributes as a means to attaining a sense of citizenship, and not just as an index of employability. This may seem an attractive and attainable prospect through the enhancement of learning via various Web 2.0 tools. After all, the hallmark of these is their openness, scope for collaboration, and creativity. There are differing stages in the adoption of these across higher education institutions, but it is clear that the "virtual university" is with us to some extent or another. If we are therefore to avoid the reduction of student learning to corporate ends and a concern solely with "future workers," then it is clear we must harness the capabilities of the web in such a way that scholarship is made the engine of the focus on the personal.

Beer and Burrows (2007) point the way for us to consider a sociology of and in Web 2.0. This kind of reflexive project is one that both educators and students can engage in as an enterprise in scholarship. As they put it:

> There seems to us to be at least three interrelated issues that the Web 2.0 phenomenon invoke that require sociological engagement: the changing relations between the *production and consumption* of content; the mainstreaming of *private information posted to the public domain*; and, our main focus here, the emergence of a *new rhetoric of 'democratisation.'* (para. 3.1; italics in the original)

This affords the opportunity for the consideration of personalisation in a completely new way, one that not only involves the development and archiving of skills, but also a reflection upon the public actions being performed. In this way, students can consider what the act of posting personal information signifies. It is here that students could be encouraged to move into realms of beyond a psychological notion of "development" to one that looks at the how social practices are themselves developing via the web. This is one of the great advantages of the sharing capacity of the Web 2.0 phenomenon. The blurred relationship between consumption and production of wikis, social networks, blogs, mash-ups, etc. throws into relief questions about what kinds of information are routinely posted, accumulated, traded, and shared. Of particular interest from the point of view of personalisation is the way in which what was previously considered private information is now made public in an increasing trend of the codification of habitus (Burrows & Gane, 2006). However, despite an accompanying rhetoric of empowering and democratic openness, Beer and Burrows also add a counterpoint for consideration. This is primarily an issue concerning access and surveillance: Who is watching? The university? Future employers? And is this developing or empowering anyone?

This affords the opportunity of not only an engagement with the technology, but also about what kinds of personal profiles and social practices students share; a vernacular sociology of the kinds of things that people find interesting about one another (Hardey & Burrows, 2008). This is indeed an education for personal development as well as being about the relationship between the self and the social world through the intermediary of the web; an examination of life within media as an aspect of global citizenship.

It is evident that higher education is having to adapt rapidly to the challenges of a global digital knowledge economy and society. In taking up Baudrillard's concept of implosion, there is a sense in which boundaries are collapsing between the legitimacy of knowledge gained from higher education institutions and the "outside" digital world. However, there is something of a tension given the current socio-cultural and economic climate in that the hyperreality of higher education is continually referenced to the notion of consuming education in order to "future-proof" oneself through the process of self-realisation. However, that very consumer culture calls into question the assumption that the world of higher education has a monopoly of knowledge.

In the world of simulacra and the power that comes from creating images of reality, higher education is faced with seeking to maintain authenticity of information and knowledge. Offering students a means of engaging in this task through a reflexive examination of life within media means that they can at one and the same time operate within a digital mediated world, but nonetheless consider its role in their own and others' lives. In so doing, higher education can hang onto the concept of merit by acknowledging a commitment to citizenship and critical thinking that is beyond the image of authentic self-realisation as performativity in relation to the standards of the market.

Conclusion

The emergence of a discourse of personalization has intensified in the world of higher education in recent years. On the face of it, this may at first appear as a welcome development in terms of student engagement and the focus on employability. This has particular resonance in light of the effects of the current economic recession and the legitimation of higher education as being able to deliver the sorts of people who are "adaptable," "motivated," and "entrepreneurial" in terms of being able to persevere and thrive in these difficult times. If, after all, the focus of the educational process is "student-centred" or "personalized," then, it is argued, this will lead to a greater level of motivation, commitment, and self-awareness. This has been accompanied by an elaborate apparatus to "capture" this reflective process, often through virtual learning environments. This, in turn, is related to a wider curricular and pedagogical framework such as the development of the student identities in terms of GAs and the drive to encourage authentic self-realisation.

Watts' (2008) engagement with Baudrillard's (1983, 1993, 2004) notion of simulacra has questioned the mediated nature of higher education through considering the policy of widening participation as third-order simulacra and therefore in the realm of hyperreality. His argument that widening participation is something of a rhetorical reality that has taken on a life of its own is perhaps giving way to the notion of authentic self-realisation through the acquisition of graduate attributes. The idea that higher education is now engaged in the engineering of identity has taken hold as the dominant rhetoric in relation to employability and "the market." There is little doubt that higher education is in that market, like it or not. However, higher education is not there simply to respond to the drive for performativity and the standards of the market. Institutions of higher education are engaged with the learning communities, and on several levels: within the physical space of a campus, with that of larger society, and more broadly in terms of a commitment to citizenship within a globalised digital culture.

This is still a challenge in terms of how educators help students to acquire not only subject content, and not merely attributes, but a critical engagement with the consumption of digital media in relation to issues of citizenship. Brabazon may well be right in her assessment of *The University of Google* (2007), but it is also the case that we are all part of that digital culture and the consumption of signs. The challenge for the future is in integrating that culture into higher education experience in such a way as to permit a reflexive engagement of life within digital media. We cannot set back the clock, so to speak, to a world of slow learning; but it is still possible to create spaces for critical thinking, scholarship, and reflection in a hyperreal world.

References

Barnett, R. (2007). *A will to learn: Being a student in an age of uncertainty.* Maidenhead, United Kingdom: McGraw-Hill/Open University Press.

Barnett, R. (2009). Knowing and becoming in the higher education curriculum. *Studies in Higher Education, 34*(4) 429–440.

Barrie S. C. (2004). A research-based approach to generic graduate attributes policy. *Higher Education Research and Development, 23*(3), 261–275.

Barrie, S. C. (2006). Understanding what we mean by generic attributes of graduates. *Higher Education, 51*(2), 215–241.

Barrie, S. C. (2007). A conceptual framework for the teaching and learning of generic graduate attributes. *Studies in Higher Education, 32*(4), 439–458.

Baudrillard, J. (1983). *Simulations.* New York, NY: Semiotext(e).

Baudrillard, J. (1988). *The ecstasy of communication* (B. Schutze & C. Schutze, trans.). New York, NY: Semiotext(e) Foreign Agent Series.

Baudrillard, J. (1993). *Symbolic exchange and death.* London, United Kingdom: Sage.

Baudrillard, J. (2004). *The Gulf War did not take place.* London, United Kingdom: Power.

Beck, U. (1992). *Risk society: Towards a new modernity.* London, United Kingdom: Sage.

Beer, D., & Burrows, R. (2007). Sociology and, of and in Web 2.0: Some initial considerations, *Sociological Research Online, 12*(5). http://www.socresonline.org.uk/12/5/17.html

Boltanski, L., & Chiapello, E. (2005). *The new spirit of capitalism.* London, United Kingdom: Verso Books.

Bourdieu, J. (1977). Cultural reproduction and social reproduction. In J. Karabel & A. Halsey (Eds.), *Power and ideology in education.* New York, NY: Oxford University Press.

Bourdieu, P. (1996). *The state nobility.* Cambridge, United Kingdom: Polity Press.

Bourdieu, P., & Passeron, J. C. (1977). *Reproduction in education, society and culture.* London, United Kingdom: Sage.

Brabazon, T. (2007). *The University of Google: Education in the (post) information age.* Hampshire, United Kingdom: Ashgate.

Burrows, D., & Gane, N. (2006). Geodemographics, software and class. *Sociology, 40*(5), 793–812

Chiapello, E., & Fairclough, N. (2002). Understanding the new management ideology: A transdisciplinary contribution from critical discourse analysis and new sociology of capitalism. *Discourse and Society, 13*(2), 185–208.

Davis, S. M. (1987). *Future perfect.* Reading, MA: Addison-Wesley.

Elliot, A. & Lemert, C. (2006). *The new individualism: The emotional costs of globalization.* London, United Kingdom: Routledge.

Hardey, M., & Burrows, R. (2008). Cartographies of knowing capitalism and the changing jurisdiction of empirical sociology. In N. Fielding, R. M. Lee, & G. Blank (Eds.), *The Sage handbook of online research methods.* London, United Kingdom: Sage.

Klinkenborg, V. (2010, May 29). Further thoughts of a novice e-reader. *New York Times.* www.nytimes.com/2010/05/30/opinion/30sun4.html

Marques de Oliveira, S. (2012). E-textbooks usage by students at Andrews University: A study of attitudes, perceptions, and behaviors. *Library Management, 33*(8), 536–560.

Petersen, A. (2011). Authentic self-realization and depression. *International Sociology, 26*(1), 5–24.

Sennett, R. (2006). *The culture of new capitalism.* New Haven, CT: Yale University Press.

Watts, M. (2008). Higher education and hyperreality. In P. Smeyers & M. Depaepe (Eds.), *Educational research: The educationalization of social problems* (pp. 141–155). New York, NY: Springer.

Watts, M. (2010). Capability and the language of educational research. In P. Smeyers & M. Depaepe (Eds.), *Educational research: Proofs, arguments, and other reasonings* (pp. 93–107). New York, NY: Springer.

Part Three. Mediated Life and Death in Arts and Entertainment

8

"Infinite Deaths": The Death of and by the Media in David Foster Wallace's *Infinite Jest*

MARTIN LÜTHE

In the face of the globalized and globalizing market of literature(s) as just one segment of the globalization of media and media cultures, a literary-studies stance towards the pivotal question of a dys- or utopian scenario of a possible life without media seems long overdue. However, the institutionalized disciplinary distinction between media (culture) studies and the "traditional" literary studies departments appears to have impeded a debate about the specific quality of fictional literatures as media and case studies regarding the global dissemination of literature. Critical and crucial work is currently being conducted in the field of literary and postcolonial studies, as cultural studies approaches and those having emerged in the field of what could be labeled a sociological study of literatures take hold in departments of literary studies around the globe (cf. Williams, 2004; cf. Jahraus, 2007). Taking these recent approaches as a meaningful point of departure, this contribution seeks to enhance an understanding of questions concerning the specific quality of the medium called the novel in contemporary globalized media cultures, especially in its single most self-reflexive form: a novel concerned with its own quality as a medium and a novel about the quality of media in a broader sense.

The novel that immediately comes to mind for scholars of American literatures—with its own interesting history of global dissemination—is David Foster Wallace's 1996 novel *Infinite Jest.* Only recently have more academic texts been published that target and interrogate Wallace's lengthy novel; a fascination that seems itself related to the literal (early) death of the author (cf. Howard, 2011). In numerous instances, David Foster Wallace's longest novel reveals its own fear of and fascination with the media cultures it must be considered a part of; however, we find this general unease most straightforwardly expressed in a passage 620 pages into the novel:

> And (get this) 94% of all O.N.A.Nite paid entertainment now absorbed at home: pulses, storage cartridges, digital displays, domestic décor—an entertainment market of sofas and eyes. Saying this is bad is like saying traffic is bad, or health-care surtaxes, or the hazards of annular fusion: nobody but Ludditic granola-crunching freaks would call bad what no one can imagine being without. (IJ, 620)

The passage makes the strong case with regard to the "reality" of the novel that it would simply make no sense to imagine a world without the powerful impact of home entertainment through the use of media and media interfaces; however, the text's own dystopic vision is grounded in an evolution of media—a figurative death of traditional media forms such as network broadcasted television—on the one hand, and the imminent threat of the end of all human beings through the deployment of an unbearably entertaining, infinite mediated joy as an ultimate terrorist tool.

It is safe to say that the underlying question of this edition, of a "life without media" and what that could/would look like, provides one of the main narrative themes in Wallace's novel. In order to establish the novel as a meaningful, if fictional and utopian, contribution to said question, the argument provided in the course of this essay is structured as follows: (1) it provides the reader with a specific synopsis of David Foster Wallace's novel through the prism of the central role of media and media addiction the text itself provides, before it (2) analyzes the significance of media production, media theory, and the text's own medial materiality as they emerge in the novel; and in conclusion (3), I propose the text requests and calls for an understanding of contemporary globalized media culture(s) and its theories through a Deleuzian lens as self-destructive, as in a sense always already dead.

Media and Media Addiction in *Infinite Jest*

Despite the fact that Wallace's novel is clearly set in a dystopian future, its dystopian sentiment is still grounded in a setting reminiscent of our current "reality," especially with regard to its pivotal theme of media and media use as Scott Esposito reminded us recently:

> With fifteen years hindsight we can see that *Infinite Jest* . . . anticipated so many of the faultlines that no writer could have known about in 1996, things that will define our world for the rest of our lives: the comglomeration [sic] of big media at the birth of the world's new medium of exchange; transnational terrorism; the triumph of willful political ignorance and American plutocracy. (Esposito, 2011, par. 6)

The somewhat polemic tone of Esposito's observation aside, he still makes a strong and convincing point about the relevance of what he calls "the conglomeration of big media at the birth of the world's new medium of exchange" for both the narrative of the novel itself and the immediate future, in which the novel came to be read by a global audience. Although the novel clearly relies on extensive use of parody and caricature, specifically in the depiction of the nexus of media and transnational terrorism, the narrative strain foregrounding the effect of the entertainment industry of the dystopian setting of the novel sounds much less parodist than, for example, the idea of a terrorist organization of Quebecois separatists in wheelchairs.

For the sake of simplicity, it makes sense to conceive of the pivotal and gruesome deaths occurring in the novel that are and could literally be brought about by the media and media use as the narrative's most important strain regarding my argument here. The oftentimes gruesome and shocking depictions of death inflicted by media use resemble horror-novel and horror-film strategies to describe the threat and harm of the horrifying Other; in the case of *Infinite Jest* said Other is simply an "unlabeled entertainment cartridge" (IJ, 42). The cartridge—as the vehicle of the narrative and an unstable center of the narrative web—is unlabeled and remains so during the novel for good reason; an observation I will return to and elaborate on. The narrative web consists of three separate, yet interconnected, grand narrative strains: the first of which is set in a tennis academy and centers on the lives of the students and one student in particular, Hal Incandenza, whose family also runs the academy. The second plot is set around the corner, or rather at the foot of the hill from the tennis academy, and zooms in on an Alcoholics Anonymous–like, rehab facility called Ennet House, focalized chiefly through one of the staff members of the facility by the name of Don Gately. The third part of the narrative features an extended meeting and dialogue between two agents, a cross-dressing U.S. intelligence agent, Hugh/Helen Steeply, and a quadruple-agent wheelchair terrorist, Remy Marathe, from Quebec, set on a desert hill outside Tucson, Arizona. The three narratives are all interconnected, if in a bricolage fashion, by the above-mentioned piece of Entertainment—always spelled with a capital E in the novel. As the plot unravels, it becomes clear that the Quebecois separatist group as well as the Hugh/Helen Steeply's O.U.S—the Office of Unspecified Services—have a keen interest in locating the master copy of the Entertainment cartridge, which as we find out in the course of the narrative contains a movie filmed and produced by the late James O. Incandenza, a deceased filmmaker, Hal Incandenza's father, and the founder of the tennis academy. His widow and two of his sons still live in the tennis academy; the oldest son has moved out, earns his living as a punter for a football team in Arizona. His function in the narrative is to further establish interconnections between the different narrative strains, mostly through his romantic and erotic activities: he flirts with the cross-dressing agent, engages in libidinal activities with a female spy (possibly hired by the Quebecois separatists), and is the ex-boyfriend of the female lead of his late-father's final piece of Entertainment (sic!).

The novel introduces the theme of media addiction almost en-passant. However, the reader gains an awareness of the fatal potential of the Entertainment, as the novel keeps returning to the scene of its original consumption through short narrative snapshots; the person introduced as the first victim in the novel is a "one-half ethnic Arab and Canadian by birth" medical attaché for the "Saudi Minister of Home Entertainment" (IJ, 33). It is only through coincidence that he finally decides on the fatal cartridge. Home alone, he finds it lying around the house, only because he is not familiar with programming the dystopia's version of the Internet called InterLace, as "the specific spontaneous pulses from the service are so technologically and cryptographically complex that the attaché has always left the whole business to his wife" (IJ, 35). Foreshadowing the impact the cartridge will have on the attaché as well as on the evolving narrative of the novel, the passage leaves the reader with the following close-up of the attaché's living room: "When he settles in with the tray and cartridge, the TP's viewer's digital display reads 1927h" (IJ, 37). The next time the narrative revisits the living room the following is what the novel lets us know:

> The medical attaché at their apartment, is still viewing the unlabeled cartridge, which he has rewound to the beginning several times and then configured for a recursive loop. He sits there, attached to a congealed supper, watching, at 0020h., having now wet both his pants and the special recliner. (IJ, 54)

Although the brief passage depicting the attaché's deterioration first and foremost suggests the specific addictive quality of the Entertainment the attaché is watching, by extension it depicts the specific danger of the cartridge towards the general context of media use: the ambiguity of the title of the novel, which is also the title of the movie on the cartridge, *Infinite Jest* (*V*) or (*VI*); and as a much broader quasi-sociological observation regarding the role of the media for purposes of leisure in our world and the dystopian world described; as well as the quality of the paragraph as an imitation and radical transgression of a TV dinner.[1] The relevance of the passage as an observation of the possibly devastating effects of media use becomes even clearer as the text leaves the scene of the living room and alludes to the omnipresence of visual media, when the reader is told that Mario Incandenza, Hal's brother with special needs, films the tennis matches played in the academy to enhance the players' games, "[T]he reason being it's a lot easier to fix something if you can see it" (IJ, 55). This obvious contradictory assumption to the living room scene, where once you see the cartridge, you do not seem to be able to fix anything anymore, not even your appetite, illustrates the airy and naïve deployment and use of media technology. Accordingly, with the attaché still sitting on the recliner, the beginning of the next section furthermore indicates the complexity of media use in the dystopia, as it establishes a connection between the three narrative strains of tennis, the media cartridge, and addiction; it reads, "[D]rug addicts driven to crime to finance their drug addiction are not often inclined toward violent crime" (ibid.). In these sequences, the role of the cartridge as a powerful and, as we are to find out, fatal piece of media entertainment, unfolds and is linked with the narrative of addiction.

David Foster Wallace famously tackled the issue of media use, with a focus on television in U.S. society, in one of his other publications (1993), that could, if dealt with superficially, be misread as an avant-garde intellectual's criticism of the effects of television. However, the essay puts forth an elaborated discussion of the complexities of the meaning and effect of television. There, Wallace already acknowledges that "the really rabid criticism less leveled than sprayed at networks, advertisers, and audiences alike, has to do with the charge that television has turned us into a nation of sweaty, slack-jawed voyeurs" and that "[T]his charge turns out to be untrue but for weird reasons" (1993, p. 151). Wallace carefully deconstructs the notion of TV use as voyeurism, most powerfully through the observation that an unawareness of being watched on the receiving end is central to the erotic stimulation of the voyeur, which remains a shared illusion in the case of television-watching: actors act most pivotally with regard to the fact that they pretend not to be watched (cf. ibid., 153f). Still, as Wallace debunks part of the erotic pleasure of watching television as voyeurism, he also comes up with the familiar analogy between watching television and doing drugs; he claims,

> Television's biggest minute-by-minute appeal is that it engages without demanding. One can rest while undergoing stimulation. Receive without giving. In this respect, television resembles other things mothers call "special treats"—e.g.,

> candy, or liquor—treats that are basically fine and fun in small amounts but bad for us in large amounts and *really* bad for us if consumed as any kind of nutritive staple. . . . Watching TV can become malignantly addictive. (ibid., 163; emphasis in original)

While the novel certainly uses the observation above as a premise of the narrative, the novel is driven by the confluence of media as a means of terrorism or media terrorism, sounding an explicit and forceful warning. Not only is media use depicted as highly addictive, the novel presents a number of deaths related to media. First, the reader finds herself confronted with those deaths resulting from the specific Entertainment; second with a number of gruesome and grotesque deaths related to media in general; and third with the decline of the previous broadcast system as an instance of figurative death, as the following examples illustrate.

In the course of the narrative, the reader finds out about the exact nature of the Entertainment's devastating impact. When the narrative introduces Rodney Tine, the chief of the Office of Unspecified Services, the text reveals more about what Tine refers to as "[T]his unwatchable underground Entertainment-cartridge" (IJ, 548): evidently, a film

> with certain . . . "qualities" such that whoever saw it wanted nothing else ever in life but to see it again, and then again, and so on. . . . These persons now all in wards. Docile and continent but blank, as if on some deep reptile-brain level pithed. . . . The persons' lives' meanings had collapsed to such a narrow focus that no other activity or connection could hold their attention. (IJ, 548–549)

On the level of effect, then, the Entertainment immediately causes a hyper-addiction in whoever catches a glimpse of the movie. By alluding to the threat of media addiction in this radical manner, the text dances on the thin line between a dystopian vision and a parody of media cultures in general and debates about the impact of media use on members of society. In its dramatic dystopian overstatement, the novel even caricaturizes Wallace's own previous text on television in U.S. culture.

The parodist quality of the novel becomes both more obvious and complex with regard to the single most significant death in the novel: that of James O. Incandenza, which provides the narratives with a central event to connect them and thereby makes most of the novel's narration plausible in the first place; much like the novel capitalizes the E in Entertainment to drive home the larger-than-life, god-like quality of the cartridge, Hal and Orin Incandenza refer to their father mostly as "Himself." Also, the novel gives further proof of the significance of James O. Incandenza Jr.'s (or Himself's) death by having him return as a ghost/wraith, whose agenda is somewhat in the open, but furthermore contributes to interconnecting the separate narrative strains (by visiting Don Gately and one of Hal's peers in the tennis academy). The obvious allusion to Hamlet aside, a connection literally imprinted on the novel by the citation of Hamlet in the title, the image of his suicide provides a haunting image of death to be found in the text, an image that also haunts the protagonist Hal (Incandenza's son) as we find out witnessing a therapy session:

> "I didn't even think a microwave oven would go on unless the door was closed. What with the microwave oscillating all over, inside. I thought there was like a refrigerator-light or Read-Only-tab-like device. . . . As we later reconstructed the scene, he'd used a wide-bit drill and small hacksaw to make a head-sized hole in the oven door, then when he'd gotten his head in he'd carefully packed the extra space with wadded-up aluminum foil."
>
> "Sounds kind of ad hoc and jerry-rigged and haphazard."
>
> "Everybody's a critic. This wasn't an aesthetic endeavor. . . . The B.P.D. field pathologist said the build-up of internal pressures would have been almost instantaneous and equivalent in kg.s.cm. to over two sticks of TNT." (IJ, 251)

There is an obvious originality and the over-the-top quality to James O. Incandenza's suicide, which we find beautifully if ironically expressed in the therapist's assessment of it being "ad hoc," "jerry-rigged," and "haphazard." After all, the suicide seems to be an aesthetic endeavor indeed: the performative logic of the filmmaker Incandenza sticking his head into a microwave and the visual image this leaves the reader with seems to reference TV itself. Sticking his head into the visual equivalent of the "media apparatus" Incandenza produced for, literally makes his head or brain explode. After all, Incandenza's expertise and focus in making movies was not much in the realm of narration or storytelling (content), but rather on the visual quality and properties of the films—form as content. Much rather than an ad-hoc suicide, this seems like a staging and visual arrangement of Incandenza's life's pursuit, especially with regard to the Entertainment cartridge the narrative clasps around.[2] Additionally, the text bemoans the death or decline of media as we know it—the collective "we" of media users in the mid-90s, which calls the readers' attention to questions of media production, media theory, the material quality of the novel itself, and ultimately the relationship between "televisuality" and current (re-)imaginings of the American pastoral (cf. Ladyga, 2011).

Media Production, Media Theory, and the Materiality of *Infinite Jest*

Certainly one of the most impressive elements in the dystopian scheme emerging in the novel is the depiction of the future of the media as a consequence of the decline of broadcast television and the U.S. network TV system, which the reader finds carefully imagined in a paper written by Hal Incandenza. Here, the melancholic subtext regarding the transformation of the media emerges, which we find best expressed in a statement by Hal's older brother Orin, "a child raised on multichannel cable TV" in response to a questionnaire; he states: "I miss summer reruns. I miss reruns hastily inserted to fill the intervals of writers' strikes, Actors' Guild strikes. I miss Jeannie, Samantha, Sam and Diane, Gilligan, Hawkeye, Hazel, Jed, all the syndicated airwave-haunters. You know? I miss seeing the same things over and over again" (IJ, 600). And further down and as a reply to the objection that he could watch cartridges over and over again, Orin observes: "But not the same. The choice, see. It ruins it somehow. With television you were *subjected* to repetition. The familiarity was inflicted. Different now" (ibid.; emphasis in original). Here, the emphasis on "subjected" on the surface helps the reader with the intonation of the sentence, it also stresses the relationship between television and the subject, or, more precisely, the decisive role of television—and by extension, the media—in the subjectification of human identity. The emphasis on connection between repetition and subjectification in Orin's statement obviously alludes to some of the recent classics of media and cultural theory, beginning with Walter Benjamin's landmark essay on "The Work of Art in the Age of Mechanical Reproduction" to Gilles Deleuze's "Difference and Repetition"—texts that interrogate the function and meaning of repetition in and for the realm of cultural representation.

The subject-media entanglement we find frequently expressed in metaphors of subject-media object hybrids and the above-mentioned producer-consumer complication. Especially, the abundance of screens and windows as interfaces, which sometimes maintain inside-outside dichotomies, however, more often deconstruct them, functions as a constant reminder of subject-media relations. In addition to the powerful, almost visual, metaphor of the suicide achieved with sticking a head into the microwave, the novel makes use of similar visual imagery in many instances. In one of the climaxes on the final day depicted in the novel and arguably the final day for most of the protagonists, the image we are left with is both disturbing and powerful. One of the tennis prodigies has gotten stuck to a frozen window screen, and when Hal tries to pull him off, the following occurs:

> There was a horrible sound. The skin of his forehead distended as we yanked his head back. . . . The dermis of Stice's forehead was still stuck fast, but the abundant loose flesh of Stice's bulldog face had risen and gathered to stretch and connect his head to the window. And for a second I saw what might be considered Stice's real face . . . (IJ, 871)

Parts of Stice's face remain stuck on the window screen after he has been pulled off, literally glued to the screen, becoming part of an in-between space neither inside nor outside, an in-between already expressed in his name *ortho* (Greek: straight) and *stice*, the anglicized suffix of the Latin *stistere*, (Latin: standing; space), which, for example, appears as suffix in the word *interstice*. The real face of the straight-standing Ortho Stice, tellingly nicknamed "The Darkness," is only revealed as it is stuck on the window: it is here that his in-betweenness is expressed in the subject-media amalgamation, an in-betweenness that, as the book suggests, might also be related to an in-betweenness of Stice regarding the here and hereafter. After all, the novel strongly suggests that Stice is one of only two characters of the novel who see and interact with the returning ghost of the filmmaker James O. Incandenza.

These stages of in-betweenness are transposed to and can be found reflected in the novel's self-reflexive awareness of the intersection of form and content that interestingly oftentimes regards the intersection of death and media as well. In footnote 24 of 388, we find a list of James O. Incandenza's oeuvre from a fictional academic journal article entitled "The Laughing Pathologists: Exemplary Works of the Anticonfluential *Après Garde*: Some Analyses of the Movement Toward Stasis in North American Conceptual Film," which gives a "listing . . . as complete as we are able to make it" (IJ, 985). Before analyzing the deployment of footnotes as a textual strategy in and of itself, it makes sense to point our scholarly attention to the nature of double parody brought forth here: First, the apparent over-use of seeming contradictions "anticonfluential," "après garde," "Movement toward stasis," and finally "laughing pathologists" in the title of the journal article pull all our postmodernist "academic legs"; the seemingly clever title appears on the verge of imploding logically, although, as readers familiar with current academic jargon, we can make some sense of it, especially regarding the deconstruction of apparent paradoxes and the complication of dichotomous differences. Second, the footnote perfectly illustrates what Katherine Hayles and others refer to as "cycles within cycles within cycles (1999, p. 684) or a novel "run through a recursive feedback loop" (ibid.; cf. Holland, 2006). The apparatus of footnotes not only fulfills a performative function with regard to the reader; it points to the construction of the novel as novel and the relationship between text and paratext—do I read the footnotes, to what effect, why footnotes in a novel? It seems logical that the list of movies is itself a footnote taken from the scholarly text, then becomes a footnote in the novel, disrupting the reader's reading of the main text, to then be itself footnoted/annotated. Such disruption of the reading experience guarantees the readers' awareness of the material quality, the very textuality, of the entertainment they are consuming; all the while they are informed about the entertainment oeuvre and the materiality of one of the characters they are reading about.

Arguably, the 8-pages-long-footnote in the novel functions much like the film text of one of the movies Incandenza directed, *Accomplice!*, in which the exclamation of the word "murderer" is repeated "over and over, so that almost a third of *Accomplice!*'s total length is devoted to the racked repetition of this word" (946) to the supposed effect that "*Accomplice!* essential project remains abstract and self-reflexive. We end up feeling and thinking not about the characters but about the cartridge itself" (ibid.). As the discussion of the self-reflexive nature of the movie *Accomplice!* continues—focalized through Hal Incandenza's reception of it—continues, Hal speaks for the audience of the movie, raising the question whether "Himself subject us to 500 seconds of the repeated cry 'Murderer!' for some reason . . . some theoretical-aesthetic end, or is Himself simply an amazingly shitty editor of his own stuff?" (IJ, 946–947). Here, Himself could refer just as well to the author of the novel and the question of his editing process, especially when considering the length of the novel, its title, and the amount of footnotes.

This instance of what one could refer to as double self-reflexivity becomes even more obvious with regard to a movie from Incandenza's "middle period" entitled *The Medusa vs. the Odalisque*. The movie is set in a theater with the cameras capturing both the simplistic play—Medusa battling a Medusa-esque creature from Quebecois mythology in a sword and mirror vs. nail-file and makeup mirror—as well as the audience in the theater. In this, as the novel has it, "meta-entertainmentish" (footnote 223) movie, the audience members in the theater end up either as stones or gems depending on whom they catch a glimpse of. However, the audience of the film "didn't think too much of the thing, because the film's audience ends up feeling teased and vaguely cheated, and the thing had only regional release, and the cartridge rented like yesterday's newspapers, and it's now next to impossible to find" (IJ, 396). Still, as we are immediately told, "that wasn't by any stretch of the imagination the James O. Incandenza film that audiences hated the most" (ibid.). In the novel, a movie called *The Joke* wins that prize: while the premise is similar to the Medusa film, *The Joke* captures the audience in the movie theater itself, brilliantly complicating production versus consumption and seeing versus being-watched dichotomies in the media. The passage introducing the movie reads as follows:

> [T]he film started up and what was on the wide public screen was just a wide-angled binoculated shot of this very art-film theater's audience filing in with espressos and finding seats and sitting down and looking around and getting adjusted and saying knowledgeable pre-movie things to their thick-lensed dates . . . facing the screen (i.e., now themselves, it turns out) with the coolly excited smiles of highbrow-entertainment expectation, smiles which the cameras and screen's projection now revealed as just starting to drop from the faces of the audience as the audience row after row of itself staring back at it with less and less expectant and more and more blank and then puzzled and then eventually pissed-off facial expressions. *The Joke*'s total running time was just exactly as long as there were critics or film-academics in the seats, who studied themselves studying themselves taking notes with endless fascination and finally left only when the espresso finally impelled them to the loo . . . (398)

This cycle, then, at least is ruptured, when the audience-as-protagonists step outside the movie to use the bathroom. The film *The Joke* also reminds us of Wallace's observation concerning the question of voyeurism and television and the passage beautifully plays with that notion. Here, even though the people being filmed are unaware of it until they recognize the image of themselves on the screen, the voyeur and the Other of the visual object are one and the same: the "endless fascination" the novel describes in the scenario expresses the audience's, and specifically the critics', voyeuristic fascination with the self. Additionally, by using "finally" twice plus the word "endless" in a passage on a movie called "the joke," the novel's own title more than shimmers through—*Infinite Jest* becomes *Endless Joke* or vice versa—and the reader adds yet another dimension of audience to the scene.

As much as the book is about mass media, and especially the visual realm of film and entertainment, it is also about reading as medial practice. In fact, the novel we are reading carries the same title as the fatal Entertainment cartridge, which as we know is the fifth or sixth attempt: *Infinite Jest* (*V*) or (*VI*). When reading the novel, we might be holding the first *Infinite Jest* in our hands. After all, we do not know much about the "movie/book" other than that it is "black and white" and "silent" and that it is "Incandenza's unfinished and unseen first attempt at commercial entertainment" (986, same footnote). The book's own fetishization of movies is found reflected in the composition of the novel and the writing of its scenes: for lack of a better description, frequently, at the beginning and end of scenes the focalization appears to shift from camera to character and vice versa. As is hinted at in many ways and rings true for Incandenza's movies, the media here often are the message.

Multiplicities and Rhizomes: The Life or Death of Media and Psychoanalysis in *Infinite Jest*

In conclusion, this text examines the Entertainment cartridge called *Infinite Jest* (*V*) or (*VI*)—the novel remains speculative about the exact number of attempts—in order to demonstrate the ultimate confluence of death and media in the novel deploying a Deleuze-inspired reading of the film and by extension Wallace's novel of the same title. Deleuze, after all, makes a cameo-like appearance in the very discussion of the "lethal final cartridge" (IJ, 792), during which the novel reveals the form and contents of the Entertainment. Deleuze's somewhat elusive approach to an analysis of culture could inspire a reading of the novel in, at least, a threefold way: First, the novel in its recursivity and its decentering of narrative structures invites a rhizomatic reading in line with one of the central ideas of Deleuze and Guattari's *A Thousand Plateaus: Schizophrenia and Capitalism* (1987). Second, and on the level of contents, the novel and the Entertainment featured in it seem to share with Deleuze's thought a decisively anti-Freudian stance, especially with regard to the Freudian fetish of (the fear of) castration. Third, however, even though the novel shares with Deleuzian thinking a highly critical stance towards the nexus of capitalism, the media, and its meanings for life/death, here the novel and Deleuzian thinking seem to part ways. The focus of the following argument is put on the two observations concerning the contents of the novel, as exemplified by an analysis of the Entertainment cartridge and the way it is framed in the narration of the novel.

While the novel leaves the reader in the dark about the contents of the fatal cartridge for most of the novel's narrative, twice towards its end, if you read it in the classic manner from page 1 to page 983, it discloses the content and form of the cartridge; once in a technical interview from the movie's protagonist's best friend, Molly Notkin, who happens to have a PhD in film studies, and then in one of Don Gately's dreams/vision, in which the ghost of James O. Incandenza re-reveals the quality of the Entertainment. Molly Notkin describes the movie as follows:

> [I]t features Madame Psychosis as some kind of maternal instantiation of the archetypal figure Death, sitting naked, corporeally gorgeous, ravishing, hugely pregnant, her hideously deformed face either veiled or blanked out by undulat-

> ing computer-generated squares of color or anamorphosized into unrecognizability as any kind of face by the camera's apparently very strange and novel lens, sitting there nude, explaining in very childlike language to whomever the film's camera represents that Death is always female, and that the female is always maternal. I.e. that the woman who kills you is always your next life's mother . . . (788)

She continues:

> *Infinite Jest* (*V*) or (*VI*)'s [camera] had been fitted with an extremely strange and extrusive kind of lens, and lay during filming on either the floor or like a cot or bed, the camera, with Madam Psychosis as the Death-Mother figure inclined over it, parturient and nude, talking *down* to it—in both senses of the word, which from a critical perspective would introduce into the film a kind of synesthetic double-entendre involving both the aural and visual perspectives of the subjective camera—explaining to the camera as audience-synecdoche that this was why mothers were so obsessively, consumingly, drivenly, and yet somehow narcissistically loving of you, their kid: the mothers are trying frantically to make amends for a murder neither of you quite remember. (IJ, 789)

Similarly, Gately's vision lets us know that

> [t]his is why Moms are so obsessively loving, why they try so hard no matter what private troubles or issues or addictions they have of their own, why they seem to value your welfare above their own, and why there's always a slight, like, twinge of selfishness about their obsessive mother-love: they are trying to make amends for a murder neither of you quite remember, except maybe in dreams. (IJ, 850)[3]

Not only is the contents again doubled as analysis/interview and vision, a post-Freudian anti-Oedipal loop is introduced at this point of the novel, in which the Freudian trope of Oedipus is inverted to the effect of creating an everlasting, anti-Freudian loop of women killing their next life sons to the effect of an additionally everlasting schizophrenia in the mother and the son.[4]

The film studies scholar Molly Notkin introduces this complexity in her reading of the contents of the movie supporting it with a reference to Deleuze. Strikingly, even though Notkin in a single sentence summarizes some of Deleuze's intellectual project, she does so referencing a publication of Deleuze that does not exist, thereby blurring the lines between scholarship and fiction and the fact/fiction dichotomy in typical postmodernist fashion. The text she points the reader to is entitled *Incest and the Life of Death in Capitalist Entertainment* (IJ, 792)—a text that strongly echoes Deleuzian sentiment in its deployment of the nexus of capitalism, the role of entertainment, and Freudian vocabulary. The novel ironically deploys psychoanalytic and poststructuralist film and media theories frequently, at times interrogating and ridiculing the very playfulness of these theories, at times powerfully subverting them: the male gaze is now the infantile gaze and the subjective-camera's gaze seems strikingly less significant than the veiled gaze of the female mother; again to the effect of completely inverting the trope of Oedipus in the figure of the mother/son-killer. Even though, as one critic called out, the trace of suspicion of the text being caught in its own self-reflexive, ironic, and thus essentially narcissistic loop remains (cf. Holland, 2006, 218–219), the novel might propose a solution as recognition of the loop itself.

Deleuze and Guattari (1987) emphatically call for a deconstruction of Freudian dichotomies, of, for example, mother versus son, mother versus father, self versus other, for the sake of an acknowledgement of multiplicities and processes of becoming—becoming-animal, becoming-imperceptible, and becoming-many—as pivotal to understanding the processes subjectification on one of their plateaus (cf. Deleuze & Guattari, 1987, pp. 30–43). However, Wallace's novel, in its subversion of the trope of Oedipus, maintains the power of the mother/son dichotomy.[5] Here, as in many other instances, the novel's ironic and dystopian political system of (trans)national "interdependency" as a metaphor of media-subject relationship comes to mind. Even though the death of broadcasting is bemoaned, it is when the media contribute to our understanding of death that they become themselves deadly in the novel; another constructed loop that emphasizes the space of in-between and the procedural nature of subjectification: while independence emphasizes difference, interdependence might be the political manifestation of a "Derridian différance." The fact that the special lens of the film looks back at us—its audience—presumably adds to its addictiveness through its insistence on the visual matrix of postmodern cultures (cf. Pisters, 2003, 2008).

In the final climax of the novel, the trope of the Entertainment powerfully recurs: in a horrible drug binge we experience through an extended memory flashback by the possibly dying character Don Gately, in which the lack of bladder control—as in the scene that first introduces the fatal cartridge—reappears as a signifier of danger, infantilization (cf. Holland, 2006, p. 239), and ultimately death.

Evidently, the Entertainment cartridge effect mirrors the infantilizing effect of drug abuse and whoever catches a glimpse of the cartridge is in for an endless and eventually fatal binge of desubjectification. Accordingly, it is in the final scene of the novel, in which Don Gately is being forcefully drugged, that the visual media and drug abuse implode into a single signifier:

> The last rotating sight was the chinks [sic] coming back through the door, holding big shiny squares of the room. As the floor wafted up and C's grip finally gave, the last thing Gately saw was an Oriental bearing down with the held square and he looked into the square and saw clearly a reflection of his own big square pale head with its eyes closing as the floor finally pounced. (IJ, 981)

While possibly alluding to Lacan's mirror stage theory as the significant moment of subjective inscription into the symbolic order, the mirror also mirrors the other abounding screens of this final setting and the multiplication effect they produce; the window-screen and the TV-screen—the last piece of furniture in the otherwise abandoned room. The squares of the mirror additionally allude to the "undulating computer-generated squares" of the Entertainment or the veiled presence of the movie itself: Gately's passing into oblivion mirrors the anti-Freudian and "infantilization" contents of the Entertainment itself in that it is the mirror as signifier of the beginning and simultaneous end of life in the symbolic order characterized by its inherent schizophrenia. *Infinite Jest*'s venture into the heart of darkness of a postmodern North American media culture—Jonathan Franzen suggested the text could just as well be entitled *Infinite Sadness* (2012, p. 165)—would call for a rephrasing of Joseph Conrad's Kurtz's famous last words by acknowledging subjectification processes through media use as a possibly devastating schizophrenic loop caught between self and Other, between the virtual and the actual: "The mirror! The mirror!" All playfulness aside, the novel ends on a different, if likely still ironic note and leaves the reader with an idyllic image of pure, beautiful, and "unmediated" nature.

Endnotes

1. Of course, in a self-aware manner the title of the novel also plays with its own sheer length and complexity as seemingly infinite.
2. Such a reading is furthermore invited by Foster Wallace's own fascination with the look of the TV set in the essay discussed above and, again ironically, by his dismissive citation of former FCC chairman Mark Fowler, who infamously likened the TV to the toaster in its function as household appliance (cf. Wallace, 1993, 155ff). Other deaths further hint at the relationship between media (addiction) and death: the traffic helicopter that crashes on the parents of a minor character Kevin (IJ, 803) provides just the most ludicrous example. For a general discussion of addiction in *Infinite Jest*, see Aubry (2008); for more regarding the interconnectedness of play, sports, and the complexities of subjectification in *Infinite Jest*, see Bresnan (2008), Burn (2004), and

Freudenthal (2010). For an examination of forms and functions of irony and the carnivalesque in *Infinite Jest*, see Goerland (2006) and Nichols (2001).

3. In 2011, filmmakers Glenn Shephard and John Lee Matney produced an 8-minute film entitled *Infinite Jest IV* inspired by the novel and what the novel reveals about Incandenza's fatal movie on the video platform Vimeo; see: http://vimeo.com/21410100
4. For an extended comparison "between a traditional psychoanalytic approach and a Deleuzian approach to the image" (Pisters, 2003, p. 5) with regard to movies, see Pisters (2003, pp. 14ff) and Flaxman (2000).
5. In its final pages, the novel strongly suggests that the children in the tennis academy will become the victims of a terrorist attack at the hand of the Quebecois separatists and alludes to a possible entanglement of Hal's mother in the terrorist plot. Hal, who would consequently be killed by the terrorists, would then have fallen to his mother's treason and become a case in point of the anti-Oedipal narrative.

References

Aubry, T. (2008). Selfless cravings: Addiction and recovery in David Foster Wallace's *Infinite Jest*. In D. Prosser (Ed.), *American fiction of the 1990s: Reflections of history and culture*. London, United Kingdom: Routledge.

Benjamin, W. (1936/2011) *The work of art in the age of mechanical reproduction*. London, United Kingdom: Penguin.

Bresnan, M. (2008). The work of play in David Foster Wallace's *Infinite Jest*. *Critique: Studies in Contemporary Fiction, 50*(1), 2008, 51–68.

Burn, S. J. (2004). The machine language of the muscles: Reading, sport, and the self in *Infinite Jest*. In M. Cocchiarale & S. Emmett (Eds.), *Upon further review: Sports in American literature* (pp. 41–50). Westport, CT: Praeger.

Cioffi, F. L. (2000) "An anguish become thing": Narrative as performance in David Foster Wallace's *Infinite Jest*. *Narrative, 8*(2), 161–181.

Deleuze, G. (1968/204). *Difference and repetition*. London, United Kingdom: Continuum.

Deleuze, G., & Guattari, F. (1987). *A thousand plateaus: Capitalism and schizophrenia*. Minneapolis: University of Minnesota Press.

Esposito, S. (2011, June 6). Who was David Foster Wallace?—Wallace's Masterpiece. *The Quarterly Conversation*. http://quarterlyconversation.com/david-foster-wallace-infinite-jest

Flaxman, G. (2000). *The brain is the screen: Deleuze and the philosophy of cinema*. Minneapolis: University of Minnesota Press.

Franzen, J. (2012). David Foster Wallace. In J. Franzen, *Farther away: Essays* (pp. 161–168). New York, NY: Farrar, Straus & Giroux.

Freudenthal, E. (2010). Anti-interiority: Compulsiveness, objectification, and identity in *Infinite Jest. New Literary History: A Journal of Theory and Interpretation, 41*(1), 191–211.

Goerland, I. (2006). "Put the book down and slowly walk away": Irony and David Foster Wallace's *Infinite Jest. Critique: Studies in Contemporary Fiction, 47*(3), 309–328.

Hayles, N. K. (1999). The illusion of autonomy and the fact of recursivity: Virtual ecologies, entertainment, and *Infinite Jest. New Literary History, 30*(3), 675–697.

Holland, M. K. (2006). "The art's heart's purpose": Braving the narcissistic loop in David Foster Wallace's *Infinite Jest. Critique: Studies in Contemporary Fiction 47*(3), 218–242.

Howard, J. (2011). The afterlife of David Foster Wallace. *Chronicle of Higher Education, 57*(19).

Jahraus, O. (2001). American touchstone: The idea of order in Gerard Manley Hopkins and David Foster Wallace. *Comparative Literature Studies, 38*(3), 215–231.

Jahraus, O. (2007). Text, kontext, kultur: Zu einer zentralen Tendenz in den Entwicklungen in der Literaturtheorie von 1980 bis 2000.*Journal of Literary Theory, 1*(1), 19–44.

Ladyga, Z. (2011). The return of the pastoral: The televisual poetics of David Foster Wallace. In J. R. Leo & M. Paryz (Eds.), *Projecting words, writing images: Intersections of the textual and the visual in American cultural practices* (pp. 235–247). Newcastle upon Tyne, United Kingdom: Cambridge Scholars.

Nichols, C. (2001). Dialogizing postmodern carnival: David Foster Wallace's *Infinite Jest. Critique: Studies in Contemporary Fiction, 43*(1), 3–16.

Pisters, P. (2003). *The matrix of visual culture: Working with Deleuze in film theory.* Stanford, CA: Stanford University Press.

Pisters, P. (2008). Delirium cinema or machines of the invisible. In I. Buchanan & P. MacCormack (Eds.), *Deleuze and the schizoanalysis of cinema* (pp. 102–115). London, United Kingdom: Continuum.

Russell, E. (2010). Some assembly required: The embodied politics of *Infinite Jest. Arizona Quarterly: A Journal of American Literature, Culture, and Theory, 66*(3), 147–169.

Shephard, G., & Matney, J. L. (2011) *Infinite Jest IV* (video). http://vimeo.com/21410100

Wallace, D. F. (1993). E unibus pluram: Television and U.S. fiction. *The Review of Contemporary Fiction, 13*(2), 151–194.

Wallace, D. F. (1996/2006). *Infinite Jest.* New York, NY: Back Bay Books.

Williams, J. J. (2004). Toward a sociology of literature: An Interview with John Guillory. *Minnesota Review: A Journal of Committed Writing, 61*(62), 95–109.

9

The Big Screen in the Transnational Novel

JENINE ABBOUSHI

Introduction

Imagining life without media assumes technological and cultural progress in time from pre-print to print culture to the now dominant digital media. The first paradox about the rise of digital and social media in particular is that it has made writers of us all. The democratizing force of new media largely depends on the amplification of writing, a traditional media. In so many ways, digital forms do not replace traditional media, but sustain a rich coexistence, and even depend on and integrate one another. Feature film increasingly draws on fiction (the novel especially), and a new form of transnational, cinematic novel anticipates its transformation to film. This increasing interdependence calls into question some of our basic assumptions about how new media function. This chapter discusses the new cinematic novel. In so doing, it calls into question several accepted ideas about the new media: the assumption of easy transformation of "content" between media, of faceless, authorless processes of adaptation, and of the general replacement of writing and print publications by audio-visual culture. It discusses why literary forms (like the novel) often have a greater ability to generate adaptable content, and how new print and digital interdependences have opened up possibilities for artistic collaboration. Arguably, with feature film's increased dependence on the novel and the hybridization of genre, imagining life without (traditional) media would entail simultaneously imagining life without the feature-film industry. As will be illustrated in this chapter, the novel form, in transnational contexts, is growing more "cinematic," adapting to its evolving role.

Novels Written with an Eye to Cinema

While working on his first adapted screenplay for Hollywood in 1921, W. Somerset Maugham observed "all this in relation to the screen is by the way." He was happy enough to think of having "all the great novels of our literature . . . shown on the screen," but he predicted "any advance in this form of entertainment which may eventually lead to something artistic, lies in the story written directly for the projection on the white screen" (Maugham, 1921, p. 675). Yet he was to become the writer with the most literary works adapted to film, exceeded only recently by Stephen King. Maugham's success and involvement in film adaptation made it almost inevitable that he wrote, naturally or consciously, literature ideal for film adaptation. Hollywood embraced his original storylines—"the story is now all the thing," he announced (p. 673)—his striking characters, fluency in several genres and, not least, his cultivation of an elegant celebrity persona, which was "sleek and lizard like, smoking a cigarette," as a *New York Times* film critic described him (McGrath, 2006).

Maugham's forecasting an end to film's use of literature was perhaps hasty, as this relationship developed in new ways that he himself helped advance. At an early stage in film history, he developed a career model that produced a hybrid form of writing that was good for fiction and film. And this model is more recently gaining considerable currency. The increased interdependence between film and the novel exactly coincides with the remarkable rise of transnational writers in recent years, both Anglophone and translated. And many of these writers are now producing novels that are not merely picked out and adapted to film (or not), but are written with an eye to cinema. My subject is not film adaptation, but rather a new form of cinematic novel, with the big screen already written in. One medium (a written literary text) that formally anticipates transformation into another (a feature film), would be a form of hybrid, even multimedia, writing.[1] My purpose is not merely to describe a form, the cinematic novel, as a hybrid of several media in transnational contexts, but to analyze the complexity of its cultural politics.[2] Such cinematic novels are often volatile texts, not just for their often undeclared "screens" within, but because of their cultural politics.

It was not merely Maugham's Hollywood experience that encouraged him to write in hybrid form, literature somehow already adapted for film. What is more consequential is the transnational reach of Maugham, his careers, and writings. His works put to film often plot characters abandoning local lives to quest in exotic worlds, as in *The Painted Veil* (1925), *The Letter* (the play version of 1927 was itself adapted from a short story in *The Casuarina Tree* collection of 1926), and *The Razor's Edge* (1944). Maugham was immensely cosmopolitan, and necessarily developed double perspectives, at once insider and outsider, because he was bilingual and bicultural (having grown up in Paris until he was orphaned, then in England), as well as through his homosexuality and bisexuality and, undoubtedly, through his intelligence work. He led an international life: he first traveled to the Pacific islands in 1916 to prepare his novel on Paul Gauguin, *The Moon and Sixpence* (the film by Albert Lewin was released in 1942). In the following decades, he voyaged extensively in South America, Southeast Asia, the Pacific Islands, India, and China, chronicling late imperial worlds, and collecting information and experiences that shaped much of his writing. Many of his encounters were of hardship or high risk: in the East End working as a doctor (traveling without leaving London), then as a British Red Cross ambulance driver in France; in Tahiti he contracted tuberculosis, which he cured in a Scottish sanatorium; as a British spy in Russia during World War I, he was sent to help stave off the Bolsheviks; then, in fleeing the Nazis from his posh villa on the French Riviéra, "Maurèsque," he was trapped for weeks in a barge unfit for passengers, many of whom died of hunger and thirst. Maugham often described adopting a kind of cinéma verité to his writing method, claiming that he recorded unusual encounters with little alteration.

Maugham's contemporary counterparts are bicultural, bilingual, or multilingual writers who anticipate and even collaborate on film versions of their works. The new film-literature interdependence most often depends on writers with bicultural, inside-outsider perspectives (sometimes native informant, even spy), and who produce writing that traverses international contexts, offering local, even inaccessible, insider experience and knowledge that is then translated to international audiences. This kind of content, perspective, and agility advances both literary and film production that increasingly anticipate and cater to global audiences.[3] In 2008, the morning after Aravind Adiga won the Booker Prize for *White Tiger*, a *Guardian* interviewer asked where he gets "the nerve . . . to write about the experiences of the Indian poor" when Adiga is privileged; the interviewer questioned how Adiga could "understand what [his] central character, the downtrodden, uneducated son of a rickshaw puller turned amoral entrepreneur and killer, is going through." Adiga responded sensibly that "for me the challenge of a novelist is to write about people who aren't anything like me" (Jeffries, 2008). One gets the feeling that both the question and the response circle around a fraught issue, a central dynamic of transnational culture. I will return later to this question and to the novel and film option of *White Tiger*.

Arguably, the transnational underpinnings of recent, and successful, cinematic novels are no coincidence, but instead are organic incarnations of both the novel and film genres—the dominant cultural forms of our time. In both *Orientalism* (1979) and *Culture and Imperialism* (1994), Edward Said defines the novel as the cultural genre of empire par excellence. Literary critic Margaret Cohen more recently (2010) links the novel's beginnings and development not with domestic middle classes, nations, or even territories, but with seafaring. Similarly, new understandings of the nature of film, expressed by practitioners, confirm this idea of displacement. In an interview with *The Guardian*, Indian filmmaker Mira Nair observes: "I feel very much that cinema is born as a medium to capture exile. The idea of going out of your hotel in Mississippi and looking out of your window and seeing your garden in Kampala. This something that cinema lends itself to brilliantly, almost as much as literature" (Greer, 2002). Nair chose to adapt Jhumpa Lahiri's *The Namesake* because it "so closely reflects [Nair's] own experience," that of the immigrant where "you might physically be in one particular space yet you feel like you are some place else in your soul." Lahiri reiterates that her central characters lack "the luxury of completely possessing and belonging to the place where [they] live" (Leyda, 2011). Nair and Lahiri did not directly collaborate on the film *The Namesake* (although Nair spent days talking to Lahiri's family and cast over 20 family members in her film). This is likely because Nair felt the story to be almost her own, as if written by her ("my most personal film"), expressing a new correspondence between literary and cinematic authorship.

The ironies of these formal and cultural transfers are intriguing. Central to both genres, novel and film, is "freak displacement," to borrow a term from Homi Bhabha (1997), in terms of development but not necessarily in terms of consumption. Nair regards the consumption of literature as enabling one "to travel the world without moving an inch" (Rivera, 2007). Paradoxically, in their rising celebrity, bicultural novelists and filmmakers often describe an observant immobility. British writer Hanif Kureishi remarked in a recent interview that the immigrant experience in London is not as isolated as it once was, and writing about it does not involve displacement because London has become a city of immigrants. He describes himself as a "local writer" who need not "go out of his way to do research" for his plays, novels, screenwriting; he just looks out of the window and writes "about the clothes, the politics, the local scene" ("I haven't seen a white English person in West London for years," he quips). An Indian journalist asks. "How about getting a room in India and looking out of the window to write a book?" "Well, you just might have something there," he responds (Majumdar, 2010). Mira Nair imagines the seeds of her career in cinema were sown by her experience as a child looking out of the car window during long trips from North to East India to visit relatives (Greer, 2002). Adiga, however, regards this sort of motionless, out-the-window watching as disadvantageous for his writing after *White Tiger*, and feels the longer he stays in his middle-class life in Mumbai, the less he is capable of seeing other worlds even directly surrounding him (Sharp, 2009).

Two in One: The Transnational Cinematic Novel

This characteristic displacement at the center of both film and novel perhaps enables the new cinematic novel, but the enterprise of merging the two forms, to facilitate adaptation, is often hidden.[4] For the growing number of transnational cinematic novels with the big screen already "written" in, the film in the novel is to be discovered (or not),[5] and is not necessarily an openly declared literary-cinematic enterprise, as was, for example, Alain Robbe-Grillet's *ciné-romans* of the 1950s and early 1960s. As film theorist Robert Stam (2005) points out, the work of Robbe-Grillet cannot be understood in terms of film adaptation, but rather collaboration between writer and director, Alain Resnais, and their roles "intermingled" (p. 260). The more integral or collaborative is the novel-film enterprise, the more conscious and innovative the cultural politics and product.

Likewise, the transformation to film of novels written with an eye to cinema cannot be understood in terms of film adaptation.[6] Classic adaptation has existed since the beginning of film's hundred-year history, and we now know it was not only a way for producers to target ready publics who consume literary classics and best-sellers. Early on, it became clear to producers and filmmakers alike that a striking story, vivid characters, and memorable dialogue are key to successful feature films, and trying to draw this out of straight-up screenwriting often does not work as well. Yet the experiment, for example, of sequestering F. Scott Fitzgerald in Hollywood to write screenplays in the late 1930s was largely disappointing (Krystal, 2009). And good novelists who are equally good scriptwriters are rare (several exceptions are John Sayles, Richard Price, and Hanif Kureishi).

So despite the merging of novel and film genres in what I am calling the new transnational cinematic novel, the two genres, separately conceived, are by all accounts radically different, even incompatible. Fiction and screenplays have in common, ideally, strong, distinct characters, sharp dialogue, and an unusual story line, which is commonly considered, unproblematically, detachable from its medium. In media, the story is called "content" when transformed (or rather transferred, as the process is imagined) between media, a process Simone Murray calls "the traffic of content" (2012). Incompatible or not, film and fiction are becoming increasingly interdependent. To make a feature film, a work of fiction is often (and more often, as we move into the future) mined. The variety of audio-visual entertainment is one reason why good storylines, or content, are increasingly in demand. Stories sold often get transformed into several media, from film to video game (so there is even a *Beloved* and the *Color Purple* interactive videogame, for example [Hutcheon, 2006, p. 87]). In our "hypermedia space," there are no more discrete media; they are now supposedly "linked together into a single seamless web of digital-electronic-telecommunications" (Deibert, 1997).[7] This new media environment is increasingly participatory, the roles of producer and receiver often indistinguishable, and authorship in new social media, for example, often anonymous (Kraidy & Mourad, 2010).

The ostensible seamlessness and even facelessness of the speedy transfer of "content" across media does not seem to hold in the transformation of print to digital and audio-visual formats. To explain the interruption and difference that print formats make in particular, it is worthwhile to briefly note the well-known differences between novel and film, for this purpose imagined as discrete media. A screenplay is "a giant memo," as Richard Price put it, and "there's no writing, there's no author—it's just dialogue and stage direction" (Michod, 2008). Description, character development, the internal thoughts of characters, temporal shift, metaphor, allusion, if integrated from fiction to film, normally must be represented by techniques specific to film: camera work, use of lighting, and sound. Novels often have the mark of the author (a novel can be identified as one by Mahfouz, Camus, or Woolf); films have the mark of the director. For the screenplay, one rarely can identify the style of a particular author. But herein lies the feature film industry's continuing reliance on fiction for screenplays. Apparently screenplays can lack soul and depth if not drawn from fiction. In fact, many writers of novels and screenplays are asked to write a novel first, and then transform it (as does John Sayles, for example). More interesting still, the growing practice of "novelization" (read often on the Internet) feeds viewers' desires for background description of characters, and to enter into their thoughts (what fiction typically can provide). Novelization is largely considered commercial, but in the new director-writer collaborations, this genre is developing rapidly.[8] Indian Canadian director Deepa Mehta adapted Pakistani novelist Bapsi Sidhwa's *Cracking India* for her film *Earth* and, in a second collaboration, Sidhwa novelized Mehta's film *Water* and both were released simultaneously in 2006. According to both Mehta and Sidhwa, their projects involved hours of discussion, cooperation, exchange of material and ideas, and their roles converged (Reeves, 2006).[9] So it is precisely the novelty of story and character complexity from print formats that interrupt the declared seamlessness and facelessness of the new hypermedia space.

The resulting multimedia texts (novel and screen) are manifestly Barthesian, with multiple meanings, frames, and references read into them.[10] And these transformations and multiple frames of meaning, when explicit and even collaborative, can be rich. As Tomas Leitch puts it, texts remain alive to the extent that they can be rewritten (2007, 12–13). In the Mehta–Sedhwa collaborations, the production of both print and audio-visual texts merge, and they engage fully in cross-media practices.[11] Not only do media critics refer to the story as "content" that can be transported between media, an unspoken assumption underlies cross-media adaptation and production: the notion that any medium can produce such "content." But in the production of content, some mediums are often richer and more versatile than others. Furthermore, content does not necessarily transform smoothly between media. Surprisingly, adaptation between more compatible media, like television series and feature film, is rarely successful (Telotte & Duchovnay, 2012). Apparently feature films need the relatively unfettered imaginative terrains that enable fiction writers to produce surprising stories with unpredictable dimensions, ones ideally challenging for filmmakers to explore through film language. Starting with novel writing instead of script writing, remarks Malcolm Bradbury, lets you sit in a taxi with "the meter switched off" (not worrying about practicalities and cost), so "you can write what you like, have Buenos Aires, have the moon, have anything you want."[12]

Adaptation continues fairly steadily since the beginning of film history, as it can between the two genres separately conceived. However, in the last two decades, between 45–60 percent of feature films are based on works of fiction any given year.[13] This sharp increase relates to the rise of translated and global literature in recent decades, and to new developments in multimedia writing. This can be specifically attributed to the increase of literature ready-made "translatable" into film, and attractive to audiences in global contexts. Hanif Kureishi implicitly makes this connection between Indian films and novels: "Films about India are popular these days. . . . Along with it, Indian novel writing seems to me to be the primary brewing industry in the third word" ("Hanif Kureishi," 2010). He regards this as a good development, as "a culture, a literature survives, because there are new voices speaking into it. You can't just read Dickens and Henry James forever" (ibid.). And particularly in the cases where literature written with an eye to cinema is an explicit project, an open, multimedia text, with this increase comes diversity and innovation. Collaboration and the open intent of writing a big screen into a novel may bypass the pitfalls of "fidelity" criticism ("the book is better than the movie").

The novel has been ritualistically declared dead for almost as long as it has existed. Those pronouncing the death of literature generally imagine it in doomed competition with technology, particularly the rise of audio-visual culture and the communications revolution. Dreary topics about "the future of the book," or "the future of literature" (akin to the "the decline of Western civilization") persist in academic forums. Not surprisingly, in these requiems, critics rarely explore or even question the relationship between literature and audio-visual culture—the two are kept separate. The simplistic idea is that the one has replaced the other: "in" with the audio-visual means "out" with literature. Yet print and digital media coexist and converge, much in the same way that old and new audio-visual and digital media sustain a messy coexistence. [14] In the context of the rise of translated and Anglophone literature, the transformation and staying power of the novel does increasingly depend on its vital link to audio-visual media, particularly to film. How novel writing, publishing, and reading in global contexts changed with the film industry's increasing demand for and consumption of novels (and short stories, to a lesser degree) has not been questioned at all, to my knowledge. We need to explore how this increasing demand for novels in the film industry has changed not only the life of novels after they are written, but while writers write them, conceive of them. The film industry is very aware of the advantages of adapting literature to film, and has always been proactive in obtaining fictional stories (novels usually) to transform into screenplays. We cannot assume, particularly with the boom of translated and Anglophone literature, that writers are oblivious to the possibilities of producing narratives that could undergo audio-visual transformation. The obvious ones very aware of this process would be bestselling authors whose works are already "major motion pictures." The *Harry Potter* director says he would be "crucified" if he didn't follow the texts closely, and Rowling's awareness of this dynamic, undeniably influenced the series as it was being written. More interesting are aspiring writers in transnational contexts who write with an eye on cinema.

Eighty-five percent of films winning Oscars for best picture as early as 1992 were based on novels (Hutcheon, 2006, p. 4), so it would be odd indeed if there were *not* novelists writing with an eye on cinema. We may imagine this is a commercially minded enterprise. Perhaps it is in many cases, but my interest is in the innovative possibilities and cultural politics of this new terrain. In terms of artistic intent and process, if writing novels with an eye to cinema is openly intended, a conscious, multidimensional project, it could develop new aesthetic forms. Indeed, this hybrid terrain, literary-cinematic, is very rich, and open collaborations may produce unconventional forms, particularly if the process is collaborative and experimental. About transforming *Naked Lunch* to film, David Cronenberg felt obliged to "fuse [his] own sensibility with William Burroughs and create a third thing that neither . . . would have done on his own."[15] Resnais' instructions to Duras for *Hiroshima, mon amour* are intriguing, and they hardly suggest a linear development from fiction to film (a basic assumption underlying film adaptation criticism). He instructs her: "Pretend you were annotating not a future film, but a finished film."[16] Yet detached from a larger literary-cinematic project, writing for cinema likely produces conventional fiction (and often conventional film) to feed the beast. I will discuss an example of each.

The Kite Runner's Big Screen

There is a big screen in *The Kite Runner*, by the Afghani Californian writer Khaled Hosseini. It is an international bestseller (2003) transformed into an acclaimed and commercially successful film. That the novel was intended as a "fiction to film" adventure becomes clearest midway through, with the second grand appearance of Assef (who raped the family boy-servant Hassan, the protagonist Amir's friend and kite-flying buddy). Until this point, the novel portrayed the world of the writer's childhood in Afghanistan with interest and color: Hosseini's spare prose, clear storyline, well-drawn characters, and quick narrative pace make for a good read (and a good work to transform into a screenplay—although this did not occur to me at first). When Amir's dying uncle bids him to return to Afghanistan to fetch Hassan's boy, Sohrab, from an orphanage in Kabul, Amir finds Taliban officials took him to serve as an enslaved boy-toy. We reencounter a blue-eyed, fascist Assef, and Assef the Taliban is willing to hand over Sohrab to the now American, childless Amir (who can, by taking Sohrab back, partly make up for standing by during the rape of Hassan at age 12). But Assef gets out his brass knuckles to attack Amir, telling him if he gets out alive, he can have the boy, bells on his ankles (Sohrab recalls the boy on the cover of Edward Said's *Orientalism*).

The characterization of Assef as Taliban lord is heavy-handed. The narrative takes one sensationalist turn after another (this is the culminating one), and the violence is gratuitous. It is in reading the latter half of *The Kite Runner* that I realized it was written for Hollywood. There is nothing wrong with this, necessarily. But I must admit that I liked the novel less from this point, as it becomes less subtle, to put it mildly, losing the rich interest the story of his childhood in Afghanistan that

Hosseini offers in the beginning. There is a gratuitous repetition rape of a whole series of little boys: Hassan, then when he is killed by the Taliban, Hassan's son, by the same Assef; then the boy Kamal, whom Amir and his father encounter in their getaway truck fleeing the Russian invasion. (Kamal dies shortly after being gang raped, and his heartbroken father shoots a bullet into his own mouth.)

The Kite Runner has all the classic features that would make it readily translatable into a screenplay: little representation of interiority (Amir feels shame or fear, but otherwise narrates events and scenes), plain prose, fast action (in the second half especially), frequent dramatic turns in the plot, a strong storyline, from one hellish experience to the next. The novel sustains a consciousness of and fascination with cinema, with many references throughout (Hosseini is a cinephile): there are references to Al Pacino in the first *Godfather* film (p. 297); the gel in Assef's hair makes him look like Clark Gable (p. 286); Amir notes that if the parting of Hassan and his father from Amir's family were a scene in a Hindi film, at that moment he would race after the car in the rain, and pull Hassan back (p. 108).

Interestingly, Marc Forster's film adaptation cuts much of the excess the novel offers up (depicts one boy rape instead of three or four, for example), offering staid, even austere interiors of an elite family home life before the Soviet invasion, unspoken emotion, repressed experiences. And yet the film highlights the public stoning of a fallen woman (surrounded by spectators), red blood stains blooming on a pink chador that collapses onto the dirt, as Amir (yet again) looks on, even if ashen-faced. In the film, Assef is even made the head henchman. Many critics attacked the film for pandering to stereotypes but ignore how some aspects of the novel invite this. Hosseini's subsequent novel, *A Thousand Splendid Suns*, narrates the story of the forced marriage of an illegitimate adolescent, Mariam, to a man 30 years her senior. The story reads almost like a laundry list of all possible cruel turns of fate suffered by a stereotypical Afghani woman, or Muslim woman, including abandonment by family members, forced marriage, full chador, physical abuse because of fertility problems (with repeated miscarriages, her husband knocks out her teeth and forces her to swallow them).

Novel/Film Collaborations: Bowles and Bertolucci on *The Sheltering Sky*

A second example is of literary-film collaboration. *The Sheltering Sky* is an interesting case not of a novel written for cinema (it was published in 1949), but of an author-director collaboration, a re-engagement with the novel so that, in the best sense, we perceive meaning in the novel we would not otherwise see. Bob Stam explains that "adaptation is potentially a way of one medium seeing another through a process of mutual illumination" (2005, p. 365). Bernardo Bertolucci's *Sheltering Sky* is something in between adaptation and a collaborative project. Author Paul Bowles is cast as narrator, sitting in Tangiers' Café de France in two sequences framing the film, and leaves an indelible mark on the fantastic music selections and, more importantly, the complex juxtaposition between sound and theme, and between sound and characters' interiorities. (Bowles was a well-known composer; he wrote the score for Tennessee Williams' *Glass Menagerie*, and other well-known musical scores, as well as successful chamber compositions. He was also a prolific archivist of North African music, and his rich collection of Moroccan music, the most complete available, is held at the Library of Congress.)

Bowles writes in the preface of the 1986 reprint of *The Sheltering Sky* that Doubleday originally commissioned him to write it, and then refused to publish it, arguing that it was not a novel. Of the film, Bowles wrote: "the less said the better." *The Sheltering Sky* has uniquely novelistic features that would be difficult to put to an audio-visual medium, dwelling for pages on characters' interiorities, flow of consciousness, thoughts, and sensory experience. A central concern of the novel is death, or rather existence on the edge of death, where life can sustain indefinitely in the immediacy of the present, unmarked by surroundings, cause, and the passage of time. To get at the elemental core of human existence, "beingness" (the novel is marked by existentialist thought, experiment, and notions of the absurd), place, movement, and the terms of communication are stripped down, reduced. Kit and Port come to North Africa from New York somewhat by chance, wherever a boat would take them (and they almost continue to Istanbul), wanting to find a country untouched by the war. They were travelers with "no plan," no beginning or end to their voyage, seeking to sustain the immediacy of the present.

Bowles' interest is in exploring and philosophizing the depths of different states of non-being, of drifting in and out of consciousness, out of space and time. In the opening, Port wakes up slowly into a stupor, disoriented (and Bowles describes waking from a heat-induced siesta in a hotel in Fez in 1947, and beginning to write the novel). In later mapping out Port's experience of typhoid fever and subsequent death, slowly slipping into "an existence of exile from the world," Bowles wanted to describe dying "as experienced from the inside." During Kit's desert wanderings with a tribe, she lives the same day over and again, engages in "motionless travel," observing the infinitude of sand dunes, and experiences the visual disorientation of the desert at dusk or at dawn, when a nearby ridge could also be a distant mountain range. By asking, "am I dead?" she knows she is not.

Bertolucci deftly portrays this traditionally untranslatable interiority (and its dependence, in the novel, on place, on a particular landscape and colonial history). The success of the magnificent cinematography of *Sheltering Sky* is how it highlights the lush continuum of organic and inorganic, of natural and humanly contrived. As Kit and Port walk, the camera pans desert, dunes, bright sky, rock formations, and settles on tombs strewn over a hill, unmarked by date or regularity. The music and script highlight this seamless continuum between the characters' sustained present and the landscapes around them, but also interrupts the reign of the present. The staccato of untranslated Moroccan Arabic (Darija), like "achkoun" (who is it?) or francophone French "Qu'est-ce que ti fi la?" (What are you doing here?), in film and novel, erect barriers.

The music—sitar, horn, heavy percussion, urgent tempo—reassert, for Kit and Port, the passage and even heady crescendo of time and place moving in on them. In the film (and not in the novel), when Kit is turned away from the Hotel du Ksar because of a cholera epidemic in the town, she finds Port in a typhoid delirium with musicians clamoring about him. She screams "arretez!" and pays them to stop; Port, in turn, pays them to continue. Chabba Zahouania's raspy, melodious voice (singing "Gulu Limmak"), provides an aural counterpart to Port's emotion during the scene where he visits a prostitute, as does the Issawi music that envelops him, as he watches a woman sway herself into a trance.

The music in the film provides not a counterpart but an interruption to the character's desired states outside of place and time. Likewise, the camera holds a close-up on Bowles' 80-year-old face, and we see his gentile figure seated in front of the art-deco mirrors and wood paneling of Café de France in Tangiers. Bowles' voiceover tells of the illusions of travel, of existence within landscapes of infinitude:

> Because we don't know when we will die, we get to think of life as an inexhaustible well. And yet everything happens only a certain number of times, and a very small number really. How many more times will you remember a certain afternoon of your childhood, an afternoon that is so deeply a part of your being that you can't even conceive of your life without it? Perhaps four, or five times more? Perhaps not even that. How many more times will you watch the full moon rise? Perhaps twenty. And yet it all seems limitless . . ."
>
> (This text is inscribed on Brandon Lee's tombstone, to bespeak his precipitous death.)

The collaboration between literature and film, conceived as a hybrid artistic enterprise, as Stam argues, ideally pushes both film and literary language and meaning further than either genre can sustain. In his discussion, Stam imagines the two genres initially autonomous. In the case of Hosseini, the film is already written into the novel, and there was no collaboration with director Marc Foster. The Bowles-Bertolucci collaboration enabled Bowles himself to contribute to the film, largely by his extra-literary talents as a composer, but also through his knowledge of Morocco, the Moroccan dialect of Arabic, Moroccan francophone expression, and his significant historical and cultural knowledge. His insider/outsider perspective, as a multilingual, cosmopolitan, multi-talented, and homosexual writer who adopted Morocco as his home and artistic terrain, was written both into the novel and then into Bertolucci's film. It is precisely in such transnational contexts, firmly rooted in such complex perspectives, that such hybrid forms and collaborations are enabled.

The New Transnational Cinematic Novel: *The White Tiger*

A final example of a cinematic novel is Aravind Adiga's *White Tiger*, which won the Man Booker award in 2008. The rights were purchased by John Hart (Smuggler Films), and Hanif Kureishi was commissioned to write the screenplay. Kureishi notes its "cinematic scope" (Majumdar, 2010). *White Tiger* is a cinematic novel, likely written with an eye to cinema. It would be hard to prove this, as if it were an accusation. Nevertheless, Adiga intimates this possibility, "even before *Slumdog*... was made I had said that my novel is multi-layered and while it is surely material for film, it needed a serious filmmaker to do justice to it" (Pais, 2009). Indeed, the action moves at a fast clip; there are memorable, remarkable characters, and the structure, epistolary, letters of an upwardly mobile rickshaw driver addressing the Chinese ambassador, easily represent dialogue and monologue almost entirely, and with almost no interiority. Balram's thoughts and narrative are communicated to the ambassador—a frame that is referenced, rather artificially, at points in the novel, and it reads as monologue and dialogue with other characters. Simone Murray recently wrote about literary prizes and adaptation, and her prime example is the Booker Prize, recognized as one of the surest conduits for film options (one out of four prize winners are adapted to film, and often prize-winning films at that), a process openly recognized by the Booker establishment.[17]

It would be difficult to untangle the process by which this happens: did Adiga consciously write a cinematic novel? Did his novel win not only because of literary merit, but because it is cinematic, this being the new, unspoken project of the Man Booker Prize? One problem with such questions is they assume this process of writing a cinematic novel, which then gets optioned, is somehow linear. Yet it is not, as made clear in the discussion about *White Tiger*'s precursors and contemporary counterparts. *White Tiger* has all the features of the new transnational cinematic novel as discussed in this chapter: written by a bicultural, Anglophone writer who lives a cosmopolitan, international life, cultivates insider knowledge of an "exotic locale" (to much of his Western readership), and imaginatively narrates existences hidden behind barriers of culture, race, and social class—normally inaccessible to his reading publics. Adiga's multicultural, multilingual identity and personal geography (his places of belonging) make it difficult to name him a latter-day Maugham or Bowles. There are sharp differences. The new cinematic novel's postcolonial "moments," in the sense that Stuart Hall gives the term,[18] set Adiga's production quite apart from these writers and even farther apart from Hosseini, all of whom largely addressed Western audiences.

In contrast to Hosseini, Adiga anticipates transnational publics in *White Tiger*, including Indian.[19] Arguably, the directness of his approach in writing a cinematic novel (not simply because he openly writes with an eye to cinema, but because he clearly imagines multiple, even contradictory publics), makes Adiga's work more akin to transnational literary film projects like the Deepa-Sidhwa film/novel/novelization collaborations, or to the work of Hanif Kureishi, who writes brilliantly for print, film, stage, and who adapts hybrid genres, as he is commissioned to do with *White Tiger*. Film adaptations of transnational fiction, if successful, can provoke uproars, like *The Slumdog Millionaire*, particularly if implicated publics are disregarded, instead of directly anticipated, addressed, even challenged.[20]

Future Novel/Cinema Combos

The new cinematic novel is written in transnational, not "local" contexts (unless they are of immigrant communities, like Kureishi's North London). What do feature filmmakers use for screenplay material (stories, "content") in regions that have very different literary histories, where there are not large fiction-reading publics or frequent bestsellers? In considering the growing number and quality of feature films in countries where the novel is not an indigenous form (like Lebanon or Palestine), has a shorter history, is largely a *muthaqafin* (intellectual's) genre instead of a popular one, the possibility of film-novel collaborations could develop very differently. It would be interesting to find out if, like Hollywood producers and directors, filmmakers from this part of the world "need" novels to transform into screenplays, or better yet, anticipate more writer–cineaste–visual artist collaborations like *Three Posters*, video and live performance by writer Elias Khoury and artist Rabih Mroué.

Perhaps the strong tradition in serial literature and cinema has often made the Egyptian novel so adaptable (the realist and serial popular press tradition of Naguib Mahfouz), and Egyptian cinema was the largest and most opulent in its heyday. Drawing on this tradition, Ala' al-Aswany's *Yacoubian Building* is easily adapted to film, not necessarily because it was written with this objective, but because it grows from a prose-fiction tradition that typically takes serialisable form (in newspapers and television serials). The development of the Egyptian novel should be formally related to the enormously popular and influential Egyptian cinema and television serials.

If the pattern of translated novels often gaining writers fame in their own countries (following translation) creates a fairly recent phenomenon of writing for translation, it is likely that the "translation" of novels to film influences how they are written, and creates a phenomenon of fiction writers writing for film or multimedia. As an often hidden process, this enterprise is accompanied by equally fraught transnational cultural politics. Novelist Bapsi Sidhwa explains that the sexual candor in her first novel, *Cracking India*, offended the Parsi community in Lahore, but protests against this content ceased once the novel gained international recognition, and was adapted to film (Soofi, 2007).

Clearly, we have not arrived at a moment where only novels that can be transformed into film are the ones that gain popularity globally. Gabriel Garcia Marquez' writings are famously "untranslatable" into film; among Anglophone authors, Arundhati Roy's novel, the internationally successful *The God of Small Things*, is also not readily adaptable to film (as a Man Booker winner, a thoroughly explored possibility). The Indian diplomat Vikas Swarup, who wrote *Q&A*, the novel adapted to *Slumdog Millionaire*, intriguingly quips, in a *Guardian* interview, "I am no Arundhati Roy," meaning that his novel is not meant as "social critique" (Jeffries, 2009). His remark also cuts a cultural and political divide between cinematic and non-cinematic Anglophone fiction. To survive, then, must the novel develop in directions that fit the requirements of audio-visual translation? Must the novel also conform to dominant global cultural politics, the same indirectly suggested by Swarup? Probably not, as the media revolution ensured such a fluidity of form and content that the cultural politics of transnational cinematic fiction is not entirely predictable. Yet the more this genre gains ground and transforms, the more innovative and open it will become. The narration and stories of both Adiga's and Roy's fiction (cinematic and almost anti-cinematic, respectively) are shot through with irony, brilliantly and humorously (and both deploy irony with serious consequences), at once targeting indigenous, traditional, Western, and Westernized personages, practices, and everything in between. The good and the beautiful that are imagined and spared irony, in these novels, have no predictable cultural affiliation or geography (as they do in the fiction of Hosseini, the son of a diplomat, for example, who does not often use such irony).

The attack on fidelity criticism offers convincing arguments why film adaptations need not be comparable to original texts, can take strange liberties, become largely unrelated and even surpass them. In the new transnational, cinematic novel, the relationship between form and content is fluid. A "book and movie" comparison is difficult to make if the comparison does not assume distinct genres. Indeed "content" in transnational adaptation is increasingly rendered fluid, like Walter Salles' film *Behind the Sun*, set in Brazil, which adapts of Ismael Kadare's *Broken April*, a story about a blood feud set in Albania. This radical cultural transposition in some respects formally parallels "copycat TV," in which television formats are adapted in far-flung countries and languages globally, sometimes superficially "nativized" by cultural experts, and for unrelated audiences.[21] The only difference is an important one: Salles' film is not an instance of globalizing (here, in the sense of homogenizing, flattening out) "content," in this case, of Kadare's novel; rather, each is grounded in cultural specificity (of Albania and Brazil, respectively). It is hard to categorize Salles' film as classic adaptation in such a transposition.[22]

However far afield are adaptations, and however convincing the arguments against fidelity criticism, audiences cannot be stopped from comparing "the book and the movie." The mass practice of reading and viewing in tandem is hardly in decline.[23] But the "book to movie" pairing in the case of Salles and Kadare, or in writer-director collaborations, like Sidwa and Mehta, becomes intriguing, new. Perhaps Folio Cinéma anticipates the future of such ensembles. It currently markets "limited" book and DVD combo editions in a glossy, attractive, faux bookbound box. There are classics, like Michel Déon's *Un taxi mauve* and Yves Boisset's film, and more recent adaptations like Fernando Meirelles' *La Cite de Dieu* packaged with Paulo Lin's novel of the same title. This attractive commercial format could easily accommodate the new fiction-cinema hybrids and collaborations in their multiple forms, and into the future.[24] This is a prime example of traditional and new media, increasingly hybrid in form, yoked in dependent and creative coexistence.

Endnotes

1. See Peeters (2010), who argues for the hybridity of the current media field, " . . . obstructing neat allocations of particular texts to particular media" (p. 122).
2. My use of the term "hybrid" concurs with Marwan Kraidy's conception of it beyond "cultural description," to include "communicative practice" with political impact (2002).
3. See Kraidy (2002), who examines how the global marketplace dictates studio practices, and how reception is a "space of hybrid creation" that transnational media corporations do not entirely control (pp. 328–332). See also Murray (2008), who notes that for both the novel and film, "the route to globalizing periphery cultural content appears to involve the bypassing of national structures in favor of 'international' networks" (pp. 15–16).
4. A distinction should be made between transnational novels that are written with an eye to cinema (the genre under scrutiny here), and novelists who experiment with cinematic techniques. The latter is not new; modernist writers in particular openly experimented with cinematic writing, as Virginia Woolf claimed (Cartmell & Whelehan, 1999). See Ouditt (1999), who studies the example of *Orlando* to explain how Woolf grew increasingly frustrated by the novel form and instead adapted cinematic techniques in her narratives.
5. See Murray (2008), for an interesting case study of *Eucalyptus*, a would-be novel to film adaptation. She discusses how and why certain texts are taken up for global circulation and are selected for adaptation whereas others are not.
6. For studies of adaptation that acknowledge and explore a dynamic interplay between print and screen forms, production and reception, see Hutcheon (2006), Stam (2005), and Stam & Raengo (2005).
7. Quoted in Kraidy & Mourad (2010).
8. For a good historical account of the evolution of novelization, an analysis of the constraints of the genre, and the more recent "highbrow novelization," like Manuel Puig's *Kiss of the Spiderwoman*, and *Christopher Priest*, Cronenberg's "somewhat" highbrow novelizer for eXistenZ, see Baetens (2010).
9. Jonathan Hardy (2011) calls this "transmedia storytelling," but he discusses such phenomena in the context of "commercial intertextuality."
10. See Barthes' *Image, Music, Text* (1977).
11. Literary texts published online are increasingly participatory productions. See Zhao's fascinating discussion of how Qidian, a Chinese original literature site, changes the way literature is produced and consumed (2011).
12. Quoted in Hutcheon (2006), p. 87.
13. See Whelehan (2012), who discusses how the two forms are have "become more and more interdependent through the course of the twentieth century" (p. 5). Also Murray writes about this increasing interdependence (2012).

14. See Jenkins (2006), who notes how the increasing little black boxes in his living space, each with necessary usages, caused him to finally give up on the "Black Box Fallacy," which has it that all media will converge in a do-it-all in one box.
15. Quoted in Zurbrugg (1999), p. 100.
16. For an analysis of this collaboration, see Davies (2010).
17. Murray (2008), pp. 103–110.
18. Hall conceives of postcolonialism in terms of contradictory cultural politics, with clear binary political divides between first and third worlds no longer possible. What defines, for Hall, this complexity are the ironies of increased third-world reactionary (as opposed to revolutionary) movements, or "postcolonial events" like the Gulf War, where opposition to American military intervention in Iraq includes opposition to Saddam Hussein's regime (1996).
19. Adiga explains in an interview that he learned from his work on an earlier novel that "Indian writers [in India] don't get the respect Indian writers in America get. That is why I looked around for an agent in America for *The White Tiger* and had the book sold abroad first." He notes his work was far better received in India than amongst Indians in America, whom he described as largely adhering to rightwing religious ideology (Pais, 2009).
20. In India, the scandal involved considerable controversy and public protests against the title of the film.
21. See Moran (1998) for a full account of this process, its history, variations, and particularly the issue of cultural transfer.
22. See Da Cunha (2005/2006) for an analysis of the two works, and the extent of authorial collaboration.
23. The increasing numbers in 2012 of novel/cinema productions created quite a media buzz. See Brody and "2012 Year of Book-to-Film Adaptations." This industry accompanies new and lucrative global foreign relations scandals. The controversy over the current filming of *Midnight's Children* succeeding *Slumdog Millionaire*. See Burke.
24. Not all novel/film combos could form such a neat package. The most recent example is *Cloud Atlas*, the unwieldy adaptation of David Mitchell's equally unwieldy novel, spanning centuries and vast geography, and which caused controversy and provoked humor by featuring white American actors playing multiple roles and races. See Brooks (2012), Lane (2012), and Travers (2012).

References

2012 year of book-to-film adaptations. (2012, August 2). *International Business Times* http://au.ibtimes.com/articles/369478/20120802/perks-being-wallflower-mortal-instruments-great-gatsby.htm

Adiga, A. (2008). *The white tiger.* New York, NY: Free Press.

The art of adaptation: The name sake. *The Writing Studio.* http://www.writingstudio.co.za/page1620.html

Baetens, J. (2010). Expanding the field of constraint: Novelization as an example of multiply constrained writing. *Poetics Today, 31*(1), 51–79.

Barthes, R. (1977). *Image, music, text* (selected and translated by S. Heath). Glasgow, Scotland: Fontana.

Bhabha, H. (1997). The world and the home. In A. McClintock, A. Mufti, & E. Shohat (Eds.), *Dangerous liaisons: Gender, nation, and postcolonial perspectives.* Minneapolis: University of Minnesota Press.

Bowles, P. (1949). *The sheltering sky.* New York, NY: HarperCollins.

Brody, R. (2012, August 7). Movies from books. *The New Yorker.*

Brooks, X. (2012, October 26). *Cloud Atlas* under fire for casting white actors in "yellow face" makeup. *The Guardian.*http://www.guardian.co.uk/film/2012/oct/26/cloud-atlas-under-fire-yellowface

Burke, J. (2012, September 9). Salman Rushdie film courts Indian controversy. *The New Yorker.* http://www.guardian.co.uk/books/2012/sep/09/rushdie-film-india-controversy-book

Cartmell, D., & Whelehan, I. (1999). Adaptations: The contemporary dilemmas. In D. Cartmell & I. Whelehan (Eds.), *Adaptations: From text to screen, screen to text.* New York, NY: Routledge.

Cohen, M. (2010). *The novel and the sea.* Princeton, NJ: Princeton University Press.

Da Cunha, M. (2005/2006). Two narratives, multiple spaces: The literature of Ismail Kadaré and the cinema of Walter Salles. *http://cpd1.ufmt.br/meel/arquivos/artigos/127.pdf*

Greer, B. (2002, June 12). Mair Nair (Interview). *The Guardian.* http://www.guardian.co.uk/film/2002/jun/12/guardianinterviewsatbfisouthbank1

Hall, S. (1996). When was the postcolonial? Thinking at the limit. In L. Curti & I. Chambers (Eds.), *The postcolonial question.* London, United Kingdom: Routledge.

Hanif Kureishi at the Jaipur literature festival 2010. (2010, February 1). *Black and White Fountain.* http://blackandwhitefountain.blogspot.com/2010/02/hanif-kureishi-at-jaipur-literature.html

Hardy, J. (2011, February). Mapping commercial intertextuality: HBO's *True Blood. Convergence: The International Journal of Research into New Media Technologies, 17*(1),

Hosseini, K. (2003). *The kite runner.* New York, NY: Penguin.

Hosseini, K. (2007). *A thousand splendid suns.* New York, NY: Penguin.

Hutcheon, L. (2006). A theory of adaptation. New York, NY: Routledge.

Jeffries, S. (2008, October 15). Roars of anger. *The Guardian.* http://www.guardian.co.uk/books/2008/oct/16/booker-prize/print

Jeffries, S. (2009, January 16). "I'm the luckiest novelist in the world." *The Guardian.* http://www.guardian.co.uk/books/2009/jan/16/danny-boyle-india/print

Jenkins, H. (2006). *Convergence culture: Where old and new media collide.* New York, NY: New York University Press.

Kadare, I. (1982) *Broken April.* London, United Kingdom: Saqi Books.

Kraidy, M. (2002, August). Hybridity in cultural globalization. *Communication Theory, 12*(3), 316–339.

Kraidy, M., & Mourad, S. (2010). Hypermedia and global communication studies: Lessons from the Middle East. *Global Media Journal, 8*(16), 1–19.

Krystal, Arthur (2009, November 16). Slow fade: F. Scott Fitzgerald in Hollywood. *The New Yorker.*

Lane, A. (2012, October 29). Lost: "Cloud Atlas" and "This Must Be the Place." *The New Yorker.* http://www.newyorker.com/arts/critics/cinema/2012/10/29/121029crci_cinema_lane

Leitch, T. (2007). *Film adaptation and its discontents: From* Gone with the Wind *to the* Passion of Christ. Baltimore, MD: Johns Hopkins University Press.

Leyda, J. (2011, January). An interview with Jhumpa Lahiri. *Contemporary Women's Writing, 5*(1), 66–83.

Majumdar, A. (2010, January 25). Hanif Kureishi has something to tell you. *Indian Express.* http://www.indianexpress.com/story-print/571264

Maugham, W. (1921, May). On writing for the films. *The North American Review, 213*(786), 670–675. http://www.jstor.org/stable/25151139

McGrath, C. (2006, December 10). Another encore for the most adaptable of authors. *New York Times.* http://www.nytimes.com/2006/12/10/movies/10chip.html

Michod, A. (2008, May). Richard Price. *The Believer.* http://www.believermag.com/issues/200805/?read=interview_price

Moran, A. (1998). *Copycat TV: Globalisation, program formats, and cultural identity.* Lutton, United Kingdom: Lutton University Press.

Murray, S. (2008). Phantom adaptations: *Eucalyptus,* the adaptation industry and the film that never was. *Adaptation, 1*(1), 5–23.

Murray, S. (2012). *The adaptation industry: The cultural economy of contemporary literary adaptation.* New York, NY: Routledge.

Ouditt, S. (2012). *Orlando*: Coming across the divide. In D. Cartmell & I. Whelehan (Eds.), *Adaptations: From text to screen, screen to text.* New York, NY: Routledge.

Pais, A. (2009, April 22). Indian writers in India don't get the respect Indian writers in America get. *Rediff Movies.* http://movies.rediff.com/report/2009/apr/22/aravind-adiga-on-the-white-tiger.htm

Parkes, W., McDonald, L. [Producers], & Foster, M. [Director]. (2007). *The kite runner.* United States: Dreamworks.

Peeters, H. (2010). Multimodality and its modes in novelizations. *Image & Narrative, 11*(1), 118–129.

Reeves, H. (2006, June 5). Translating the subcontinent: From books to film and back again. *Indo-American Arts Council.* http://www.iaac.us/BS_Water/press_release.htm

Rivera, A. (2007, March/April). Mira Nair: Interview from Bengal to the Big Apple. *Mother Jones*, 32(2), 82–83. http://motherjones.com/media/2007/03/mira-nair

Said, E. (1979) *Orientalism.* New York, NY: Vintage.

Said, E. (1994). *Culture and imperialism.* New York, NY: Vintage

Sharp, S. (2009, June 19). Mojo Interview: Aravind Adiga. *Mother Jones. http://www.motherjones.com/media/2009/06/mojo-interview-aravind-adiga*

Soofi, M. (2007, June 13). Interview with Bapsi Sidhwa. *Books, interviews/permalink.* http://gbytes.gsood.com/2007/06/13/interview-with-bapsi-sidhwa/

Stam, R. (2005). *Literature through film: Realism, magic, and the art of adaptation.* Malden, MA: Blackwell.

Stam, R., & Raengo, A., Eds. (2005). *Literature and film: A guide to the theory and practice of film adaptation.* Malden, MA: Blackwell.

Telotte, J., & Duchovnay, G. (Eds.). (2012). *Science fiction film, television, and adaptation across the screens.* New York, NY: Routledge.

Travers, P. (2012, October 25). Cloud Atlas [Review]. *Rolling Stone.* http://www.rollingstone.com/movies/reviews/cloud-atlas-20121025

Zhao, E. (2011). Social network market: Storytelling on the web 2.0 original literature site. *Convergence: The International Journal of Research into New Media Technologies, 17*(1), 85–99.

Zurbrugg, N. (1999). Will Hollywood never learn? David Cronenberg's *Naked Lunch.* In D. Cartmell & I. Whelehan (Eds.), *Adaptations: From text to screen, screen to text.* New York, NY: Routledge.

Part Four. Journalism and Public Relations in a Changing Media Sphere

10

Life Without a "Liberal Representative" Journalism: Towards a Professional Deontology with a Deliberative Turn

MARÍA LAMUEDRA GRAVÁN

Life Without a Liberal Representative Public Sphere

Life in modern societies requires complex institutions of mediation. In fact, the development of media is linked to the emergence of modern societies (Thompson, 1998). Informative media are thought of as great contributors to the "public sphere," a Habermasian concept according to which, in modern times, political systems and civil society are connected via the media, along with other cultural agents. Without media, people in different cities, villages, and social classes would not be connected to a similar notion of "what is happening," i.e., to the threats, challenges, and opportunities of societies within a national state (see Splichal, 2006, p. 708; Nieminen, 2009, p. 21; Trenz, 2009, p. 39).

In postmodern times, the current globalised economy (and its institutions such as the IMF or the World Bank) is exerting pressure on modern nation states, state sovereignty (Appadurai, 2000, p. 16), and therefore, democracy. In this context, civil society does not have a way to connect to this new supranational political system through a cosmopolitan public sphere (see Splichal, 2006, p. 702) (although much faith is placed on the Internet in this regard). There is not even a healthy European public sphere. Theorists argue whether the European democratic deficit can only be eliminated if a European public sphere comes into existence, or if the causal direction between democracy and publicness should be reversed (see Karppinen, 2009, p. 64; Splichal, 2006, pp. 296–298; or Trenz, 2009, p. 49).

In this context, movements that question the legitimacy of political representation in mature democratic societies have emerged, and they also strive for what Appadurai called "globalization from below" (2000, pp. 15–18). The so-called New Social Movements of the 1970s have shifted, evolved, and found new ground in recent movements such as Occupy Everywhere, or the Spanish 15M (Juris, 2012, p. 260). They are searching for ways to overcome these obstacles, and call for a more participatory, deliberative, and democratic society with more participatory media, and which also have an international ethos. As Hardt and Negri (2004, p. 307) have posited, modern representative democracy requires a re-birth to recover its radical, utopian meaning of "the rule of everyone by everyone."

This chapter, therefore, assumes that if life in modern societies needs mediation, such need is even greater in postmodern neoliberal and globalised societies. However, the informative media, which assured some level of democracy in the so-called advanced democratic nation states, and created a specific kind of public sphere, offer insufficient instruments for democracy under the pressure of neoliberalism and a globalization understood mainly in economic terms. For this reason, this chapter deals with the kind of informative media, and journalism, necessary for a more participative public sphere and democracy: a deliberative public sphere in a deliberative democracy. It does so by analyzing viewers' perception of representativity in public service news, as well as the professional ethics associated with this perception. It also explores how journalistic ethics should adapt to a deliberative concept of democracy.

Demands for Citizens' Participation in Media and Democracy

Since May 2011, just after the Arab Spring revolutions, the Spanish 15M movement along with many citizens have been organizing protests, spreading the initiative around the world. Labels such as "Occupy" not only question political representation and demand higher levels of participation, they are also developing an assembly-style (*asamblearian*), horizontal organizational culture for which the global justice movement was a significant predecessor (Della Porta, 2005, pp. 73–94). Romanos (2012, pp. 3–7) defines this asamblearian way of decision-making on Plaza del Sol in Madrid (among other public squares in the world) as horizontal, inclusive, and transparent.

Something similar can be applied to media. According to Carroll and Hackett's study conducted in the United Kingdom and the United States (2006, p. 85), activism for democratization *through* the media and *by* media can be considered emergent. Some of the media, including Indymedia, are again linked to the global justice movement. They not only denounce the alliance of media conglomerates to the agents of economic globalization, and the crisis of representation in corporate media, they are also primarily horizontally organized, often in cooperative lines in contact with the community they serve (see also Haro Barba & Sampedro Blanco, 2012, p. 161; Juris, 2012).

These new participative practices and diagnoses have many similarities to media academics' and theorists' concerns when describing ongoing trends in journalism and democracy during the last decade. Herman and Chomsky (1988) explained how the media serve the interest of political and economic elites, and in doing so developed Antonio Gramsci's notion of popular cultural products of the 1930s as one of the domains where ruling elites gained consent for their projects. More recently, Castells (2010) has also described how the media have become the arena where political and business power strategies are played out. Herman and McChesney (1999; McChesney, 2008) argue that the majority of newsrooms are in the hands of large economic groups for which neither the democratizing role nor public service is a priority. Almirón (2010) affirms that the commercial media have become financialized, since unprecedented progressive borrowing, the disembarking of actors related to global finance (i.e., investment banks) in the ownership structure of the chief communication groups, and the direct influence of financial institutions on boards of directors have all become part and parcel of their commercial activities.

In the area of theory of democracy, there are also numerous and qualified experts concerned with current deficits in democratic societies, who call for a more participative democracy, a tendency that has been called "the deliberative turn" (Dryzek, 2000). John Rawls, Jürgen Habermas, and Hannah Arendt are the three most influential theorists who have advocated for a system in which the public use of reason is exercised by society at large, and in which public issues are agreed upon by deliberation among all social agents taking part in each issue (Velasco, 2009, pp. 26–77).

One of the main barriers for the possible application of this deliberative democratic ideal is that the frames in which public opinion and participation are formed are constructed by the same media which cause so much concern Velasco (2007, pp. 41–42) and Nino (1997, pp. 224–228) explicitly mention the poor quality of social debate created under the above-mentioned media conditions.

The lack of homogeneous theory linking the role of media, journalists, and citizen within democracy (Carpentier, 2007, p. 157) has been seen as an additional obstacle faced by a media model more attuned to deliberative democracy ideals. Public journalism theory, however, must be considered an exception. Haas and Steiner (2006, p. 238) explain that the public journalism movement emerged in the United States in the early 1990s in response to two widening gaps of "crisis" proportions: between government and citizens, and between news organizations and their audiences. In response, and inspired by the Habermasian public-sphere ideal, certain media theorists, such as J. Rosen, J. Carey, T. Glasser, and M. Schudson, along with many news organizations, opened a public debate and began to experiment with ways to enhance civic commitment and participation in democratic processes and to rethink their relationship to their audience. Many pioneering initiatives for journalism were undertaken that promoted rational debate on social problems in local communities. During this process, as Rosen notes (1999, p. 33), both academics and journalists broke the "fortress" in which they separately undertook their professions, and engaged in public discussion.

Public journalism took it upon itself to reflect seriously upon journalism in relation to democracy: "Journalism and politics cannot be thought of as two separate domains of activities . . . they can only be known via their mutual and active adaptations which are cooperative and antagonistic by turns. In fact, every conception and practice of politics is simultaneously a conception of journalism" (Carey, 1999, p. 51). Even the term "deliberative democracy" was not absent from the public journalism debate. For instance, in 1995, Cole Campbell, editor of the *St. Louis Post Dispatch*, is quoted to have said in a forum on public journalism "we are coming to realize that deliberative democracy may hold more possibilities than representative democracy" (Rosen, 1999, p. 36).

Currently, a similar and related field of research and theory is being built in the supposedly participation-enhancing Internet era. Dan Gillmor (2006), Nico Carpentier (2005, 2007), and Nick Couldry (2005) are currently working in this field, which is being revitalized by the analysis of new media's influence in organizing social protests (for example, see Juris, 2012; Haro Barba & Sampedro Blanco, 2012; Skinner, 2012). This chapter contributes towards—as well as helping to foster in Europe—the aforementioned debate, and reflects upon a possible transformation of journalism theory in line with deliberative democracy.

James Carey (1999) argues that:

> the view of the press as the representative of the public and the effectiveness of its watchdog and adversary roles—in tune with a traditional representative democracy—could only be sustained if the following conditions were met: (1) The public had to believe that the press was authentically their representative and therefore in a responsible and fiduciary relation to it; (2) the public had to believe that the press was not in cahoots with the state, with the most powerful interest groups or both; and (3) the public had to believe that the press was capable of representing the world, that is, of rendering a reasonable, unbiased true and factual account of it. In all these senses of "represent." (p. 57)

This chapter strives to make a contribution to exploring whether the public believes that the above-mentioned three conditions are met, through the data obtained in 60 interviews with Public Service Television (PSB) news viewers in Spain and the U.K. in 2009. In particular, as regards their concept of the news, data obtained suggest that even before *indignados* and Occupy protests took place, most people questioned the classic view of media news as representing the world, often expressed through the metaphor of media or the news as a window to the world, through which citizens just need to quietly observe politicians' acts and vote every four years (that is the view of the media role in current liberal representative democracies). The first part of this study explores the way in which citizens perceive "media reality" in relation to their own way of perceiving reality in their daily lives. This is relevant to assess their perception of media as representing the real.

The second part of this chapter deals with the hegemonic discourse of journalism that renders it "representative." The deontological principles of objectivity and impartiality are associated with this role of journalism as the "invisible medium" for this window, which have been subjected to journalistic and academic criticism even before it was adopted (Schudson, 1967, pp. 144–155). However, empirical work with readers shows that the notions of objectivity and impartiality are still a central reference for quality journalism. For all these reasons, it is argued here that no alternative view of the role of journalism in democratic societies (to that of a window to the world) appears to be available to viewers, according to the interviews. These findings further emphasize the need for media theorists to propose and contribute towards an alternative theory of the news media's mission (see Ettema, 2007, pp. 143–160). Finally, the third part of the chapter provides a small contribution to this alternative theory, in tune with the idea of deliberative democracy.

BBC and TVE News Viewers Talk About the News: The Notion of Representation Is Challenged

First, this section offers some context information on study methodology and BBC and TVE news programmes. Second, it insists on the relationship between the model of journalism "as a window" and a liberal representative public sphere. And third, it analyses whether the views held by TVE and BBC interviewees on the news are in line with the window model. Later, we'll look at those views as they relate to the window model deontology.

The Methodology of the Study and the News on BBC and TVE

The qualitative study is based on 60 interviews—30 with TVE viewers and 30 with BBC viewers—conducted between 2006 and 2007, with sufficient diversity as to sex, age, and socio-demographic profiles. The interviews took place in several locations in the United Kingdom (London, and the mainly rural Devon area) and Spain (Madrid, Segovia, Seville, and Granada), and participants were selected using snowball sampling techniques. The TVE sample interviews were conducted by trained professionals living in Spain and the BBC sample interviews by professionals living in the U.K. They lasted 40–100 minutes and were semi-structured, although interviewers were instructed to make sure the conversation included the following eight areas or themes: their general habits of television consumption; their particular habits of news consumption; their likes and dislikes about different elements of BBC/TVE news programmes (such as issues, anchors); the relationship between the reality as perceived by viewers and the news world; discourses about the public service; possibilities of improving the news programmes; the coverage of burning issues at the moment of interviews; and discourses about sports.

Until September 2012, the Spanish Public Service Broadcasting (PSB) television was the most popular channel, with a comfortable 20.3 percent of the audience share, followed by the commercial channels Telecinco, with 16.7 percent, and Antena 3, with 13.7 percent (EGM, 2011). After leading the ranking for the last five years, with over five points of share ahead of its closest competitor.

The commercial channel Telecinco, according to Kantar Media, has recently taken the lead as a result of retrograde institutional changes introduced by the conservative party in government since April 2012 (see Bustamante Ramírez, 2012[1]). The BBC is considered a central social and cultural institution in the U.K., and

BBC1 is also the most popular channel in the U.K., with 21 percent of the share, followed by ITV1, with 15 percent, according to BARB figures for April–June 2011. BARB figures show that BBC news programs are the most popular of their kind. As regards news programmes on all channels, only BBC News occupied positions in the BARB ranking of the 50 most popular programmes; for example, 10 positions in the week ending on 17 April; 12 positions in the week ending on 22 May; and 10 positions in the week ending on 19 June, almost all in the lower half of this ranking.

The Window Metaphor and Liberal Representative Public Spheres

Liberal-representative democracies like ours assume that in a democratic system, political decisions must respect citizens' interests, as well as the processes by which the will of citizens is formed. This typically happens at election times; for citizens to be able to make informed decisions, they need to be aware of all competing actors in power, and the actions and laws that have been implemented since the last elections. Under this model, the public sphere[2] is created when citizens are well-informed, can exercise their free will, and can control the political elite. The public sphere is, thus, the system of citizen observation (Gerhards, 1997 and 2002, in Thomas, 2010, pp. 63–67). The members of the political elite, on the other hand, are aware that the citizens observe them, take into consideration their attitude, and therefore orient their actions towards citizens' expectations. This process requires a high degree of transparency and should ensure that the elite respond to the will of citizens. Of course, in contemporary representative democracies, this process is mediated and the public sphere is basically one created by the media, because immediate contact between citizens and the elite is no longer possible.

Transparency has traditionally been associated with the idea that media are a window to the world, in which journalists are "the windowpane," mere transmitters of information. The so-called journalistic autonomy applied to journalists, which encompasses values such as balance, fairness, and objectivity (McDevitt, 2003, p. 156), lends credibility to this metaphor. However, one of the chief problems of the current media system lies in the fact that the elite's sources have priority over those of civil society to such an extent that it is possible to argue that there is a re-feudalization of the public sphere (Manning, 2001, p. 5).[3] And, yet, this trend (among others) has become paradoxically invisible. Moreover, the media also function as the representative of the public, which tend to make citizens believe that just by watching or reading the news they are taking part in democracy (Lazarsfeld

& Merton, 1948 in Wolf, 1987, p. 76) and there is no need to take further action. In other words, the current functioning of news media masks power imbalances in the public sphere and works as an obstacle for social participation.

At an epistemological level, the representative public sphere is in keeping with a positivist view of reality, represented as being external to us, and which can be reflected and controlled, providing that suitable procedures are used. According to David Harvey (1990, pp. 28–29), positivism was already being questioned by artists and intellectuals such as Baudelaire or Manet after 1848. Now in the realm of communication research, authors such as Fishman (1980), Gans (1979), and Tuchman (1978), who conducted participant observation in the media, developed the theory of news-making. They described how information is created from elements of "reality," which are chosen and focused in accordance with a series of previously established news routines and values and end up conditioning the flux of social reality: roughly speaking, these routines and values end up favouring the version of the elite, and news centred on conflicts, about which barely enough contextual information is provided for an in-depth understanding. As will be shown, viewers who thought of the news as a window to the world held a positivistic view of reality, while those who questioned the window metaphor were more aware of how media influence shapes our views and our social system.

The Citizens' View: Closer to the Window Metaphor or to the Constructed Nature of News?

Based on the interviews, an attempt was made to analyze to what extent the citizens' view of reality coincided with the metaphor of the media as a window to the world. One of the main issues analyzed here relates to the following question posed to interviewees: does the reality that you perceive on a daily basis coincide with that of the news programmes of TVE/ BBC? In addition, in many cases, interviewees talked spontaneously about this issue without prompting. The coverage of the most burning current issues was also included in interview themes in order to improve "vividness, nuance and detail" (Rubin & Rubin, 1995, pp. 78–81). As will be seen, the answers to questions about current news provided some interesting insights because the interviewees with a view closer to the window metaphor tended to identify news with reality. On the other hand, those more aware of the dynamics involved in the media, who questioned the window model, tended to centre their arguments on the news coverage itself; in other words, they did not talk about news and reality as if it were the same thing.[4]

The results are shown as a continuum: at one end, a group of British and Spanish interviewees shared views coinciding with the window metaphor; others, whose discourse has been defined here as an "imperfect window," showed a certain degree of reflection; while a third group rejected the model. Nonetheless, the interviewees comprising this last group were frequently aware of the fact that it was impossible for them to escape from media effects and whose reasoning was consistent in this respect. The findings are shown in the following table.

Table 1. Viewers' discourses and their relationship with the window view

	BBC sample	TVE sample
"Window view"	4	10
"Imperfect window"	5	5
"Questioned window view"	21	15

Sample: 30 TVE and 30 BBC viewers

Window View

The following extracts illustrate the views of those for whom the media system was "a window to the world":

> I think that they keep us fairly well informed. I don't have a problem with that, at all. They cover everything. There is very little in the world that isn't covered. I'm quite satisfied. There's not much more to be told. I say this because I watch the news and read the newspaper." (Shop Assistant, 58. BBC sample.)
>
> I believe that it's fairly real because in reality, well . . . they simply have to keep us informed about everything that happens at each moment and every day, about everything that is a current issue. (Real Estate Agent, 44. TVE sample.)

Among the TVE viewers sharing this standpoint, there was a majority of older people, with a lower level of formal education, something that could not be confirmed in the British sample.

Two of the interviewees from the United Kingdom who fit in with this model, only did so during most of their interview. One of them was Social Worker, 56, born in the Dominican Republic. She reflected on how coverage of third-world countries, like her own, tended to be negative, a view that did not coincide with her own notions of such countries. However, this did not stop her from talking about news programmes, at least, the televised kind, as a window to the world:

> When news programmes are broadcasted live, that is what is happening now in a certain part of the world . . . for example, the news broadcasts from Afghanistan. . . . I can see the reporter, I can see the soldiers in the background, it's possible to see a certain area that they are attacking or whatever . . . that's the image that I have. (Social Worker, 56. BBC sample.)

This extract is a reminder that television can be seen as the triumph of the myth of objectivity (Ferrés, 1994, pp. 61–75).

Imperfect Window

Another group defended a position that is still closer to the window metaphor, although imperfect because they maintained that in the content selection process, unnecessary news items were included and others left out, or that the approach used was unsuitable. For example, among the BBC viewers, two of the interviewees, Job Centre Worker, 35, and Teacher, 42, believed that if the editor did not edit so much and showed more footage, a certain amount of partiality that they had noted in international news could be somehow eradicated. This indicated a certain amount of reflection, although they continued to believe that the footage itself represented the reality, thus demonstrating a positivist idea that the reality is out there and can be shown.

Journalism as a Building Agent of Social Reality? Discourses Questioning the Window Model

The largest group of interviewees proved to have a view much closer to the idea that the media contribute to shaping the notion citizens have of what happens, and in this way, exert an influence on "social reality." This view is illustrated by the following extract:

> Sometimes, I think that the news makes people believe that they know what is really happening, but this isn't true. Sometimes, news stories exaggerate how badly we live, the crisis in Spain, I think that journalists exaggerate a bit or try to get the most out of the story. In reality, things are different from what they are saying . . . that gives a bad image of the country. . . . I don't think it's good for

people. People who don't know differently will think everything's like that. (Shop Assistant, 38. TVE sample.)

Again, Shop Assistant, 38, thought that this coverage was not positive for the majority of citizens. Among the BBC interviewees, the discourse most commonly used to explain why news stories were a long way from "reality" as they perceived it revolved around the idea that the BBC's international coverage was partial and too Anglo-centric. This was the discourse used by 19 interviewees, 16 of whom proved to have a concept closer to construction and three to the imperfect window. Among immigrants and international sector workers, there was an absolute consensus on this issue. Besides these two groups, this discourse was shared by another 11 interviewees, seven with higher education and four with vocational training.

Lawyer, 48, a BBC viewer, and Audiovisual Art Researcher, 39, a TVE viewer, illustrate how this worldview affected their own view and how they tried to limit its impact:

> You know about what they show you . . . your worldview. . . . I think it's very much shaped than it should be, so I think there's a dangerous thing about that, because the BBC's so English-centric . . . if you watch Al Jazeera News every day, then you would have a very different view of the world. (Lawyer, 48. BBC sample.)

> Although we don't want to, we are all influenced—including me—by the media, inevitably, but I try to be aware of it and fight against it. But when you're in a system, you're part of it and repeat a lot of what it shows you. (Audiovisual Art Researcher, 39. TVE sample.)

Music Doctoral Programme Student, 27, reflects on journalistic coverage based on events and suspects that there exist reasons of an organizational nature for this, although she is unable to identify them:

> The impression I have is that we are kept more informed when something happens, but not in the meantime. So, no one really knows how it works, what's happening, what's at the heart of that, and we're not informed about that. I don't know if it's because no one has information or because it can't be given. . . . I don't know what channels there are in between, but what I do understand as a viewer is that I only get to know about bad things, that is to say, when there's a terrorist attack, and about what there is underneath, not a lot. (Music Doctoral Programme Student, 27. TVE sample.)

In the case of the BBC viewers, three-fourths of the interviewees with a view very different from the window metaphor were middle class with a university education. As regards the Spanish interviewees, there were two clear-cut groups: one with a much more structured discourse, comprising people with a solid education (like Music Doctoral Programme Student, 27, above), and another group, made up of people who had a generally poor discourse and basic education, but who said similar things. Among the Spanish interviewees, there were answers in which a certain degree of resignation could be detected, as if at some level of awareness they perceived news reality as an imposed one. Housewife, 76, seemed angry at the fact that, although she did not trust it, she finally had to accept it as real.

> Sometimes I get angry [laughter], I become quite annoyed. That I don't like some things . . . and we have to swallow them. . . . I believe that there are some things that are a bit of a lie, or highly exaggerated, or they don't tell it as it should be told . . . but it's their lookout, they can do as they please. We believe it, those of us that are listening. (Housewife, 76. TVE sample.)

The case of City Worker, 35, a BBC viewer, requires further consideration and calls for comparative research on those working in the financial sector and other sectors of society, for instance, those with a public service ideology. His discourse distinguished itself from the rest. On the one hand, City Worker, 35, was at the very least distrustful of media coverage: "They show you what they want you to see . . . they don't probably show you what is truly happening all the time." On the other hand, he objected to the way the BBC broke the news about the bank Northern Rock, because in some way he seemed to think that the media should grant priority to companies over the public:

> I think, yes, the BBC News has probably been seen as a public service programme, I think when the BBC broke the news about Northern Rock. . . . I think that if the BBC had been more sensitive about how they approached this story, Northern Rock maybe wouldn't be in the position it's in today. . . . I think the people have a right to know, but I think that ultimately, it's the government's responsibility and maybe the BBC is like the government, you know . . . , instead of just saying, you know, your savings are at risk, etc., etc., you should manage the people better. (City Worker, 35. BBC sample.)

This implies that he was aware that news stories have an effect on reality; for example, they had affected the fall of a bank. However, due to something akin to his "class interests," he preferred that public service put the welfare of the sector in which he worked before that of citizens in general.

This analysis suggests that most interviewees have their doubts about whether or not the media serves as a true window to the world. The majority of the viewers in the Spanish and British samples—above all in the latter—questioned the editing and media influence in society. At the same time, the general consensus was that the media constitute the frame of reference for citizens (developed from the work of McCombs & Shaw, 1972). This idea was even expressed by interviewees with poorly structured discourses. The interviewees with more structured discourses raised the issue of how they could overcome the unavoidable influence of the media on their frame of reference. The analysis also suggests other conclusions:

- In the poorly structured discourses included in the TVE sample, this impression, normally associated with the suspicion that the media serve other interests, came hand in hand with impotence: "we have to swallow them."
- In the case of the BBC, the belief of the viewers in the honesty of the public service limited the importance of this suspicion, which was only voiced as regards foreign news coverage.
- Those interviewees with the highest qualifications had a more developed discourse as regards selection processes, edition, interpretation of materials, and influence on society, although they did not seem to understand the whole process and its implications.

Despite the questioning of the window model, it may come as no surprise that no alternative model was clearly detected. If such an alternative journalistic model is to be developed by media theorists, it is advisable to take into account the criticism that both journalists and academics have levelled at the window model deontology. Later, this will be compared to the deontological values that, according to TVE and BBC viewers' data, are identified with quality journalism.

Professional Deontologies and New Forms of Journalism

> Journalists offer conventional explanations on how they identify the truth, which tend to consist of quick answers given in interviews or discourses, or what is worse, in mercantile slogans, based on mere metaphors. The press is "the mirror of society" . . . , "journalism is the reflection of daily passions" . . ."anything outstanding on a particular day." The aforementioned explications make journalists seem passive, mere recorders of the latest news, rather than selectors and editors of information. . . . More than defending our techniques and methods for discovering the

> truth, as journalists we have had to deny its existence . . . this is one of the reasons why the debate on the objectivity of journalists has become a trap. (Kovach & Rosenstiel, 2003, pp. 58–59).

In the 1950s or thereabouts, the social responsibility theory certified the social demand that news media observe a deontological code (McQuail, 2001, pp. 201–202). In the United States, however, the debate about adopting the notion of objectivity as a deontological reference had been taking place since 1920. For Walter Lippmann, what had to be objective was the journalistic method to know the facts, but despite this, the ideal of the "objective journalist" ended up being that deontological anchor, even if it had already been subjected to criticism (Schudson, 1967, pp. 144–155). Besides, it will come as no surprise that there has been a long and well-established tradition of academic criticism of the notion of objectivity (and to a lesser extent, impartiality) applied to journalists (see, for instance, Tuchman, 1978; Ferrés, 1994; Muñoz-Torres, 2000; O'Donnell, 2007).

Journalists' associations have been working for decades in a similar direction: the rejection of objectivism was central to the New Journalism movement that became popular in the United States in 1960s. Moreover, nowadays neither objectivity nor impartiality appears in the deontological code of the Pew Project for Excellence in Journalism, or, for that matter, in that of the International Federation of Journalists (IFJ), which has recently launched its "Ethical Journalism Initiative" (EJI), which, along the same lines of the Pew Project, aims to reform journalistic values.

The Pew Project for Excellence in Journalism code is among the most influential nowadays. It is described in the book entitled *The Elements of Journalism* (*Los Elementos del Periodismo*) by Bill Kovach and Tom Rosenstiel (2003). The code itself was agreed upon after intense research[5] and deliberation by journalists. The book implies that a healthy practice of journalism requires clear and shared deontological values, as well as clear and shared work methods, and news companies with a public service-centric structure. According to this code, quality is related to the notions of truth and loyalty to citizens and must be made visible so that it can be assessed through vigorous research, verification methods, and the will to explain them to citizens (the code will be addressed further later). The Pew Project, therefore, supports Lippmann's view of deontology as based on objective methods, not objective journalists.

Despite all these considerations, the notions of objectivity and impartiality applied to the journalist still have some social hold. And this happens even under the current pressure that the new social uses of blogs, social networks, and the demand for citizen journalism are bringing to bear on the social role traditionally given to journalists, who are increasingly asked to stop working as a content managers, isolated from the public, to become collaborators or facilitators, and to connect virtual citizen spaces created using new media with the public sphere (Díaz, 2009).[6]

Some analysts have described the news diet as being influenced by this trend (see Gillmor, 2004; Noguera, 2008; Varela, 2005). The most visible symptoms are also the most recent ones, such as the unleashing effect that social media is said to have had on the Arab Spring revolutions (see Skinner, 2011; Mendez Muros and García Estevez, 2011, pp. 9–11) show how during the first week of 15M protests in Spain, in May 2011, the mainstream press did not consider it a privileged news event. According to Ferreras's study (2011), the 15M protest was not only born out of an organization created thanks to new media activity, e.g., on Twitter; what was also remarkable was that during the week of protests, the information spread via the new media grew exponentially. This put pressure to the mainstream media to cover the protests as the main news event in the following weeks. However, most theorists, at least until having had the opportunity to analyze these new processes in a systematic manner, agree that despite the fact that new Internet uses contribute to greater social participation, this does not replace the social mission that a healthy professional journalism can accomplish in society (see Gillmor, 2004, pp. xvi–xvii; Díaz, 2009).

Key Deontological Principles for BBC and TVE viewers

Regarding ethical principles, the study aims to identify all those values associated with the metaphor of journalism as a window mentioned by interviewees, such as those related to journalistic autonomy, objectivity, impartiality, fairness, and neutrality; on the other hand, attention has also been paid to values that could represent journalism as a participative agent in the construction of reality, as opposed to "a sphere of observation." These are the values that make the practice of journalism visible in the public sphere. In this section, professionalism, diversity, and citizen-centricity are taken into account. A minority call for more participatory news can also be identified. A data analysis follows:

Table 2. Deontological principles of journalism appearing in viewers' discourses

	BBC sample	TVE sample
Autonomy	Balance/fairness: 11 Impartiality: 11 Credibility: 12 Objectivity: 4 Independence: 3	Impartiality, neutrality, or independence: 10 Objectivity: 5 (as demanded of public service broadcasting), and 5 (as a quality of TVE reporting)
Use of autonomy to evaluate news coverage	Impartiality: 12	Impartiality: 22
Values in tune with journalism as an agent that constructs social reality	Professionalism: 21 Quality: 21 Diversity of views: 6 Citizen-centric: 8 Deeper and broader information on BBC website: 4 Honest: 3 Committed: 3 Considerate: 1	Professionalism: 2 Extensive coverage: 3 Inclusive: 1 Citizen-centric: 1
Call for more participatory news	Depth and complexity, nuance, and commitment: 7 Social content: 2 Public participation: 2	Depth and complexity, nuance, and commitment: 7 Sources, pluralism, and social content: 5
Other values	20	8

Values Associated with Journalistic Autonomy (The Window Model, and Liberal Representative Democracy)

Impartiality, neutrality, and independence were the values to which the BBC and TVE viewers alluded most. In the TVE sample, these values were used both as public service ideal values, as well as for rating the journalistic performance of TVE news programmes: the majority still believed that the news programmes were partial to the government, a large number opined that they were still partial but less so than in the past or to a lesser degree than the news programmes of its competitors, and a small number regarded them as being so inherent to a state news programme that they did not even criticize them.

As to the BBC interviewees, the concepts of balance/fairness, impartiality, and credibility—a concept also associated with the broadcasting company's reputation and tradition—were the most popular. A smaller group of interviewees valued the BBC for its independence and for acting as a counter-power. For instance, Programme Coordinator for Latin America, 53, used as an example and milestone the war in Iraq, and Fundraiser, 30, the Palestinian problem.

When criticizing the BBC, the most mentioned concept was also its partiality. As mentioned above, a part of this group considered that the channel's international news was too Anglo-centric and served national interests. Other viewers mentioned the Conservatives, the government and the establishment as other beneficiaries of this alleged partiality. It is worth noting that the deontological value of objectivity was cited less frequently by both the British and Spanish interviewees.

Values of Journalism as Constructor of Reality

The BBC viewers appreciated, to a great extent, the PSB news programmes for the principles covered in this section. Professionalism and news programme quality elicited the greatest consensus. Along these lines, some of the values appreciated by the interviewees included its correspondent network, good reporters and reporting, the presence of experts with a sound judgement in news programmes, and the maturity of the presenters and their capacity to pose good questions.

Other values mentioned were the diversity of points of view or the inclusion of information on issues not on the main news agenda of the BBC, and the fact that issues relating to the international political arena, which received scant coverage in the more general news programmes, could be read about on the BBC's website. Other interviewees claimed that the news programmes were more citizen-centric due to the issues they covered and their approach, with the accent on highlighting the implications of news stories for citizens. This view is compatible with other adjectives, such as "honest" or "upright," "considerate" or "committed." For instance, Fundraiser, 30, stated that "the BBC news programmes served the purpose of making things matter to people."

In comparison with BBC interviewees, fewer TVE viewers referred to these kinds of values as qualities of TVE news coverage: some of the values mentioned included more extensive coverage, professionalism and experience, inclusiveness, and public-centricity.

With regard to the most popular demands, the interviewees called for news with a greater depth and complexity, nuance, or commitment. The majority of these interviewees were those with the highest qualifications and whose discourse was highly structured as regards the role of the media in society, both in the TVE sample and in that of the BBC. They were referring to how news programmes centre on conflicts, thus depriving them of elements of analysis of their causes and context. Several of the BBC viewers—the sample with the largest number of interviewees with higher education—made a number of specific requests with an eye to counteracting this: more research, a more in-depth analysis, more air time for correspondents, longer news programmes, and generally, more awkward issues.

Some interviewees called for substituting impartiality with commitment. Likewise, some TVE interviewees claimed "more sources," "greater pluralism," and "more social or grassroots content." Some of the BBC interviewees also seconded this request, along with greater public participation.

In the analysis of discourses, other categories also emerged. The most significant being "resistance to commercialism," which refers to the belief that TVE and BBC public news programmes were more serious than those of the commercial channels, in the sense that they were less inclined to commercialism. Excessively general, vague values, such as "the explanatory dimension of the news," as well as issues relating to format, such as the sobriety of TVE's news programmes, compared to the commercial channels, also cropped up in the interviews.

The analysis of the deontological values frequently found in the discourses of the British and Spanish viewers suggests that:

- On the one hand, there is a strong discursive presence of values related to the autonomy of the media, such as impartiality, neutrality, balance, fairness, or independence, values which are in tune with the idea of the media as representatives of society, and as the "invisible pane" of the window to the world, in an observation system for citizens in a liberal representative democracy. This occurred despite the fact that most viewers interviewed question the window-to-the-world metaphor of the media.

- On the other hand, the discourses show some awareness of the importance of values such as diversity or citizen-centricity. In Spain, the discourses were more a call than an acknowledgement, while in the United Kingdom the opposite tended to be true. Among the British interviewees, it is also worth mentioning the wide consensus on the professionalism of the news programmes, which highlights the BBC as an agent that contributes to news-making. However, viewers did not seem to be aware of the importance of verification methods, as established by the Pew Project deontological code.
- Moreover, those interviewees with a high level of education in both samples called for principles and practises along the following lines: more complex and honest information, based on ample research, less oriented towards explaining conflicts, and with more contextual information, above all as regards international issues.
- Although this may be regarded as an "expected" outcome, it is worth noting that not even the discourses of the most qualified tended to grasp the epistemological implications of each discourse: the window model is consistent with a positivist concept that the reality is out there, and the need for a more iterative view of social reality, which requires greater commitment and collaboration of all the social agents, including journalism.

So far, it has been argued that there is wide concern among protesters, as well as media and democracy theorists about both institutions' deficiencies and widening gaps with citizens. The study analysis also suggests that British and Spanish PSB news viewers at least question the journalism model associated with liberal representative democracy, the one represented by the metaphor of news as a window to the world. However, they still value the deontological principles of impartiality, neutrality, and objectivity associated with such a conception of journalism. Likewise, they also value and call for other principles that would be necessary for a more participatory conception of journalism, although without establishing a clear reference of an alternative journalism model. The following section argues that deliberative democracy could be this alternative reference, and reflects on the professional deontology that could operate in this model.

Life with Another Kind of Journalism: Journalism and Journalism Ethics in a Deliberative Democracy

Martí (2006, pp. 13–14), in his exhaustive study on deliberative democracy, explains that the current model of democracy is "mercantilised" and political parties compete for citizens-consumers' votes, paying less and less attention to their real problems. Citizens understand that beyond the elections, important political decisions do not consider their interests. The underlying problem is that our current system assumes that in democracy, each agent defends its particular interests. And the value of democracy is to limit the damage caused by this "natural tendency" (Nino, 1997, pp. 102–124). However, in the end, those agents that can defend their interests in a more forceful way by organizing themselves in lobbies obtain greater profit from the system than most citizens, and this dissolves the moral sense of democracy.

Deliberative democracy theory intends to re-activate community bonds and self-government ideals and to separate public matters from egoistical interests by individuals or groups (Martí, 2006, pp. 13–14). It springs from the idea that public use of reason not only makes it more difficult to defend egoistical interests that, in consequence, prejudice the common good, but also activates a process that improves the moral quality of social debate.

For deliberative democracy, citizen participation cannot only be channelled through the election of political representatives every four years. Therefore a deliberative public sphere cannot just be a system of observation, but should constitute the arena where communication about the common good takes place, where citizens are central actors, without whom this model is unworkable. Citizens act within groups or NGOs and want all decisions to be informed by the arguments exchanged, before all interests are considered. Moreover, the character of the discourse is a central element in the deliberative model. It requires a well-conducted exchange of information and reasoning between the acting groups and political parties.

Once it has been acknowledged that reality is not "out there," but constructed and that the media constitute a first-rate agent, the deliberative public sphere then calls for a process of shaping social reality which is participative, rational-argumentative, and centred on the common good.

Professional Journalism Deontology and Values in a Deliberative Democracy

Journalists working in a deliberative democracy cannot be invisible mediators, but should play the part of public collaborators who care about the public relevance and truth of the information available in the public sphere, the quality of the discussions that arise, and make sure that the public sphere remains an inclusive space. Nico Carpentier's (2005) work on the identity of the (professionals of) journalistic models helps to illustrate this difference. Carpentier identifies four pairs of opposing key nodes[7] that make it possible to distinguish a common hegemonic and counter-hegemonic identity (see Table 3):

Table 3. Pairs of opposing postures in the discursive dimensions of the nodal points put forward by Nico Carpentier (2005) for analyzing the identities of professional journalists

Hegemonic identity	Counter-hegemonic identity
Relationship with the medium (professional elite)	*Relationship with the public (citizen representation)*
Management (gatekeeper)	*Collaboration (gate-opener)*
Autonomy	*Dependence*
Objectivity	*Subjectivity*

The hegemonic identity can be associated with traditional journalism suited to liberal representative democracies, while the counter-hegemonic tendencies offer ground to reflect upon which qualities would be suited to a deliberative democracy.

On the one hand, traditional journalism views journalists as content managers who have to work with autonomy (independency, neutrality, objectivity). This autonomy is so central to the model that journalists' standards relate more to their superiors and colleagues than to the citizenry (Gans, 1979, p. 230; Hagen, 1999, p. 132; Lamuedra & Lara, 2009, pp. 42–49). On the other hand, the orientation towards the public and collaboration is much more adequate in a system that has as its central feature public dialogue and collaboration among social agents done in an iterative and visible manner, towards the common good. Therefore, a deliberative public sphere is better suited to enlarging the scope and quality of sources that the so-called citizen journalism has to offer, and is also in line with several alternative media, based on an ideology of direct democracy or "alterglobalization," which, like Indymedia, have gained a foothold in the global media system (Juris, 2004, pp. 54–57).

However, the dependency and subjectivity that today operate in these new media are not compatible with professional journalism: alternative media or citizen journalism are valuable sources (and agents in an eventual deliberative public sphere). Despite the fact that the progressive adoption of a discursive ethic and public use of reason can influence the kind of subjectivity of these (and other) social agents, the practice of journalism would still benefit from a deontological code that guides the daily routines of journalists, always under the pressure of meeting deadlines. The Pew Research Project on Journalism's ethical code, which is covered in detail in Kovach and Rosenstiel's (2003) *The Elements of Journalism*, is certainly up to the challenge. What follows is an overview of some of the proposed deontological principles.

The first principle is truth, which is regarded as the fundamental one and is defined as practical and functional. So as to defend themselves against the problems of truth caused by the rupture with positivism, which problematizes the existence of an "essential truth" (although the authors do not explain it in this way), they indicate that journalists must look for a journalistic truth, similar to the kinds of truth that operate in the educational system which allow students to learn, for example, a consensual version of history, or in the legal system which allows for criminals to be arrested and brought to trial. On the other hand, journalism cannot be limited to reporting on what sources say, without delving deeper. This requires the professional practice of honesty and reflectivity.

The second principle that they evoke is loyalty to citizens. In pursuit of an alleged independence and neutrality, they argue, many journalists isolated from their social function unwittingly serve the interests of economic groups. In order to counter these problems, the authors propose that owners and managers of media companies build an organization geared to citizen service and scrutiny

The third basic principle is verification. Kovach and Rosenstiel (2003, pp. 99–129) argue that "the impartial voice frequently employed by many media is a useful device that they make the most of to highlight the fact that they are trying to produce something obtained by means of objective methods. Hence, journalists that use it without verification methods are immersed in a form of deception." The authors explain that, although the idea of the objective method exists among journalists, it appears in a very fragmented way and no one has yet consolidated a valid standard method as in law or scientific research. The alternative answer given by Kovach and Rosenstiel to the question of autonomy is to have diverse newsrooms, so that an active confrontation of perspectives can limit the (relative) dependency that all information is bound to have on journalists' own backgrounds, class, sex, race, and personal experience.

The Table 4 synthesizes and pools together the aforementioned approaches:

Table 4. Features of Representative and Deliberative Public Spheres

	Representative public sphere	**Deliberative public sphere**
Metaphor	Window	Space of public negotiation/construction
Function of the media	Show the world	Allow participation and promotion of rational collective debate
The role of the media as	Content manager	Collaborator
Professional values	Objectivity, impartiality, independence (applied to journalists)	Truth, through: a) Honesty, transparent research, edition, and interpretation. A consensual process of *verification*. b) Newsrooms with a structure geared to public service, loyalty, independence, and diversity.
Other values of the public sphere		Honesty, argumentative capacity, common good, participation

We believe that insisting on verification methods would not only lead to a journalism less dependent on press offices, but also a journalism based on methods approved by a greater consensus and with a greater transparency in the eyes of the general public. This could break with the metaphor of journalism as a window to the world and the passivity that this provokes. Furthermore, it puts the accent on an organizational structure keyed to public service. The more visible the whole structure is, the less valid the image of journalists as mere objective mediators would be.

Unsurprisingly, in the interviews with viewers there was a noticeable absence of some of the journalistic and general values that could be necessary for a deliberative public sphere, such as the obligation of the media to promote rational and argumentative collective debate, and how important it is that newsrooms acquire a structure oriented towards public service, or the necessity of agreeing upon a journalistic work methodology and ensuring its transparency. Neither an argumentative capacity nor an orientation towards the common good was detected in the discourses of the majority of the interviewees. However, if a deliberative public sphere were to be implemented in the media, these shortcomings would need to be addressed.

In closing, we would like to argue that there is an increasing social demand for another form of political and media system, with more ample space for citizens' participation and deliberation. This happens at the same time that the principle of representativeness in politics, but also in the media, has been called into question in a context in which democracy and state sovereignty have come under pressure by the globalised economy. It has been argued that the concept of the media as a window to the world, creating an observation system that offers grounds for citizens to decide on whom to vote for at election times, doesn't allow us to face the aforementioned challenge. This is because the sheer extent of the window metaphor eclipses the mediation of news, thus preventing viewers from noticing the impact of the economic, political, cultural, and professional variables that determine which kind of information appears in the media agenda and which perspective it holds. This encourages viewers to identify watching the news with taking part in democracy, legitimating social conformism and inaction.

Activist use of social media and media activism are already changing the media sphere by opening spaces of deliberation through the use of blogs, Twitter, and Facebook, a reality that's become particularly evident in social movements such as a Occupy Everywhere. Thus, further research is needed into how these new deliberative practices are transforming the social understanding of media in life. If journalism is to follow and change in line with a deliberative public sphere, this would in turn entail a transformation of journalistic deontology.

Acknowledgments

This work is part of a larger research and development project undertaken by a group of Spanish researchers on Public Service Television called GITEP, in which the following have taken part: Agustín G. Matilla as the leader, Tiscar Lara, Alejandra Walzer, and Jessica Retis. The questions addressed by this work have emerged in the late stages of the process of this larger project, which also included an analysis of 40 interviews with news professionals working for TVE and BBC (see Retis, Lamuedra, & Matilla, 2010).

Miguel Vázquez Liñán, Fernando León-Solís, and Hugh O'Donnell have also contributed to this chapter with their sage advice. I would like to thank them all for sharing their talent and time with me.

Funding Acknowledgments

This work was supported by the Spanish R+D authorities. Ministerio de Educación y Ciencia, Plan Nacional de I+D+I (SEJ 2005–03839).

Endnotes

1. Bustamante´s artcile is available at http://www.teledetodos.com/component/k2/item/457-las-actuaciones-del-gobierno-rajoy-sobre-rtve
2. Jürgen Habermas' theory of the public sphere was mainly set out in *The Structural Transformation of the Public Sphere* (1989). Habermas argues that in 18th-century London, the public use of reason started to be exercised in tea and coffee houses. This contributed to the emergence of the notion of public opinion and is also related to the development of the press, still partisan at that time. The whole process in which the public sphere was shaped contributed to the English parliamentary system. The public sphere, according to Habermas, is inclusive and oriented towards deliberation and opinion formation.
3. A term which had also been used by Habermas (1989).
4. It has to be said that the interviewees were not consistent in their views all the time, some of them even contradicting themselves at different points. For instance, in the TVE sample, Manager of a Travel Agency, 40, claimed that "the world we see through the news, well, it's the world they want us to see" and she used an example from her experience as a travel agent: if the conflicts in a country received news coverage, her clients did not want to travel there, something that did not occur with other destinations where there were also conflicts that did not receive news coverage. However, on the subject of the specific coverage of terrorism and politics, which are burning issues in Spain, instead of talking about news coverage, she talked about them as if they occurred in a "reality" detached from mediation.
5. The Committee of Concerned Journalists (CCJ), which developed the Pew Project for Excellence in Journalism, convened 21 public forums attended by more than 3,000 people, in which the evidence of 300 professionals was examined, among other studies (Kovach & Rosenstiel, 2003, pp. 14–17).
6. For a wider debate, see Lamuedra, 2011; Lamuedra & Lara, 2009.
7. Carpentier (2005) begins by stating that the identities are determined by some discourses and positions that we adopt as subjects and that (in the abstract) they provide

us with multiple points of identification; although they acquire a certain degree of stability when they position themselves and start to circulate in the social framework, that is, the public sphere. Among these elements, there are some that are especially significant and which the author calls "nodes."

References

Almirón N. (2010). *Journalism in crisis: Corporate media and financialization.* Cresskill, NJ: Hampton Press.

Appadurai, A. (2000). Grassroots globalization and the research imagination. *Public Culture, 12*(1), 1–19.

Bustamante Ramírez, E. (2012). Las actuaciones del gobierno Rajoy sobre RTVE. *Teledetodos.* http://www.teledetodos.com/component/k2/item/457-las-actuaciones-del-gobierno-rajoy-sobre-rtve

Carey, J.W. (1999). In defense of public journalism. en T. L. Glasser, *The idea of public journalism.* Nueva York: The Guilford Press.

Carpentier, N. (2005). Identity, contingency and rigidity. *Journalism, 6*(2), 199–219.

Carpentier, N. (2007). Coping with the agoraphobic media professional: A typology of journalistic practices reinforcing democracy and participation, en Cammaerts, B. y Carpentier, N. (Eds). *Reclaiming the media: Communication rights and democratic media roles.* Bristol: Intellect Books, pp. 157–175.

Carroll, W. K., & Hackett, R. A. (2006). Democratic media activism through the lens of social movement theory. *Media, Culture & Society, 28*(1), 83–104.

Castells, M. (2010). *Communication power.* Oxford, United Kingdom: Oxford University Press.

Couldy, N. (2005). The extended audience. In M, Gillespie (Ed.), *Media audiences* (pp. 184–196; 210–220). London, United Kingdom: Open University Press,

Della Porta, D. (2005). Making the polis: Social forums and democracy in the global justice movement, *Mobilization,* vol. *10,* pp. 73–94.

Díaz A. R. (2009). Periodismo cívico vs. periodismo ciudadano, *Observatorio de Medios de Comunicación y Sociedad* (Madrid), *1,* 9–15. http://www.1mayo.ccoo.es

Dryzek, J. S. (2000). *Deliberative democracy and beyond.* Oxford: Oxford University Press.

Estudio general de medios (Octubre de 2010 a Mayo de 2011). Associacion para la Investigacion de los Medios de Communicacioc amc. Available at www.aimc.es

Ettema, J. S. (2007). Journalism as reason-giving: Deliberative democracy, institutional accountability, and the news media's mission. *Political Communication, 24,* 143–160.

Ferreras, E.M. (2011). Telos: Cuadernos de comunicación e innovación, Nº. *89,* pp. 61–73.

Ferrés, J. (1994). *Televisión y educación.* Barcelona, Spain: Paidos.

Fishman, M. (1980). *Manufacturing the news.* Austin: University of Texas Press.

Gans, H. (1979). *Deciding what's news: A study of CBS Evening News, NBC Nightly News, Newsweek and Time.* New York, NY: Pantheon Books.

Gillmor, D. (2006). *We the media: Grassroots journalism by the people, for the people.* Sebastopol, CA: O'Reilly Media.

Haas, T., & Steiner, L. (2006), Public journalism: A reply to critics. *Journalism 7* (2), 238–254.

Habermas, J. (1989). *The structural transformation of the public sphere.* Cambridge, United Kingdom: Polity.

Habermas, J. (2001). Warum braucht Europa eine Verfassung? (Why does Europe need a constitution?). *Deutschland, 6,* 62–65.

Hagen, I. (1999). Slaves of the ratings tyranny? Media images of the audience. In P. Alasuutari, *Rethinking the media audience.* London, United Kingdom: Sage.

Hardt, M. and Negri, A. (2004). *Multitude: War and Democracy in the Age of Empire.* (New York: Penguin. 2004)

Haro Barba C., & Sampedro Blanco, V. (2011). Activismo político en Red: del movimiento por la Vivienda Digna al 15M. *Revista Tecknocultura, 8*(2), 167–185.

Harvey, D. (1990). *The condition of postmodernity.* Malden, MA: Blackwell.

Herman E. S., & Chomsky, N. (1988). *Manufacturing consent: The political economy of the mass media.* New York, NY: Pantheon.

Herman, E. S., & McChesney R. W. (1999). *Los medios globales: Los nuevos misioneros del capitalismo corporativo.* Madrid, Spain: Cátedra.

Juris, J. (2004). Indymedia: De la contrainformación a la utopia informacional. In V. Mari Saez (Ed.), *La red es de todos* (pp. 154–177). Madrid, Spain: Editorial Popular.

Juris, J. (2012, May). Reflections on #Occupy Everywhere: Social media, public space, and emerging logics of aggregation. *American Ethnologist, 39*(2), 259–279.

Karppinen, K. (2009). European public sphere and the challenge of radical pluralism. In I. Salovaara-Moring (Ed.), *Manufacturing Europe: Spaces of democracy, diversity, and communication* (pp. 53–67). Göteborg, Sweden: Nordicom.

Kovach, B., & Rosenstiel, T. (2003). *Los elementos del Periodismo.* Madrid, Spain: Santillana.

Lamuedra, M. (2011). Medios de servicio público, periodismos alternativos y esfera pública deliberativa, en Chasqui Ciespal, edición 113.

Lamuedra, M., & Lara, T. (2009). La crisis de identidad de los periodistas en las televisiones públicas europeas: Comparación entre BBC y TVE. *Estudio sobre el Mensaje Periodístico, 15,* 33–60.

Manning, P. (2001). *News and news sources: A critical introduction.* London, United Kingdom: Sage.

Martí, J. L. (2006). *La república deliberativa.* Madrid, Marcial Pons.

McChesney, R. W. (2008). *The political economy of media: Enduring issues, emerging dilemmas.* New York, NY: Monthly Review Press.

McCombs, M. E., & Shaw, D. (1972). The agenda-setting function of mass media. *Public Opinion Quarterly, 36,* 176–187.

McDevitt, M. (2003). In defense of autonomy: A critique of the public journalism critique. *Journal of Communication, 53*(1), 155–160.

McQuail, D. (2001). *Introducción a la teoría de comunicación de masas.* Barcelona: Paidós.

Mendez Muros, S., & García Estevez, S. (2011, December) *Sociedad civil y redes sociales: Democracia Real Ya en Sevilla como estudio de caso* (Civil society and social networks: Democracia Real Ya in Seville as case study). Actas III Congreso Internacional Latina de Comunicación Social. Santa Cruz de Tenerife, Spain: Universidad de La laguna. http://www.revistalatinacs.org/11SLCS/actas_2011_IIICILCS/004_Sandra.pdf

Muñoz-Torres, J. R. (2000). Concepciones epistemológicas implícitas en los libros de estilo de El País, El Mundo y ABC. *Revista ZER, 9.*

Nieminen, H. (2009). The European public sphere as a network? Four plus one approaches. In I. Salovaara-Moring (Ed.), *Manufacturing Europe: Spaces of democracy, diversity, and communication* (pp. 19–35). Göteborg, Sweden: Nordicom.

Nino, C. S. (1997). *La constitución de la democracia deliberativa.* Barcelona: Gedisa.

Noguera, J. M. (2008). *Blogs y medios.* Madrid, Spain: Libros en Red.

O'Donnell, H. (2007). *Noticias y ciudadanía: El telespectador, el poder y el debate público.* Madrid, Spain: Ediciones de la Torre.

Retis, J. M., Lamuedra M., & Matilla, A. G. (2010). *Los informativos diarios en TVE y BBC.* Madrid, Spain: Ediciones de la Torre.

Romanos, E. (2011, November 18). El 15M y la democracia de los movimientos sociales. *Books&Ideas.net.* http://www.booksandideas.net/El-15M-y-la-democracia-de-los.html

Rosen, J. (1999). The action of the idea; Public journalism in built form en Glasser, T.L. *The idea of public journalism.* Nueva York. Guilford.

Rubin, H., & Rubin, I. (1995). *Qualitative interviewing: The art of hearing data.* Los Angeles, CA: Sage.

Schudson, M. (1967). *Discovering the news: A social history of American newspapers.* New York: NY Basic Books.

Skinner, J. (2011). Social media revolution: The Arab Spring and the Occupy Movement as seen through three information studies paradigms. *Sprouts: Working papers on Information Systems, 11*(169), 11–169.

Splichal, S. (2006). In search of a strong European public sphere: Some critical observations on conceptualizations of publicness and the (European) public sphere. *Media, Culture & Society, 28*(5), 696–714.

Thomas, B. (2010). PSB and the European public sphere. In P. Iosifidis, *Reinventing public service communication: European broadcasters and beyond* (pp. 63–76). London, United Kingdom: Palgrave Macmillan.

Thompson, J. B. (1998). *Los media y la modernidad: Una teoría de los medios de comunicación.* Barcelona: Paidós.

Trenz, H.-J. (2009). Uniting and dividing: The European public sphere as an unfinished project. In Salovaara-Moring (Ed.), *Manufacturing Europe: Spaces of democracy, diversity, and communication.* Göteborg, Sweden: Nordicom.

Tuchman, G. (1978). *Making news: A study in the construction of reality*. New York, NY: The Free Press.

Varela, J. (2005, October 1). Blogs vs. MSM. Periodismo 3.0, la socialización de la información. *Telos. Cuadernos de información e innovación.*

Velasco, J. C. (2007). *Deliberación y calidad de la democracia* en *Claves de la Razón Práctica, 167*, pp. 36–43.

Velasco, J. C. (2009, July 17). Democracia y deliberación pública. *Confluencia XXI. Revista de Pensmiento Político:* 70–79.

Wolf, M. (1987). *La investigación en comunicación de masas*. Barcelona, Spain: Paidós.

11

Issues Management as a Mediated Activity in a Changing Media Sphere

KATHY MATILLA AND GUILLEM MARCA

Introduction

This chapter proposes a bibliographical study of a communication tool that permits organizations to manage potential conflicts proactively: issues management. Starting with a description of the origins of the object of study, we proceed to the definition of the concept of an "issue," in order to then establish the types and stages in the life cycle of issues management, and, last, we define the management process.

We present a personal contribution that opens a new perspective to the study conducted on this subject, consistent with overcoming the canonical idea of prospecting applied exclusively to issues management and introducing a guide for the identification of opportunities which may arise in the field, very useful for the proactive, strategic planning of corporate public relations.

However, the world is changing dramatically and, therefore, we propose a dual question: what would be the role of issues management against a backdrop of profound change in the public sphere? Would it be at risk of survival in a world without media?

The Origins of Issues Management

The situation of a turbulent environment, saturated with critical movements of citizens against large corporations, has been extensively discussed in the literature, as well as the activity of issues management, which is configured as one of the basic obligations of the leadership role of anticipatory guidance of corporate public relations from the last quarter of the 20th century. Wilcox, Cameron, Ault, and Agee (1989, p. 168) introduced an idea closely linked to strategic planning: the planning of issues management. Under the view that the identification and management of potential conflicts is an important element in strategic planning, the authors defined this activity as an active and systematic approach (Thayer, 1968), which allowed professionals in corporate public relations to predict problems, anticipate obstacles, minimize surprises, solve various unforeseen issues, and prevent crisis situations.

Corporate public relations should be considered as a mediating activity, which manages the conflicts between various organized groups (Ehling, 1975, p. 20), and issues management is the organized activity to identify emerging trends, problems, or issues that may affect the organization in the coming years, and develop broader and more positive responses from the organization in the future (Coates, Jarrat, & Heinz, 1986) that solve potential problems for the early detection of signs that issues may arise. The emphasis on issues management is extended proactively, in an effort to detect "any subject" (legislative, economic, political, or social, in its broadest sense) that may pose a problem, acute or chronic, for the future of the organization.

Many authors have worked on the concept of issues management: Bryan (1997); Chase (1977, 1982a, 1982b, 1984); Chase and Jones (1979); Coates, Coates, Jarratt, and Heinz (1986); Ewing (1979, 1980a, 1980b, 1981, 1982, 1987a, 1987b, 1990a, 1990b, 1997); González Herrero (1998, 2003); Grunig and Repper (1992); Heath and Nelson (1986a, 1986b); Heath (1988, 1992, 1997); Heath and Cousino (1990); Hirsch (2002); Matilla (2007, 2009); Poors (1997); Reynolds (1997); Simcic Bronn and Bronn (2006); or Thomsen (1995), among others. Gaunt and Ollenburger (1995, pp. 65–82) link issues management to the concept of forward planning. It could be a useful proactive technique that would try to identify emerging issues that may have some influence on an organization, before they affect it negatively.

In its origin, issues management was strongly linked to the management of crises, which had a markedly reactive nature, making it necessary to react once the crisis had erupted. The introduction of issues management could help to prevent the emergence of a future crisis, if the possible causes are identified in advance.

Polysemy of the Concept Issue

Heath (1997) writes that "issue" has become a term with different meanings, placing its initial scope of action within the framework of risk and crisis communication, which would be established by Grunig and Repper (1992) as the backbone of the strategic process of corporate public relations, understood as the problems created by an organization that is perceived by their publics and that puts the "issue" as an already existing conflict, framed and in a reactive vision. To Plowman et al. (1995, p. 238), issues management would manage a conflict occurring between an organization and its stakeholders, an opinion also held by Ewing (1997, p. 173). Grunig and Repper (1992, pp. 134, 147) define "issues" as political or social problems, which create conflict in the political or social system.

The first professionals who specialized in issues management in the United States were W. Howard, B. L. Jones, and H.W. Chase. They understood the concept as a proactive management process that identifies issues that potentially could lead to the political arena, with laws or regulations; analyzes these issues; establishes priorities for action; develops strategic action programs; implements a communication program according to the strategy; and evaluates results. The innovation introduced by Chase focused on the idea that the task of observation associated with issues management should become a systematic and continuous effort in order to detect internal and external matters that could affect the company in the future, in a proactive manner, as an and the proactive nature of it, in the initiative taken by the organization to participate in the political debate before circumstances forced them to it.

During the 1970s, corporate strategic planning and surveillance or monitoring of the environment became inseparable partners. Later, authors such as Post (1979) and Buchholz (1989); Buchholz, Evans, & Wagley, (1985) published works defending the need to recognize the importance that politics and public debate play in strategic planning efforts. Taylor, Vasquez, and Doorley (2003) consider that research on issues management can be found in political science, futurism, business management, public policy, communication, corporate public relations, strategic planning, management information systems, and business ethics, since each organization is influenced by its map of publics and the relationships established with the stakeholders (Pfeffer & Salancik, 1978).

Jones and Chase (1979) developed the model: communication is a resource for testing messages, target audience analysis, and message channel selection in the later stages of the issues management process to earn the public support for corporate policy. The core concept is strategic issues diagnosis (SID), and strategic issues are events, developments, or trends that are viewed as having implications for organizational performance.

To Taylor et al. (2003), Crable and Vibbert (1985) made a new contribution to the state of the art, identifying some problems in the five-step Chase-Jones Model: on one side, organizations only have the authority to influence the creation of public policies and not create them on an equal footing with political power, as assumed the reference model, and therefore, issues management would be the process in which they could exercise such influence; Chase and Jones viewed an issue as an unsettled matter ready for decision. Thus, Crable and Vibbert defined an issue as a question. In addition to the three types of strategies in the Chase-Jones Model (reactive, adaptive, and dynamic), Crable and Vibbert (1985, p. 12) incorporated a fourth: the "catalytic" strategy in an organization attempts to take an issue through its life cycle (of status) so that it can be resolved in favorable directions to the organization; thus, issues management would be a genuinely proactive activity in influencing and formulating public policy.

Taylor et al. (2003) advocate considering a new vision of the concept based on active dialogue between an organization and its publics, that will be more effective if issues are handled in ways that consider and integrate stakeholders in corporate decision making, anticipating their needs (Grunig, 1992, 1995, 1997; Lauzen, 1997; Lauzen & Dozier, 1992, 1994), in line with the input taken by some scholars since the end of the 1990s (Broom, Casey, & Ritchey, 1997; Huang, 2001; Hon, 2001; Karlberg, 1996; Ledingham & Bruning, 1998, 2000; Ledingham, Bruning, & Wilson, 1999). They estimated also that should not be considered solely as public advocacy groups and lawmakers who build public policy, because the relationship with the stakeholders should continue to develop throughout the process, even once the issue is resolved, to establish long-term relationships and ongoing assessment and measurement (Cuenca, 2010; Marca, 2011).

Issues Management: Types and Life Cycle

Scientific procedures for identifying conflicts are the analysis of the trend impact and its extrapolation, with complex and high-cost techniques (Pasquero, 1989, pp. 116–128), especially with regard to the sophistication required to deal with quantitative and qualitative analysis. Some researchers have provided their own methodologies of "environmental monitoring" (Simcic Bronn & Bronn, 2006, pp. 247–258), helping to achieve the proper suitability of the stage of identifying potential conflicts, which constitutes the keystone of the arch of the management process. In this line, Xifra (2005, p. 230) explains that Pasquero (1989) defends the thesis that an issue or public conflict rests on the basis of the existence of specific demands, posed to organizations by certain segments of its environment. The life cycle of a conflict, from its communicative perspective, will comprise four stages:

1. The latent period
2. The period of emergence
3. The period of implementation
4. The period of recovery

Renfro (1987, pp. 545–554) also describes the issues management process as a cycle of four stages, but as follows:

1. Birth
2. Mediation and amplification
3. Organization
4. Resolution

To Xifra (2005, p. 231), Ewing (1987b) considers the life cycle of issues management as an integral part of public policy (Business Ethics), since the turbulence environment experienced by organizations requires the adoption of diverse corporate public relations strategies, which can range from generating expectancy inaction, the adaptive reaction to change or the proactive in influencing change, to the collaboration with various actors involved in the process. Based on the Chase-Jones Model of five stages, Ewing (1997, pp. 181–183) established another model, adding two stages:

1. Issues identification
2. Issue analysis
3. Development of corporate policy position on the issue
4. Development of specific action plans (tactics)
5. Implementation of action plans
6. Review of reaction, adjustments responding to legitimate objections, and negotiation
7. Keeping management and staff's attention focused on the issue

According to Xifra (2005, pp. 231–232), the contribution of Crable and Vibbert (1985) and of Taylor et al. (2003) is that a potentially controversial topic or issue is generated at the instant that one or more human agents give meaning to a given situation, or when they perceive a problem. So there are four stages, which run parallel to those established by Pasquero (1989):

1. Potential status
2. Imminent status
3. Current status
4. Critical status

Also, potential conflicts, considered as both subject and outcome of a public discussion and inserted within the media agenda, may exist with varying degrees of intensity depending on the stage of the life cycle, and their presence will be measured in forums beyond the media, such as at conferences and in seminars. The phases of emergency, diffusion, establishment, and erosion of an issue are directly related to its life evolution, and its pass from one stage to another reflects its social penetration:

- Issue emergency. The germinal stage where the conflict exists as a large emerging trend, only identified by experts and think tanks, and therefore still unknown by most of the various social partners and public opinion. As the issue is advancing in its emergency phase, there is a particular interpretation of social reality that sets the heart of a potential conflict. According to Xifra (2005, pp. 232–233), Fink (1986) advocates the idea that it is the generation of the feeling of need that will provide meaning at this stage, which will be introduced across multiple channels.

  At this and during the following stages of the life cycle, the conflict involves the presence and active participation of intermediaries, exercising great influence on how the issue will penetrate to social reality. The more the debate is polarized, the easier the protagonists and antagonists can be identified in each of its stages. According to Coleman (1993), they are the groups or individuals who have authority and sufficient leadership to define the issue.

  In the emerging phase, the fundamental concept is often accepted very quickly, although, because it's usually debated by experts, there's a high degree of complexity. The experts express their opinions amid much discussion. According to Xifra (2005, pp. 234–235), journalists then reduce the concept to a single opinion, or two, at most, as a counterproposal.

- Issue diffusion. Those affected by the issue play a starring role in spreading news of the issue. The antagonists clearly and unambiguously define their positions. The conflict spreads to neighboring territories. Unlike what occurred in the previous phase, variables are now easily communicated.
- Issue establishment. The issue is disclosed and can reach large sectors of civil society: it is generalized. Social organizations often have the most influence. They frequently take over as the leading voice in the media, which may lead to polarization in the public debate.
- Issue erosion. The erosion of a potential conflict comes with its loss of relevance and the stagnation of public interest, especially following related legislative action or policy changes. The actors involved in earlier discussions will lose significance, as will the issue, which, if discussions arise again, will only occur among a small group of stakeholders with a high command of the subject.

  Issues management, initially based on simple observation of the environment, gives way to a new alternative vision that places the momentum within an organization, rather than outside. This involves a substantial turning point, since it implies that the organization accepts responsibility for the generation of conflict, or at least a portion of it.

In the mid-90s, researchers in the U.S. began to apply techniques of prospective dimension, especially in the field of crisis prevention, in which issues management played a key role (Wimmer & Dominick, 1996; Hiebert, 1988). Along the same lines, Lerbinger (1977) conducted methodology research as it applied to auditing:

- Environment monitoring
- Public relations audit
- Communication audit
- Social audit (perceptions and attitudes)

Xifra (2005, pp. 215–216) emphasizes the fundamental role of the management model for managing issues proactively in corporate public relations, in the broader context of public policy: the practice of civil society participation in public affairs becomes one of the scenarios in which dialogue and communication are essential.

Lobbying Versus Issues Management

In recent years, social movements have led to the creation of multiple associations of shared interests (lobbies), which has led to corporate public relations as a form of corporate governance, as they have fully integrated into the scope of decision-making processes of public action (Xifra, 2005, p. 216). The public, legislators, senior officials, responsible interest groups (lobbies), and journalists, among others, set priorities for a corporation's strategic plans. This is because the political dynamics have become an important and often critical component of the environment configuration.

Fostered from the high dome of corporate governance, public relations strategies involve the media, lobbying, and the dissemination of defensive issue management, as an ongoing form of communication. Xifra defines this discipline as targeted action to identify potential or emerging issues (legislative, political, and social), which can affect the life of an organization, mobilizing available resources in order to strategically influence the issues, and wherever possible, seek to benefit the organization driving the communication.

For Chase (1984), a potentially contentious issue is the space or distance between effects resulting from the performance of an organization and the expectations of their publics. This gap can strongly influence the corporate strategy and have draft implications in fulfilling its mission and its organizational goals and objectives. Hence, corporations must be strategic in identifying, analyzing, and responding to issues and trends, in order to build an agenda of potential conflicts, and through their proper management, facilitate the anticipation of change.

The emphasis on issues management now extends to a company's ability to be proactive in detecting issues (legislative, economic, political, or social, in its broadest sense) that may pose a problem for the future of the organization. Fahey (1986) states that a potentially contentious issue can be fully classified as public if it

- is part of a public policy or public affairs management
- is any event, controversy, or development of public policy that may affect the organization
- originates in a social, political, administrative, or judicial environment; even so it should be clarified that the trends, understood as patterns of events, conditions, attitudes, and opinions of the publics, and shaping their expectations, should be considered as distinct from potential conflicts.

The process of generating public policies (pre-legislative period) is the natural field of action of an organization's strategic plan; therefore, the five stages of issues management are:

1. Issues or problem identification. In this stage, an issue goes from the private to the public sphere, and private interests must be articulated. Participation is achieved through communication and relational techniques specific to corporate public relations, including proactive issues management and lobbying as reactive management:

- Perception processes
- Definition processes
- Aggregation processes
- Processes of structures organization
- Processes of interest representation
- Defining the public agenda as a fundamental process to analyzing how authorities set the agenda or identify the problem, with the goal of building an action plan in which communication plays an important role as the public agenda refers to public debate among citizens, lobbyists, political parties, companies and organizations, journalists, etc., setting the stage for their relative strength or influence.

2. Program development.
3. Program implementation.
4. Program evaluation.
5. Program end.

As a technique for corporate public relations strategic planning, issues management develops prospective research programs so organizations can:

- Identify emerging issues that may influence the organization's interests
- Identify early signs of potentially conflicting issues and environmental trends to anticipate, predict, prepare for, and avoid crisis situations
- Catalog conductive trends and key drivers
- Assess potential and real opportunities and threats in their emergent stages, as well as their probabilities, grades, and intensities
- Assess the organization's vulnerabilities and strengths

- Set priorities and direction, define positions, establish response and planning schedules, and link communication with the strategic goals of the organization
- Adapt corporate organization objectives to each of its stakeholders, depending on the nature and the involvement level of these with the issue
- Customize the behavior of the organization to the corporate interests that will determine future public decisions on the matter and bring those decisions to the corporate organization interests
- Design a corporate response, through action and communication, to influence and redirect a given performance of the key audiences, or to avoid a potential conflict from becoming public (strategic planning)
- Establish partnerships and possible strategies, and when appropriate, build coalitions
- Assess, monitor, and evaluate (Marca, 2011) the progress of potential conflict and the strategic efficacy of the organization

The Issues Management Process

The process of issues management is circular (Morley, 2002, pp. 82–83): potential conflicts are identified, prioritized, managed, observed, and re-examined to adapt the strategy to new situations by redefining the position, modifying the plan action, or eliminating the potential conflict on the agenda, among other possibilities (Xifra, 2005, pp. 226–227). Buchholz (1989) linked the life cycle of potential conflicts in the process of formulating public policy based on three stages:

1. Formation of public opinion
2. Development of public policy
3. Implementation of public policy

Prospective Research and Issues Management

Issues management requires that companies and institutions develop applied research, prospective in nature, in order to obtain information on future trends, emerging issues, and stakeholders. However, as Matilla advocated in 2007, all this is insufficient for appropriate and comprehensive strategic planning, since information about "future possibilities" obtained about issues, trends, and key publics should be incorporated on an ongoing basis, which will determine the dynamics of possible alternative scenarios for the future where new trends can be developed and evaluated by the stakeholders who will interact with them. The prospective research that shapes the field of issues management will allow organizations to seize strategic information about the future, and to implement appropriate policies and corporate plans, which will allow them to compete with the best guarantees of success in their market segment, to adapt to new needs arising from evolving technological, social, economic, political, and demographic characteristics generated from the environmental turbulence so typical of the 21st century.

Thus, we can conclude that investing in applied research information for "future possibilities" is key to a much more refined approach in strategic definition, and it becomes increasingly necessary, if not imperative, for companies, institutions, governments, and political parties, especially in these times of financial, economical, social, and values crisis, to create innovative resources and policies that enable these organizations to cope with emerging paradigms.

We note that since issues management focuses on identifying emerging trends, we consider the concept of "trend" as a behavioral pattern in future events, conditions, attitudes, and public opinions, which shape society's expectations. Constant monitoring and analysis are critical to the detection of emerging issues that are initially visible only to skilled, forward-looking groups.

We think of governance as the tool used by public decision makers (governments) to generate public policy, defined as anything that an authority has legitimacy and power to do, or not to do. Its key elements are:

- Content or concrete measures that form the core of politics
- Program or general framework in which public policy is developed (electoral programs, laws, government program, and so on)
- Policy guidance (interests, values, goals)
- Coercion factor derived from the exercise of legal authority
- Social competence (interests, perceptions, and behavior of citizens or those who are "managed")

Issues Management: A New Perspective

Issues management was born closely linked to risk and crisis, from its anticipatory and proactive approach. As a result, when analyzing the environment, special attention is given to those issues that can cause conflict with or within the organization. It's logical to conceive issues management as a predictive tool that allows organizations to anticipate scenarios facing adversity and/or weakness, coupled with the detection of elements of maximum vulnerability and weakness.

We propose to dilate the field of view and introduce a new perspective that goes beyond the academic vision and development, based solely on the identification of potentially conflicting situations, which were the ones that initially formed the leitmotif of historical overview of the canonical theory of issues management. The same prospective effort allows one to focus beyond the environments that can create clearly threatening issues, to those that potentially may pose opportunities for an organization. Thus, the same investment in qualitative and quantitative research, from the perspective of establishing lasting relationships of trust with the strategic publics of an organization, opens a new dimension where the corporate public relations manager can tackle issues management. Thus, issues management expands beyond the constrictive vision that placed it in the realm of vulnerability, risk, and crisis communication, and even beyond its anticipatory (proactive) perspective that has been under consideration in recent times.

The epistemological concept proposed by G. B. McGrath (1998) opened a new dimension to the proactivity that, on our part and as stated by Matilla (2007), we understand in the broadest sense of the term: that besides identifying potential conflicts, it also identifies new opportunities and brings to the role of corporate public relations, fully and definitively, the responsibility of continuous supervision and monitoring of the environment in terms of "threats" and "opportunities," typical of the classic SWOT analysis.

We believe that today, as Matilla noted in 2007, if one identifies emerging issues or tipping points that change communication to or perceptions of key publics, potential conflicts generators and opportunities could be identified. This entails a much richer dimension to the task assigned to observing the role of corporate public relations, creating a better and wider view for proactive orientation of strategic planning. However, success will depend on whether managers and corporate public relations consultants, following the ideas advocated by Carr and Kemmis (1988) and García García (2001, p. 655), conceive our profession as technical (trade), as a practice (decisions based on experience), or as a strategy (submission of knowledge to a systematic review). That is, in our view, the major challenge faced by professionals and the academy.

From this new double anticipatory perspective, by investing in applied research prospectively—"future possibilities"—and incorporating the identification of possible scenarios proposed by Matilla (2007), organizations may use information in order to design their future corporate policies and corporate public relations and plan their strategies, given the information is accurate in terms of:

a. A concise definition of the aimed subject (issue)

b. A diagnosis of the life-cycle stage of the issue

c. The level of complexity of the concept being analyzed

d. The identification and analysis of the possible points of inflection produced in recent years around the concept under study (historical)

e. The identification of stakeholders related to the concept

f. The degree of intensity with which the social actors deal with the issue from the standpoint of communication

g. A description of the key strategic public map (designed by the issue) from the map of social actors related to the concept

h. The state of stakeholders' perceptions and key strategic publics identified, in relation to the issue

i. The degree of involvement of affected stakeholders and key strategic publics

j. The identification of the different stances (attitudes) of social actors and key strategic audiences identified with the concepts analyzed

k. Establishment of an alliances map between social actors and key strategic audiences identified, who are concerned with the issue

l. A situation diagnostic based on the analysis of the alliances map of different social actors involved and key strategic audiences

m. Identification of new possible trends that can anticipate possible new emerging scenarios, in a broad or specific sense (social, cultural, demographic, technological, economic, political, financial, etc.)

n. New trends in behavior patterns that can appear at new venues, events, under new conditions, or due to changing perceptions and attitudes of key strategic stakeholders and different social actors, which configure their expectations around the issue, in relation to futures and potentials:

- Scenarios of action
- Processes of perception
- Process definition

- Aggregation processes
- Structures organization processes
- Processes of different interests' representation
- Processes of defining the public agenda
- Setting processes of public debate
- Establishing processes of forces and/or influence correlation

o. The identification of stakeholders and future scenarios that could produce tipping points on emerging trends around the concept.

p. Probable new trends on possible future impacts on public policy, in relation to:

- Possible scenarios of political distribution of power
- Content or concrete measures that could constitute the core of public policy
- Program or framework in which to develop public policy
- Policy guidance (interests, values, goals)
- Coercion factor derived from the exercise of legal authority
- Social competence (interests, perceptions, and citizens behavior)

Is It Possible to Perform Issues Management in a Changing Media Sphere? No Life Without Media?

What we've just described is based on an assumption, stable and unchanging until recently: that issues management is set around four players that form a closed system, whose internal dynamics is its reason for being:

1. An organization that, as a subject promoter, initiates the process of trying to influence the "management of the future" and to this end, identifies emerging issues and trends, proactively managed, via mass communication
2. Some public authorities that establish the legislative and public policy regarding the issues
3. Some citizens who, through their opinions, attitudes, and actions, shape public opinion in favour or against positions on issues
4. Some media of communication which, through agenda-setting, selects and polarizes the issues, contributing to the formation of public statements

What if one of these players in the established system changed its nature? This is what has happened recently with the media, striking the structure below its waterline. Advances in information technology have led to a radical change in the monopoly in which the media were acting to recruit, select, and disseminate the news, and, now bloggers and users of Internet social networks share an active role in the selection, production, and news broadcast once reserved to journalists. The audience gradually diminishes as buying habits and information consumption are drastically modified in a world shrunk by globalization. Thus, advertising effectiveness based on audience rankings undergoes a phenomenon of fragmentation and causes a decline in investment; and the boundaries between civil society and media fade to almost nothing, confusing the classic roles of transmitter/receiver set by Lasswell from a functionalist view from a distant 1948.

In this new scenario, a total paradigm shift has been configured, which requires a comprehensive review of the concept of public sphere, and consequently, of issues management, opening doors to new questions: Is the death of traditional media a real threat? What future will this paradigm shift bring? Does issues management make sense in such a context?

There are many doubts and uncertainties about what lies ahead. At the heart of issues management, its purpose is to anticipate the future, identify issues, and manage them proactively. Should issues management be done—about issues management? Our research group will continue to seek answers to these questions.

Power, Communication, and Issues Management in a Life Without Media

The IV International Congress on Communication and Reality posed the interesting and provocative exercise that resulted in this book: to take to the extreme and reduce to the absurd a future social scene centered around the idea—certainly apocalyptic—of what would happen if the traditional mass media were to disappear.

In this context, Sáez, Sabaté Salazar, and Comas (2011, pp. 502–503) considered that the general press was not born out of technology, but because of a new social organization, and that today, it is in possible danger of extinction due to a series of technological changes that have altered the information consumption patterns of citizens. In a society where the traditional mass media seem to have less and less meaning, the authors observed that what has really changed is the social organization that led to the birth of traditional mass media, and that today, dialogue and ideology seem absent in a society that's becoming a sum of distinct groups with impermeable monolithic thoughts or contrary and discordant opinions. And with society's lack of commitment, people no longer need to consult other sources, as they act in a digital environment that promotes anonymity, causing opinions for which the issuer doesn't feel responsible. Finally, Sáez et al. conclude that the new social organization has transferred the ability to influence from traditional media to "citizen journalists" of the Internet and social networks. Thus, the society is self-represented, clearly showing that it no longer needs what media have been offering for the past two centuries. The traditional media is replaced by the new digital media, but not removed; although, as Couldry stated (2009, p. 438), "something about media is changing. At stake is not just a single relation (the 'self' versus the 'net', as Manuel Castells [1997: 3] once put it), for digital media are now integral to how selves appear at all. A deeper transformation is under way that challenges the ontology on which the mass communication paradigm was based," while new models of collaborative communication appear, which Leadbeater (2007) calls "we-think."

We link the above reflections of the British Couldry and the Catalan academics Sáez et al. with another Catalan researcher, Castells (2009), who takes the view that power is based on the control of communication and information produced by the state, media, or organizations, as he states:

> The power of communication is at the center of the structure and dynamics of society . . . [and] the essential form of power is in the ability to model the mind . . . because it is through communication as the human mind interacts with its social environment. . . . The communication process influences decisively the way to build and challenge power relations in all fields of social practices, including political practice. (2009, pp. 23–24)[1]

We started this chapter with a summary of the state of the art of issues management, including the sophisticated techniques of corporate public relations. By now we hope we've expressed that issues management research is driven by the strategist; that is to say, someone interested in anticipating events and, ergo, someone who strives to "manage the future" (Matilla, 2007). It's something we all do every day, in our individual processes of decision making. But investing in identifying trends in not-yet-visible issues, in order to manage their communication during the process leading to the issue's debate in the public sphere is, in our view, something that goes beyond the natural proactive impulse that leads all social actors to deal with the uncertainties and unknowns—and the future is, by definition. Actually, this is a very human trait, closely linked with the desire for control and power.

Sáez et al. (2011) claim that the new social network structure, acting as a new and fragmented paradigm, consists of a number of autarkic groups, immobile in their point of view, which, no longer able to dialogue with the other, even fail to lay the foundations to generate the public debate that has characterized the public sphere of the pre-digital society, where the traditional media and issues management have had their full rationale and have played, unambiguously and effectively, their role in the social game. Meanwhile, Castells (2009) defends the idea that desire for control and power are part of human nature, a view to which we align. Accordingly, we do not yet know how or when human beings—who aspire to an essential way of power—would find the formula to continue taking control of social change through influence on the collective mind through communication, and we are now concerned with exploring answers to these questions. We do not doubt that humans will overcome the obstacles created by the environment turbulence of the new social construction. We're also confident we'll find the path to the future—with or without media and with or without traditional issues management—knowing an intense craving for control will magnetize the compass to make our wish come true.

Endnotes

1. "El poder de la comunicación está en el centro de la estructura y la dinámica de la sociedad . . . [y] la forma esencial de poder está en la capacidad para modelar la mente . . . ya que es mediante la comunicación como la mente humana interactúa con su entorno social. . . . El proceso de comunicación influye decisivamente en la forma de construir y desafiar las relaciones de poder en todos los campos de las prácticas sociales, incluida la práctica política." (2009, pp. 23–24)

References

Ansoff, H. I. (1980). Strategic issue management. *Strategic Management Journal, 1,* 131–148.

Ansoff, H. I. (1984). *Implanting strategic management.* Englewood Cliffs, NJ: Prentice Hall.

Arrington Jr., C. B., & Sawaya, R. N. (1984). Managing public affairs: Issues management in an uncertain environment. *California Management Review, 26,* 148–160.

Ashley, W. C. (1983). Issue management: New tool for new times. *Bank Marketing,* 10–14.

Bartha, P. F. (1982). Managing corporate external issues: An analytical framework. *Business Quarterly, 47,* 78–79.

Bartha, P. F. (1984). Tuning in on issues management. *Canadian Business Review, 11,* 25.

Beck, U. (2000). *La democracia y sus enemigos.* Barcelona, Spain: Paidós.
Bennett, W. L., Harris, P. D., Laskey, J. K., Levitch, A. H.; Monrad, S. E. (1976). Deep and surface images in the construction of political issues: The case of amnesty. *The Quarterly Journal of Speech, 62,* 109–126.
Broom, G., Casey, S. & Ritchey, J. (1997). Toward a concept and theory of organization-public relationships. *Journal of Public Relations, 9*(2), 83–98.
Bryan, J. L. (1997, July). The coming revolution in issues management. *Communication World,* 12–14.
Buchholz, R. A. (1989). *Business environment and public policy* (3rd ed.). Englewood Cliffs, NJ: Prentice Hall.
Buchholz, R. A. (1992). *Public policy issues for management.* Englewood Cliffs, NJ: Prentice Hall.
Buchholz, R. A., Evans, D., & Wagley, D. A. (1985). *Management response to public issues: Concepts and cases in strategy formation.* Englewood Cliffs, NJ: Prentice Hall.
Camillus, J. C., & Datta, D. K. (1991) Managing strategic issues in a turbulent environment. *Long Range Planning, 24,* 67–74.
Carr, W., & Kemmis, S. (1988). Teoría crítica de la enseñanza: la investigación-acción en la formación del profesorado, Barcelona, Spain: Martínez Roca.
Castells, M. (1997). *The power of identity.* Oxford, United Kingdom: Blackwell.
Castells, M. (2009). *Comunicación y Poder.* Madrid, Spain: Alianza. (English edition: 2009, *Communication Power:* New York, NY: Oxford University Press.)
Chase, W. H. (1977, October). Public issues management: The new science. *Public Relations Journal, 33,* 25–26.
Chase, W. H. (1982a). Issues management. In J. S. Nagelschmidt, *The public affairs handbook.* Chicago, IL: American Management Association.
Chase, W. H. (1982b). Issues management conference: A special report. *Corporate Public Issues and Their Management, 7,* 1–2.
Chase, W. H. (1984). *Issues management: Origins of the future,* Stamford, CT: Issue Action.
Chase, W. H., & Jones, B. L. (1979, Summer). Managing public policy issues. *Public Relations Journal, 5*(2), 7.
Chase-Jones PR Strategy Model. Available at *file://A:Chase%20Award% 20Entry% 20McDonalds_archivos/EIRMC-chart.gif]*
Cheney, G., & Vibbert, S. L. (1987). Corporate discourse in public relations and issues management. In F. M. Jablin, L. Putnam, K. H. Roberts, L. W. Porter (Eds.), *Handbook of organizational communication.* Beverly Hills, CA: Sage.
Coates, J. F., Jarratt, J., & Heinz, L. (1986). *Issues management: How you can plan, organize and manage for the future.* Mounty Airy, MD: Lomond.
Coleman, C. L. (1993). The influence of mass media and interpersonal risk judgments. *Communication Research, 20,* 611–628.
Colman, A. M. (1982). *Game theory and experimental games: Study of strategic interaction.* Oxford, United Kingdom: Pergamon Press.

Coob, R. W., & Elder, C. D. (1983). *Participation in American politics: The dynamics of agenda-building* (2nd ed.). Baltimore, MD: Johns Hopkins University Press.

Coombs, W. T. (2002). Assessing online issue threats: Issues contagions and their effect on issues priorisation. *Journal of Public Relations, 2*(4), 215–229.

Couldry, N. (2009). Does "the media" have a future? *European Journal of Communication, 24*(4), 437–447.

Crable, R. E., & Vibbert, S. L. (1985). Managing issues and influencing public policy. *Public Relations Review, 11*(2), 3–13.

Creedon, P. (1993). Acknowledging the infrastructure: A feminist analysis of systems theory. *Public Relations Review, 19*, 157–166.

Cuenca, J. (2010). *El análisis de la calidad de las relaciones en el ámbito de las Relaciones Públicas. Aplicación de un modelo global de auditoría de Relaciones Públicas a la sociedad municipal 22@ del Ayuntamiento de Barcelona.* Barcelona, Spain: Ramon Llull University. http://www.tesisenred.net/handle/10803/21777

Dozier, D. M., Grunig, L. A., & Grunig, J. E. (1995). *Manager's Guide to Excellence in Public Relations and Communication Management.* Mahwah, NJ: Lawrence Erlbaum Associates.

Dutton, J. E. (1993). Interpretations on automatic: A different view of strategic issue diagnosis. *Journal of Management Studies, 30*, 339–357.

Dutton, J. E., & Ashford, S. J. (1993). Selling issues to top management. *The Academy of Management Review, 18*, 397–410.

Dutton, J. E., Walton, E. J., & Abrahamson, E. (1989). Important dimensions of strategic issues: Separating the wheat from the chaff. *Journal of Management Studies, 26*, 379–396.

Ehling, W. P. (1975). PR administration, management science and purposive systems. *Public Relations Review, 1*(2), 15–43.

Ewing, R. P. (1979, Winter). The uses of futurist techniques in issues management. *Public Relations Quarterly. 24*, 15–18.

Ewing, R. P. (1980a). Socio-political forecasting: Managing the black hole of the future. In F. Feather, *Through the 80s: Thinking globally, acting locally.* Washington DC: World Future Society.

Ewing, R. P. (1980b, June). Evaluating issues management. *Public Relations Journal, 36*(6),14–16.

Ewing, R. P. (1981). The uses of futurist techniques in issues management. In A. Elkins & D. W. Callaghan, *A managerial odyssey: Problems in business and its environment.* Reading, MA: Addison-Wesley.

Ewing, R. P. (1982). Modeling the process. In J. S. Nagelschmidt, *The public affairs handbook.* Chicago, IL: American Management Association.

Ewing, R. P. (1987a). *Managing the new bottom line: Issues management for senior executives.* Homewood, IL: Dow Jones-Irwin.

Ewing, R. P. (1987b). Issues management: Managing trends through the issues life cycle. In C. L. Caywood (Ed.), *The book of strategic public relations and integrated communications* pp. 173–188). New York, NY: McGraw-Hill.

Ewing, R. P. (1990a, Spring). Moving from micro to macro issues management. *Public Relations Review, 16*, 19–24.

Ewing, R. P. (1990b, Winter). The role of issues management in managing the new bottom-line. *Journal of Corporate Public Relations.*

Ewing R. P. (1997). Issues Management: Managing trends trough the issues life cycle. In C. Caywood (ed.), *The handbook of strategic public relations and integrated communications*, Boston pp. 173–188: McGraw-Hill.

Fahey, L. (1986). Issues management: Two approaches. *Strategic Planning Management, 81*, 85–96.

Ferguson, S. D. (1999). *Communication planning: An integrated approach,* Thousand Oaks, CA: Sage.

Fink, S. (1986). Crisis management: Planning for the inevitable. New York: American Management Association.

García García, F. (2001). Hacia una teoría estratégica para la acción cotidiana. In R. A. Pérez (Ed.), *Estrategias de Comunicación.* Barcelona, Spain: Ariel.

Gaunt, P., & Ollenburger, J. (1995, Fall). Issues management revisited: A tool that deserves another look. *Public Relations Review*, 199–210.

Godet, M. (1991). *Prospectiva y planificación estratégica.* Barcelona, Spain: SG.

González Herrero, A. (1998). *Marketing preventivo: La comunicación de crisis en la empresa.* Barcelona, Spain: Bosch.

González Herrero, A. (2003, April). Issues management (o la gestión de asuntos potencialmente conflictivos). *Revista del Col·legi de Publicitaris i Relacions Públiques de Catalunya, 5*, 10–12.

Gossen, R., & Sharp, K. (1987). How to manage dispute resolution. *Public Relations Journal, 43*, 35–38.

Graber, D. (1997). Media as opinion resources: Are the 1990s a new ballgame? In B. Norrander & C. Wilcox (Eds.), *Understanding public opinion* (pp. 230–251). Washington, DC: CQ Press.

Grunig, J. E. (1989). Symmetrical presuppositions as a framework for public relations theory. In V. Hazleton Jr. & C. H. Botan (Eds.), *Public relations theory* (pp. 17–44). Hillsdale, NJ: Lawrence Erlbaum.

Grunig, J. E. (ed.) (1992). *Excellence in public relations and communication management.* Hillsdale, NJ: Lawrence Erlbaum.

Grunig, J. E. (1997). A situational theory of publics: Conceptual history, recent challenges and new research. In D. Moss,, T. MacManus, & D. Vercic (Eds.), *Public relations research: An international perspective* (pp. 3–48). London: International Thomson Business Press.

Grunig, J. E. & Repper, F. (1992). Strategic management, public and issues. In J. Grunig (ed.), *Excellence in public relations and communication management.* Hillsdale, NJ: Lawrence Erlbaum.

Guth, W. D. (1976). Toward a social system theory of corporate strategy. *Journal of Business, 47,* 374–388.

Hainsworth, B. E. (1990). The distribution of advantages and disadvantages. *Public Relations Review, 16,* 33–39.

Hainsworth, B. E, & Meng, M. (1988). How corporations define issues management. *Public Relations Review, 14*(4), 18–30.

Hanna, N. (1985). Strategic planning and management: A review of recent experience. *World Bank Staff Working Paper #* 751 (pp. 59–69, 84). Washington, DC: World Bank.

Heath, R. L. (1988). *Strategic issues management: How organizations influence and respond to public interests and policies,* San Francisco, CA: Jossey-Bass.

Heath, R. L. (Ed.) (1992). *Rhetorical and critical approaches to public relations.* Hillsdale, NJ: Lawrence Erlbaum.

Heath, R. L. (1997). *Strategic issues management: Organizations and public policy challenges,* Thousand Oaks, CA: Sage.

Heath, R. L., & Cousino, K. R. (1990, Spring). Issues management: End of the first decade—progress report. *Public Relations Review. 16,* 6–18.

Heath, R. L., & Nelson, R. A. (1986a). *Issues management: Corporate public policymaking in an information society.* Beverly Hills, CA: Sage.

Heath, R. L., & Nelson, R. A. (1986b). *Issues management.* Newbury Park, CA: Sage.

Hiebert, R. E. (1988). *Courtier to the crowd: The story of Ivy Lee and the development of publics relations.* Ames: Iowa State University Press.

Hirsch, H. (2002). *Essential communications strategies* (2nd ed.). Hoboken, NJ: Wiley Press.

Hon, L. C. (2001). Demonstrating effectiveness in public relations: Goals, objectives, and evaluation. *Journal of Public Relations Research, 10,* 103–135.

Huang, Y. D. (2001). Values of public relations: Effects on organization-public relationships mediating conflict resolution. *Journal of Public Relations Research, 13*(4), 265–301.

Johnson, T. J., Hayes, C. E., & Hays, S. P. (1998). *Engaging the public: How government and the media can reinvigorate American democracy.* Lanham, MD: Rowman & Littlefield.

Jones, B. L., & Chase, W. H. (1979). Managing public policy issues. *Public Relations Review, 5*(29), 3–23.

Karlberg, M. (1996). Remembering the public in public relations research: From theoretical to operational symmetry. *Journal of Public Relations Research, 8,* 263–278.

Katz, D., & Kahn, R. L. (1967). *The social psychology of organizations.* New York, NY: Wiley.

King, W. R. (1982). Using strategic issue analysis. *Long Range Planning, 15,* 45–49.

Lasswell, H. D. (1948/1967). *Power and personality.* New York, NY: Viking Press.

Lauzen, M. M. (1995). Toward a model of environmental scanning. *Journal of Public Relations Research, 7*, 187–203.

Lauzen, M. M. (1997). Understanding the relation between public relations and issues management. *Journal of Public Relations Research, 9*(1), 65–82.

Lauzen, M. M., & Dozier, D. M. (1992). The missing link: The public relations manager role as mediator organizational environments and power consequences for the function. *Journal of Public Relations Research, 4*, 205–220.

Lauzen, M. M. & Dozier, D. M. (1994). Issues management mediation of linkages between environmental complexity and management of the public relations function. *Journal of Public Relations Research, 6*, 163–184.

Leadbeater, C. (2007). *We-Think*. London, United Kingdom: Profile Books.

Ledingham, J. A., & Bruning, S. D. (1998). Relationship management and public relations: Dimensions of an organization–public relationship. *Public Relations Review, 24*, 55–-65.

Ledingham, J. A., & Bruning, S. D. (Ed.). (2000). *Public relations as relationship management: A relational approach to the study and practice of public relations*. Mahwah, NJ: Lawrence Erlbaum.

Ledingham, J.A., Bruning, S.D. & Wilson, L.J. (1999). Time as an indicator of the perceptions and behavior of members of a key public: Monitoring and predicting organization-public relationships, *Journal of Public Relations Research, 11*(2), 167–183.

Lerbinger, O. (1977). Corporate uses of research in public relations. *Public Relations Research, 3*(4), 11–19.

MacMillan, I. C. (1978). *Strategy formulation: Political concepts*. St. Paul, MN: West.

Marca, G. (2011). *La evaluación en los modelos de planificación estratégica de las Relaciones Públicas. Análisis comparativo del uso de la evaluación de la comunicación en las redes hospitalarias de los modelos sanitarios de España, el Reino Unido y Estados Unidos*. Barcelona, Spain: Faculty of Communication, Rovira i Virgili University. http://www.tdx.cat/handle/10803/51765

Matilla, K. (2007). *Aportaciones para un modelo global de Planificación Estratégica en Relaciones Públicas y Comunicación Integral*. Barcelona, Spain: Faculty of Communication, Ramon Llull University. http://www.tesisenred.net/TDX-1001107–131810

Matilla, K. (2009). Conflicto e *Issues Management* (Gestión de Conflictos Potenciales). In *Conceptos fundamentales en la planificación estratégica de las Relaciones Públicas*. Barcelona, Spain: UOC, 109–135.

McGrath, G. B. (1998). *Issues management: Anticipation and influence*. San Francisco, CA: International Association of Business Communicators.

McGrath, J. E. (1966). A social psychological approach to the study of negotiation. In R. V. Bowers (Ed.), *Studies on behavior in organizations*. Athens: University of Georgia Press.

Millar, F. E., & Rogers, E. (1976). A relational approach to interpersonal communication. In G. R. Miller (Ed.), *Exploration in interpersonal communication* (pp. 87–103). Beverly Hills, CA: Sage.

Morley, M. (2002). *How to manage your global reputation: A guide to the dynamics of international public relations.* Houndmills, United Kingdom: Palgrave.

Marx, T. G. (1946). Integrating public affairs and strategic planning. *California Management Review, 29,* 141–147.

Marx, T. G. (1990). Strategic planning for public affairs. *Long Range Planning, 23,* 9–16.

Murphy, P. (1989). Game theory: A paradigm for the public relations process. In V. Hazleton Jr. & C. H. Botan (Eds.), *Public relations theory.* Hillsdale, NJ: Lawrence Erlbaum.

Murphy, P. (1996, Summer). Chaos theory as a model for managing issues and crises. *Public Relations Review, 22*(2), 95–113.

Nelson, R. A. (1990, Spring). Bias versus fairness: The social utility of issues management. *Public Relations Review, 18*(1), 25–32.

O'Toole, J. E. (1975). Advocacy advertising shows the flag. *Public Relations Journal, 31*(11), 14–16.

Pasquero, J. (1989). Gérer stratégiquement dans une économie politisée. *Gestion, 14*(3), 116–128.

Pavlik, J. V. (1987). *Public relations: What research tells us.* Newbury Park, CA: Sage. (Spanish edition: *La investigación en Relaciones Públicas,* Barcelona, Spain: Gestión 2000, 1999.)

Pfeffer, G., & Salancik, J. (1978). *The external control of organizations: A resource dependence perspective.* New York, NY: Harper & Row.

Plowman, K. D. (2004). Conflict strategic management and public relations. *Public Relations Review, 31*(3), 131–138.

Plowman, K. D., Revelle, C., Meirovich, S., Pien, M., Stemple, R., Sheng, V., & Fay, K. (1995). Walgreens: A case study in health care and conflict resolution. *Journal of Public Relations Research, 7*(4), 231–258.

Poors, C. A. (1997, July). How issues management turned the tide: A case study for action and results. *Communication World,* 23–24.

Post, J. E. (1979). *Corporate behavior and social change.* Reston, VA: Reston.

Rakov, L. (1989). Information and power: Toward a critical theory of information campaigns. In C. T. Salmon (Ed.), *Information campaigns: Balancing social values and social change* (pp. 164–184). Newbury Park, CA: Sage.

Ramsey, S. A. (1993, Autumn). Issues management and the use of technologies in public relations. *Public Relations Review, 19*(3), 261–275.

Regester, M., & Larkin, J. (1997). *Risk issues and crisis management.* London, United Kingdom: Kogan Page.

Renfro, W. L. (1987). Issues management: The evolving corporate role. *Futures, 19*(5), 545–554.

Renfro, W. L. (1993). *Issues management in strategic planning.* Westport, CT: Quorum Books.

Reynolds, C. H. (1997, Winter). Issues management and the Australian gun debate. *Public Relations Review,* 340–360.

Sáez, A., Sabaté Salazar, J., & Comas, E. (2011). A life without media: símptomes i primers diagnòstics. VI Congreso Internacional Comunicación y Realidad, *A life without media, Trípodos Extra* (pp. 501–511). Barcelona, Spain: Facultat de Comunicació Blanquerna, Universitat Ramon Llull.

Schneider, B. L. (1985). Issues management: It counts!. *United States Banker,* 41–42.

Shelby, A. N. (1986). *Issues management: A new direction for public relations professionals.* Meeting of the International Communication Association, Chicago, IL.

Simcic Bronn, P. N., & Bronn, C. (2006). Issues management as a basis for strategic orientation. *Journal of Public Affairs, 2*(4), 247–258.

Stanley, G. D. (1985). *Managing external issues: Theory and practice,* Greenwich, CT: JAI Press.

Taylor, M., Vasquez, G. M., & Doorley, J. (2003). Merck and AIDS activists: Engagement as a framework for extending issues management. *Public Relations Review, 29*(3), 257–270.

Thayer, L. (1968). *Communication and communication systems.* Homewood, IL: Irwin.

Thomas, K. W., & Tymon Jr., W. G. (1982). Necessary properties of relevant research: Lessons from recent criticisms of the organizational sciences. *Academy of Management Review, 7,* 345–352.

Thomsen, S. R. (1995, Fall). Using online databases in corporate issues management. *Public Relations Review,* 103–121.

Vell, S. R., & Kent, M. L. (2008, November). Issues management and inoculation: Tylenol's responsible dosing advertising. *Public Relations Review, 34*(4), 399–402.

Wartick, S. L., & Rude, R. E. (1986). Issues management: Corporate fad or corporate function? *California Management Review, 24,* 124–140.

Waymer, D. (2007). Emergent agents: The forgotten publics in crisis communication and issues management research. *Journal of Applied Communication Research, 35*(1), 88–108.

Wilcox, D. L., Cameron, G. T., Ault, P., & Agee, W. (1989). *Public relations strategies and tactics* (2nd ed.). New York, NY: Harper & Row. (Spanish edition: *Relaciones Públicas. Estrategias y Tácticas* [6ª ed.], Madrid, Spain: Pearson Educación, 2001).

Wilson, L. J. (1996). Strategic cooperative communities: A synthesis of strategic, issues management, and relationship building approaches in public relations. In H. M. Culbertson & N. Chen (Eds.), *International public relations: A comparative analysis* (pp. 67–80). Mahwah, NJ: Lawrence Erlbaum.

Wimmer, R. D., & Dominick, J. R. (1996). *La investigación científica de los medios de comunicación.* Barcelona, Spain: Bosch.

Xifra, J. (1998). *Lobbying.* Barcelona, Spain: Gestión 2000.

Xifra, J. (2003). *Teoría y estructura de las Relaciones Públicas.* Aravaca (Madrid), Spain: McGraw- Hill/Interamericana de España.

Xifra, J. (2005). Relaciones Públicas proactivas: El modelo de la gestión de Conflictos Potenciales. In A. Castillo Esparcia, *Comunicación organizacional. Teorías y estudios.* Málaga, Spain: Clave Aynadamar.

Xifra, J. (2008). *Los Think Tanks,* Barcelona, Spain: UOC.

Xifra, J. (2009). *Comunicación Proactiva. La gestión de Conflictos Potenciales en las organizaciones.* Barcelona, Spain: Gedisa.

Epilogue

EVA COMAS, JOAN CUENCA, AND KLAUS ZILLES

It stands to reason that contemplating the disappearance of the media must, on the face of it, seem irreverent and provocative. However, we have found that using the classical argumentative figure called reductio ad absurdum, whereby we set out to take the apocalyptic scenarios of the possible demise of traditional media to their limit, has stimulated a profusion of new ideas, and has spawned a fruitful, critical discussion about the possible implications of life with or without media.

The main conclusion that emerges most strongly from this discussion is that the conception and definition of what we call "communication media" is being subjected to a thorough review, a review which invariably must be couched in a comprehensive rethinking of the very political, economic, and cultural forces which afforded center stage to the so-called communication media in the first place. Indeed, representative democracy, the free-market system based on competition, and the ideal and scientific literacy derived from the Enlightenment, are based on the existence of a public agora thus far constituted by the traditional media. Thus, the very context in which the media have acted as a transmission hub is in need of a redefinition.

In the opening of his landmark work, *Technopoly: The Surrender of Culture to Technology* (1992), Neil Postman, U.S. media theorist and cultural critic, alerted us to the epistemological and linguistic changes that take place every time a new communication technology thrives and begins to impinge on the social landscape, engendering untold messages and interactions among its members. Postman claimed that communication technologies not only introduce new words, but, in turn, transform the old ones. Thus, the telegraph and the press changed what was hitherto understood as "information." Television changed the meaning of terms such as "political debate," "news," and "public opinion." The advent of computers once again changed the denotation of "information." That is to say, the words remain unchanged, but their meanings and definitions undergo re-signification whenever a communication technology reconfigures the context. And most important, says Postman, this process takes place with most of us being largely oblivious to it.

While it may seem fanciful that the word "media" should disappear from our vocabulary, or undergo significant alteration, there is evidence that its meaning and usage in modern liberal societies, which after all engender the media, is being reformulated even as we write these lines.

In the introduction of this volume we wondered whether the online environment and the new media could contribute to enhancing literacy and the enlightenment of the public, strengthen the market economy, and heighten the accountability of the representative democratic system. The gatekeeper function of guarding the boundary between the public and private was the avowed task which the "old media" were believed to carry out for more than two centuries. We wanted to know, then, if the new media could be expected to fill the "old media's" shoes. Despite failing to obtain conclusive answers to this question, we feel certain that in different areas of communication, the old ideas are fated to find new definitions of/for themselves. In the eleven chapters of *Life Without Media*, it emerges that besides "media," the terms whose meanings are clearly in flux are "citizen," "democracy," "public," "private," "privacy," "individual," "consumer," "education," and "knowledge,"—though this catalogue is far from complete.

In the first part of the book, these terms are discussed from a theoretical, epistemological, and sociological perspective. Mark Brewin's chapter gets the debate underway by drawing attention to a truly interesting aspect: our way of conceptualizing individuality, of understanding and imagining the human subject, is the result of the social organization of the public sphere and the organizing role carried out by the media. Thus, the conception of the self is the result of a particular technological, cultural, political, and economic context.

In liberal democratic society, born of the Industrial Revolution, the American and French Revolutions, and the Enlightenment, the media were, according to

Brewin, institutions with a central role, able to articulate control over their content and to mediate between the public and private sectors; and their role went beyond that of mediator. In truth, their pursuit created both a public sphere and a discrete space for privacy. As a result, human subjects relished an actual (albeit now considered illusory) sense of self, of autonomy, and a significant capacity for criticism of the environment that surrounded them, while at the same time embracing the possibility of introspection and self-criticism.

The horizontal mode of communication characteristic of the so-called new media basically sends the old media reeling from their central role. The boundaries between public and private have become tenuous at best, and the individual has become a porous, permeable being, indistinguishable from its outer surface. The mode of thinking of the human subject has become thoroughly transformed. Says Brewin:

> . . . the Enlightenment citizen, bravely confronting tradition and superstition with his individual reason and moral sensibility, no longer makes much sense. Nor does a theory of the public that both depends upon the efforts of these various reasoning, autonomous individuals to devise a way forward, and depends as well on the sense of individual freedom to ultimately justify itself.

According to Brewin, a professor at the University of Tulsa, we are in the process of repositioning ourselves from a rigid conception of subjectivity, in which the self is free, independent, and stable, to a more fluid conception of human subjectivity, linked to the unstable nature of information on the Internet, which owing to its level-plane network organization allows for many areas and varieties of relationships, thus promoting a more fluid and changeable sense of identity. In this new context, the audience becomes the producer of content, and while this is celebrated as a democratic achievement, it is not without perils. Indeed, for Brewin the Internet does not automatically constitute a locus of critical discourse in which various subjectivities cohabitate and enrich each other.

Alternatively, in Chapter 2, Nick Couldry submits a critical and more global approach in that he conceives the media from a decentralized perspective, both traditional media as well as the new online mediascape. Couldry argues the need for a broader look at media studies, beyond merely analyzing media institutions or the content they publish. This is because, for Couldry, it is essential to investigate exactly what the contributions of the media amount to regarding our knowledge of the world, our capacity of "agency," and our ethical values:

> It is important to look at our own resources, as media researchers, for reorienting critical media research towards our needs as citizens, as human beings: our need to act in the world (agency); our need to act in particular on the basis of facts and not illusion, and so to grasp the embedding of knowledge, imagination, and action in material conditions, processes, and infrastructures (knowledge); and our need, through that understanding, to address the work of power and to understand the contradictions between the work of power and a life that we might choose to value (ethics).

According to Couldry, it is essential to understand that there are powerful forces beyond media outlets such as the economic or religious institutions, which exert a critical force and which, in their own way, participate in communication transfer. But his greatest emphasis lies in critically scrutinizing the media where they interface with society in order to gauge and assess their contributions to knowledge and human life.

Richard Maxwell and Toby Miller conclude the theoretical review in the first section of the volume by turning their attention to the social and technological changes that are reshaping the central concepts in public life such as democracy and citizenship. In their research, Maxwell and Miller emphasize an aspect they feel has not been adequately addressed by utopian or dystopian media pundits, namely the environmental impact and the energy resources required and expended in the use of social media. And it must be noted that they include both new media as well as old media in their assessment:

> Media technology is yesterday's, today's, and tomorrow's news, but rarely in the way that it should be, because the prevailing myth is that the printing press, telegraph, phonograph, photograph, cinema, telephone, wireless radio, television, and Internet changed the world without changing the Earth. Yet their touchstone is environmental destructiveness, tied to the power of the military-industrial-entertainment-academic complex and managerial command over labor.

According to Miller and Maxwell, we need to find alternatives to click-capitalism and clickocracy, alternatives which must invariably entail aspects of sustainability and citizen participation guided by ethical principles: "there needs to be a discussion about the costs and benefits of electronic pleasure and participation that is neither anti-fun nor anti-reality." Taking their cue from this directive, the authors engage in a philosophical debate about the implications of these issues in terms of human subjectivity and the political concept of citizenship.

In section two of *Life Without Media*, entitled "Parenting, Schooling, and Socializing: Youth Mediatization Gone Wrong?" our authors direct their gaze to the part of the population media scholars have taken to dubbing "digital natives." Whether regarding children, adolescents, or young adults, digitization makes a crucial impact in different areas of their lives in the way they communicate and relate to their peers. The four chapters that make up this thematic section address, respectively, children as consumers, the digital divide among adults and teenagers, privacy issues in the use of social media by adolescents, and, finally, the impact of digitization on higher education.

Early on, we questioned whether the online environment and the new media can be a factor in strengthening the market economy. David Buckingham answers this question in the affirmative in regard to the children's market, albeit with the caveat that "the children's market is significantly more volatile and uncertain than adult markets. The failure rate for new products is much higher here than in the adult market." As a result, the "marketers" are trying to address the risk associated with this market, deploying techniques like advergaming, product placement, viral marketing, and social networking. Research shows that rather than adopting aggressive hard-sell techniques, marketers increasingly, and subtly, find ways around young consumers' skepticism and potential resistance.

But perhaps the most revealing aspect of David Buckingham's analysis lies in cross-examining the notion of children as consumers. Buckingham argues that it is necessary to envisage children as a consuming public beyond the polarized debate among some scholars who see children as "victims of a powerful, highly manipulative form of consumer culture" and "marketers" who "often claim that children are becoming 'empowered' in this new commercial environment." Buckingham explains that these two contrasting positions neglect the fact that "the more ubiquitous and participatory techniques that are now being used by commercial companies reflect a new construction of the child consumer (and indeed of the consumer more generally). This new construction in turn requires us to rethink the terms of the debate, and some of the basic assumptions of consumer culture theory."

We have stated repeatedly that the common denominator emerging in this volume is the need to consciously rethink and re-signify commonly accepted terms and language, which in the current technological, economic, political, and social environment have altered, if not their meanings, at the very least their connotations. Jordi Busquet and Ana Cinthya Uribe discuss the need to redefine established notions in the educational system. It is evident that while traditional education championed the one-directional transmission of knowledge, now the educational process tends to be understood as an act of collaboration and negotiation. This reformulation should be framed, Busquet and Uribe point out, in a new cultural paradigm that is no longer based on book culture, and which must be viewed in the context of the globalization process. In keeping with this new cultural paradigm, the authors posit that the use of new technologies creates a "digital divide" between adolescents and adults, be the latter parents or teachers.

Indeed, in a culture in which apparently "young people perceive themselves (and, more importantly, are perceived) as owners of skills and even 'knowledge' exclusive to them and completely alien to adults," it is necessary to rethink the use of technologies in education. Lamentably, though, according to Busquet and Uribe, what is happening in many classrooms is that the models reproduce traditional teaching with information technology affixed largely for the sake of appearances.

Revisiting the changing role of the media in creating boundaries between the private and the public sheds light on the fact that adolescents' use of social networks is an issue of extraordinary sensitivity in the sense that adolescents are actively configuring their own demarcations of privacy. And they are facing these decisions and choices during their formative years, at a time when they are experiencing drastic changes and when social interaction with peers is experienced with special intensity. In their chapter, "Connecting and Protecting? Adolescents, Social Network Sites, and Privacy," Michel Walrave, Wannes Heirman, and Ellen Van Gool point out that while social network sites like Facebook are hugely successful among adolescent users, "concerns have risen about potential privacy-related risks for adults but more particularly for adolescents, ranging from inadvertently disclosing personal data to online aggression such as harassment and cyberbullying."

In a survey among 350 Belgian youth aged 10 to 19 years, these researchers collected data about the ways young users deal with privacy issues when using social network sites (SNS). The study reveals that "peer influence is the most important predictor of teenagers' disclosure of personal information on SNS. Teenagers with high susceptibility to peer influence disclose significantly more data." The survey results also show that boys tend to disclose more personal information than girls, just as adolescents who attribute a crucial role to social networks in their lives. On the other hand, it is important to note that "parental mediation" holds no special influence on "online self-disclosure." The analysis concludes with an appeal for policy initiatives that address and regulate these issues:

> The finding that teenagers' level of privacy concern is the most important predictor of their use of privacy settings could be particularly inspiring for future policy initiatives, as it implies that helping teenagers become aware of online privacy

> could help to optimize the use of privacy settings among adolescents. As observed in the second assessment of the European Safer Social Networking Principles, major SNS are already assisting young users by grouping e-safety hints in security centres or other dedicated websites. In half of all SNS, however, this guidance is difficult to find and understand.

Returning to the institutions of learning, the fourth and last chapter in the section addresses the pitfalls of digitization in higher education. The previously invoked digital divide, which affects not only parents but also teachers and university lecturers, has resulted in a profound disconnect between instructors who view social media as a mere appendage to established teaching methods, often not recognizing that students organize their entire lives around their social networks activities. This scenario, coupled with the economic crisis, which is deeply felt in the education system, offer evidence that school and university are some of the areas in which the redefinition of the concept of "media" is of particular significance.

In "Hyperreal Higher Education," James Moir, for instance, sounds the alarm in view of an impending fragmentation of knowledge: "students now download academic material to garner specific bits of 'information' rather than to gain depth of understanding through extended reading. Such is higher education in the information age, where the agency of the student in terms of choice and selection of downloadable material overrides broader educational ends." Similarly, he deplores a reductionist view of education according to which digital technology should be introduced into the classroom to train future workers: "The assumption is that we need greater numbers of graduates who are able to operate in such an economy and who have the information literacy and technology skills to be able to adapt and future-proof their employability prospects." A trend imported from the U.S. is the increasing customization of education, which views the student primarily as a future marketable employee. Conversely, Moir advocates safeguarding the true meaning of educational institutions: "In the world of simulacra and the power that comes from creating images of reality, higher education is faced with seeking to maintain authenticity of information and knowledge."

The main conclusion to be drawn from Part Three of the book, entitled "Mediated Life and Death in Arts and Entertainment," is that while the culture of print seems to have gone into a steady decline, it is also true that it can still muster sufficient vigor to reinvent itself and devise strategies to secure a place in the new cultural, economic, and political framework. A genre very much tied to print culture, the novel is the object of two studies proposing different strategies of reinvention. The first, by Martin Lüthe, analyzes David Foster Wallace's *Infinite Jest* in order to show how the communication media can feature as the narrative backbone of fiction writing. While the narrative takes place in a dystopian future, and the use of caricature and parody are the principal recurring devices, the import exerted by the media in contemporary society as well as addiction to "the powerful impact of home entertainment" is clearly showcased throughout the story.

Jenine Abboushi explores another strategy of reinvention of the novelistic genre in her chapter "The Big Screen in the Transnational Novel." Here, the strategy of the various novelists under scrutiny does not consist of placing the communication media at the center of their plots. Rather, these writers opt for conceiving and creating narrative works that are constructed with the "big screen written in" and with a future audiovisual adaptation in mind, thus affording them a much wider, and more mediatized, audience. This type of "transnational cinematic novel," various examples of which are examined in the chapter, sheds light on "why written forms (like the novel) often have a greater ability to generate adaptable content, and how new print and digital interdependences have opened up possibilities for artistic collaboration."

Archetypal media disciplines such as journalism and public relations take up the fourth and final part of *Life Without Media*. In the field of journalism, we can see a good many signs of a new professional design. And this redefinition of journalism is closely linked to a new way of thinking about democracy. As María Lamuedra Graván observes in her chapter, different parts of the world are currently seeing political movements similar to the 15M movement in Spain, calling for a more participatory democracy and promoting a more assembly-style political culture with horizontal structures of organization. Around the year 2000, the media started calling this phenomenon "the deliberative turn." According to Lamuedra, something similar is happening in the media on account of various factors, including the emergence of social networks. Based on an in-depth analysis of the reception of news aired by two major public networks, the BBC and Televisión Española (TVE), the researcher raises the question of what kind of journalism and media will be required in a new mediascape based on deliberative democracy. She argues that "a deliberative public sphere cannot just be a system of observation, but should constitute the arena where communication about the common good takes place, where citizens are central actors, without whom this model is unworkable." In this model, the role of journalists must change, says Lamuedra, from being invisible mediators to individuals involved in the public sphere and committed to the truth of the information and its public impact.

The profound transformation facing the public sphere must of necessity affect an activity like public relations. Kathy Matilla and Guillem Marca proffer an exhaustive literature review of "Issues Management," traditionally described as a communication tool of corporate public relations that allows institutions and corporations to anticipate and manage potential conflicts. However, Matilla and Marca offer a broader view of the concept and suggest that it might be seen as a strategy to detect and investigate trends that are not yet visible:

> We propose to dilate the field of view and introduce a new perspective that goes beyond the academic vision and development, based solely on the identification of potentially conflicting situations, which were the ones that initially formed the leitmotif of historical overview of the canonical theory of issues management. The same prospective effort allows one to focus beyond the environments that can create clearly threatening issues, to those that potentially may pose opportunities for an organization.

Thus we may discern that in the field of public relations an effort is made to reformulate and resignify a term that thus far had enjoyed a well-established meaning and usage, but which now, in a time of technological, political, cultural upheaval, takes on a new significance and therefore requires new definitions.

In June 2011, we held the VI International Conference on Communication and Reality at the Blanquerna School of Communication, with *Life without Media* as our central conference topic, encouraging participants to ponder, and think through to the end, some of the apocalyptic theses claiming that the media as we have known them were destined to disappear. The debate our event generated has gone some way to show that, far from disappearing, the media, along with the professions associated with them, remain a major societal force, but their conception is being subjected to a thorough review and a search of new definitions for old words. Hopefully this book has rendered proof of this.

Contributors

Jenine Abboushi studied at Birzeit University in Palestine, and completed her Master's and PhD at Columbia and Harvard. She taught comparative literature and Middle Eastern studies at New York University, and, following a Fulbright year in Morocco, she left New York to live and write in Casablanca. She currently lives in Beirut, where she is completing a novel and teaching English and comparative literature at the Lebanese American University. She has written on the cultural politics of translation for the *Times Literary Supplement*, and has also written on aesthetics and colonial cultures, Islamism's new media, an, most recently, on film's literary dependencies and collaborations in transnational contexts.

Eva Comas is a journalist and she holds a PhD in Communication Studies from Ramon Llull University, and a B.A. in Spanish Philology from Barcelona University. She is the author of a book on radio-journalism entitled *La ràdio en essència* (Blanquerna, 2009). Between 2007 and 2010, she has worked as a media consultant both for the Catalonian government (la Generalitat de Catalunya) and for the president of Ramon Llull University. Her main research is concerned with the language in broadcast radio, though her publications explore many aspects of the mass media. The most recent publications she has co-authored are "Un mundo sin periódicos" ("A World without Newspapers") *ICONO 14* (2010) and "Advertising Characteristics and Strategies in Prime Time Sports Broadcasts," *Radio Evolution-*

ECREA (2011). In 2011 she played an instrumental part in determining and articulating the conference theme *Life Without Media* of the International Conference on Communication and Reality at Ramon Llull University. Currently, she hosts a radio show at Ràdio Onda Cero Catalunya, and she has done freelance work for radio stations and news outlets such as COM Ràdio (2011–2012), Canal 33 (2005–2007), Catalunya Ràdio (2003), Catalunya Cultura (2002–2005), Avui (2002–2006) and El País (2004–2006), to name a few.

Mark Brewin is Associate Professor of Communication and Chair of the Faculty of Communication at The University of Tulsa, in Tulsa, Oklahoma, US. His work has primarily addressed issues of political communication and history, particularly as these touch upon questions of the public sphere, media theory, and the role of ritual and religious discourse in public life. He has published in the *Communication Review, Critical Studies in Media Communication*, and the *Journal of Communication Inquiry*, among other venues. In 2008, Peter Lang published his book *Celebrating Democracy*, which dealt with the history of Election Day, and its changing status as mass mediated political ritual.

David Buckingham is professor of Communications and Media Studies at Loughborough University, U.K., and a visiting professor at the Norwegian Centre for Child Research, NTNU Trondheim. His research focuses on children's and young people's interactions with electronic media, and on media education. He is currently directing a project on learning progression in media education; and has recently completed projects on childhood, "sexualisation," and consumer culture, and on young people, the Internet, and civic participation. He's the author, co-author, or editor of 26 books, including most recently *Beyond Technology: Children's Learning in the Age of Digital Culture* (2007), *Youth, Identity and Digital Media* (2008), *Video Cultures: Media Technology and Amateur Creativity* (2009), and *The Material Child: Growing Up in Consumer Culture* (2011).

Jordi Busquet (Terrassa, 1962) holds a PhD in Sociology and a BA in Economics. He is professor and head of research at the CONinCOM Network (Conflict, Childhood and Communication) at the Blanquerna School of Communication (Universitat Ramon Llull–Barcelona). He has led or participated in several research projects in the fields of culture and communication at the Catalonian, Spanish, and European level. He was awarded with the VIII Award of Mass Communication Research by the Generalitat de Catalunya with his research work: "Culture and Mass Communication Debated: The Intellectuals and the Analysis of Culture," which was later published in Catalan with the title "The Sublime and the Vulgar."

Nick Couldry is professor of Media and Communications, and joint chair of the Department of Media and Communications, at Goldsmiths, University of London, where he is also director of the Centre for the Study of Global Media and Democracy. He is the author or editor of ten books, including most recently *Media, Society, World: Social Theory and Digital Media Practice* (Polity, 2012), and *Why Voice Matters: Culture and Politics After Neoliberalism* (Sage, 2010).

Joan Cuenca is a public relations expert and he holds a PhD in Communication Studies, a master's degree in Social Communication, and a B.A. in Advertising and Public Relations from Ramon Llull University, Barcelona, Spain. Professionally, he works as a strategic consultant in communication. In the academic field, he is a faculty member of the department of Advertising and Public Relations at the Blanquerna School of Communication Studies, where he teaches courses in advertising and corporate public relations strategy. He is a consultant for the Open University of Catalonia (UOC), besides having taught a wide range of courses at different universities and business in Spain: University of Barcelona, University of Alicante, Architecture and Engineering La Salle of Barcelona, E.A.E. Business Administration School (UPC Catalonian Tech University), Institute of Marketing of Barcelona (ESIC Business Marketing School), among others.

He is a founding member of the research group ESTISMA (Strategy and Issues Management in Public Relations and Corporate Communication). His main research is in public relations audits. Together with Klaus Zilles, he coordinates the 6th and 7th edition (2011 and 2013) of the International Conference of Communication and Reality of the Faculty of Communication Blanquerna (URL). His most recent book publication is *Auditorías de Relaciones Públicas*, UOCPress (2012). He is a member of the Association of Researchers in Public Relations of Spain, and FISEC (Latin American Forum of Communication Strategies).

Ellen Van Gool obtained a master's degree in Communication Studies at the University of Antwerp. Her graduation research project focused on adolescents' disclosure of contact details in social network sites. She is currently involved with MIOS research dealing with youngsters' self-disclosure online. Her research interests include the impact of new media, social media in particular, on children and teenagers and how they deal with this newly created online privacy.

María Lamuedra Graván is lecturer at the University of Seville. In 2004 she received her PhD in Media Studies from Glasgow Caledonian University, with a dissertation entitled "Readers, Storyworlds and the Popular Public Sphere: A Comparative Analysis of Women´s Magazines in Spain and the U.K." Her research looks into the relationship between the public sphere and some of the most influential media genres, such as the news, celebrity stories, and soaps. In 2007, she published "Aristócratas, meritócratas y famosillos': Cómo participan lectores y televidentes en las historias de famosos"(*Ediciones de la Torre)*, and "Las historias de famosos en la sociedad mediática" (*Diputación Provincial de Huelva).* Public Service Television is also an important object of her research. In this field, she has co-edited "Los informativos diarios en BBC y TVE" (2010, *Ediciones de la Torre*), and edited "El futuro de la radiotelevisión pública: La necesaria alianza con la ciudadanía" (2012, Editorial Popular). In English, she has co-authored with Hugh 0'Donnell "Terms of Engagement: East Enders, Public Service,and Cultural Citizenship" (*European Journal of Cultural Studies,* forthcoming in 2013).

Wannes Heirman is teaching assistant at the Department of Communication Studies of the University of Antwerp. After obtaining his master's degree in Communication Studies, he started conducting research with the research team MIOS. In the period 2008–2009, he worked together with other MIOS colleagues on a research report concerning cyberbullying. This report was destined for the Belgian Internet Rights Observatory and ultimately resulted in policy advice. Besides the topic of cyberbullying, he has a broad interest in research into how information and communication technologies are impacting the daily lives of children and teenagers. Currently he is conducting fieldwork for his PhD project, which aims to examine how young children and teenagers deal with their privacy on the Internet.

Martin Lüthe was a PhD fellow at the International Graduate Centre for the Study of Culture at Justus-Liebig University in Gießen (2007–2010) in the field of American cultural studies, where he finished his dissertation entitled "Color-Line, and Crossing-Over: Motown and Performances of Blackness in 1960s American Culture." From the Fall of 2010 to Spring 2013, Lüthe held the position of lecturer of American Cultural History and American Studies at Ludwig-Maximilians-University, Munich. He currently is assistant professor at the John F. Kennedy Institute of the Free University Berlin, where he teaches and researches in American culture.

Guillem Marca has a PhD in Communication from the Rovira i Virgili University (URV). He graduated in Fine Arts from Barcelona University. He has a BA in Advertising and Public Relations from the Blanquerna School of Communication and International Relations, and an MA in Management Communication from the Escuela de Administración de Empresas (UPC Catalonian Tech University).

He works as a strategic communication manager for Ala Oeste Communication Management Agency. He is currently working for several clients, such as AsInfor, Finconsum (La Caixa), Generalitat de Catalunya, Elite Electrodomésticos, Iderma (UPS Dexeus), Sage Software and Services, SEPAR (Spanish Respiratory Physicians Society), Taurus, UPC Catalonian Tech University, UPC School of Professional & Executive Development, and WinShop, among others.

He belongs to the faculty staff of the Department of Communication Studies, Rovira i Virgili University, and the Business and Communication faculty, Vic University (UVic). He is a founding member of the applied research group ESTISMA-Strategy and Issues Management in Public Relations and Corporate Communication at the Blanquerna School of Communication and International Relations.

Kathy Matilla holds a PhD in Communication from Ramon Llull University (URL). She graduated in Public Relations and in History of Art from Barcelona University, obtained a master's degree in Marketing from ESADE (URL), and a master's degree in Social Communication from Ramon Llull University.

She works as a strategic consultant in corporate public relations (lobbying, crisis communication, and issues management), and has had various clients in Spain, Europe, and the U.S., among them Akzo, Bridgestone, Bristol-Myers Squibb, Coty, Gallina Blanca, Generalitat de Catalunya, Firestone, I.T.T., Mahou-San Miguel, Hoechst, La Caixa, Legrain, Louis Vuitton-Moët-Hennesy, Nokia, Novartis, Pfizer, Pharmacia &Upjohn, Purina, Rolex Suisse, Revlon, Satéllite ASTRA, Tabacanaria, W.R. Grace, and the Democratic Party in the U.S.

She belongs to the faculty of the Blanquerna School of Communication and International Relations, where she teaches courses on corporate public relations strategy, and is a founding member and coordinates the applied research group ESTISMA-Strategy and Issues Management in Public Relations and Corporate Communication.

She has been the public relations vice dean of the College of Public Relations and Advertising in Catalonia. She is currently a member of the management team of the association of communication directors Dircom Catalonia, and the international president of FISEC-Iberamerican Forum of Communication Strategies.

Richard Maxwell is professor of Media Studies at Queens College, City University of New York. He has published widely on a range of topics, from television in Spain's democratic transition to Hollywood's international dominance, from media politics in the post-9/11 era to how big political economic forces work in the mundane routines of daily life and culture. His most recent book, *Greening the Media*, is coauthored with Toby Miller.

Toby Miller is distinguished professor of Media & Cultural Studies at the University of California–Riverside. His latest books are *Blow Up the Humanities* (Temple UP, 2012) and *Greening the Media* (Oxford UP, 2012, with Richard Maxwell), and you can follow his adventures at tobymiller.org.

James Moir is a senior lecturer in sociology at the University of Abertay Dundee, Scotland, with a research interest in the application of discourse analysis across a wide range of socio-psychological topics. This has involved the study of discourses of occupational identities; doctor-patient interactions and shared decision-making; the discursive construction of tourism as visual experience; Western discourse surrounding death and dying; higher-education policy discourse, the media and political opinionation, and in this volume, the impact of digital media in higher education. Dr. Moir was recently a senior associate of the U.K. Higher Education Academy's Centre for Sociology, Anthropology and Politics (C-SAP), and has also conducted funded projects for the Quality Assurance Agency's (Scotland) Enhancement Themes on Graduates for the 21st Century, and Developing and Supporting the Curriculum.

Ana Cinthya Uribe (Guadalajara, Mexico, 1979) is an assistant researcher at the Blanquerna School of Communication of the Universitat Ramon Llull. With a BA in Journalism and studies in corporate communication and public management, she collaborates at the CONinCOM group and is also writing her PhD dissertation on the subject of new Internet devices for democracy, specifically Voting Advice Applications. She has been founder and executive manager of the VAA (website) elecciones.es for Spain since 2010.

Michel Walrave is an associate professor at the Department of Communication Studies of the University of Antwerp. He leads the research group MIOS that conducts research on, among others, children's and adolescents' ICT uses. His research focuses on ICT-use-related privacy risks. He has conducted several research projects on e-marketing, social networking sites, privacy, and cyberbullying, among other topics. He teaches marketing communication, e-marketing, and governmental and social-profit communication at the University of Antwerp and is a guest lecturer in several other universities. Michel Walrave was appointed as an expert involved with the first and the second assessment of the safer social networking principles for the EU. He is a member of the Expert Commission on governmental communication of the Flemish Parliament and involved in the Internet Rights Observatory. Michel Walrave holds a master's degree in Communication Studies, a master's in Information Science, and a PhD in Social Sciences.

Klaus Zilles is an associate professor at the Blanquerna School of Communication Studies and International Relations at Ramon Llull University in Barcelona, Spain. A graduate of Heidelberg University (Germany), he has also studied at the University of New Mexico at Albuquerque, and studied and taught at the University of Illinois at Urbana–Champaign. In 1998, he earned his PhD in English and German Philology from the University of Heidelberg. His doctoral dissertation on Chicano writer Rolando Hinojosa was published in 2001 by the University of New Mexico Press under the title *Rolando Hinojosa: A Reader's Guide*. In 2008, he co-edited, with Fernando Clemot, *En la frontera: i migliori racconti della narrativa chicana.* (Milan: Gran Vía Edizioni). Klaus Zilles writes and publishes on Chicano literature, literature and film, and identity politics in the media. Together with Joan Cuenca, he has coordinated the 6th and 7th edition (2011 and 2013) of the International Conference on Communication and Reality at Blanquerna.

Index

A

B

C

N

O

P

Q

R

V

W

Y